REBUILDING AFTER COLLAPSE

REBUILDING
AFTER
COLLAPSE

POLITICAL STRUCTURES FOR CREATIVE RESPONSE TO THE ECOLOGICAL CRISIS

EDITED BY

JOHN CULP

PROCESS
CENTURY
PRESS

ANOKA, MINNESOTA 2018

Rebuilding After Collapse: Political Structures for Creative Response to the Ecological Crisis

© 2018 Process Century Press

Process Century Press
RiverHouse LLC
802 River Lane
Anoka, MN 55303

Process Century Press books are published in association with the International Process Network.

Cover: Susanna Mennicke

VOLUME XVII: TOWARD ECOLOGICAL CIVILIZATION SERIES

JEANYNE B. SLETTOM, GENERAL EDITOR

ISBN 978-1-940447-34-6
Printed in the United States of America

TABLE OF CONTENTS

PART 4

ACTUALIZING POSSIBILITIES THROUGH ELECTIONS, VOLUNTEERS, AND TECHNOLOGY

SERIES PREFACE:
TOWARD ECOLOGICAL CIVILIZATION

We live in the ending of an age. But the ending of the modern period differs from the ending of previous periods, such as the classical or the medieval. The amazing achievements of modernity make it possible, even likely, that its end will also be the end of civilization, of many species, or even of the human species. At the same time, we are living in an age of new beginnings that give promise of an ecological civilization. Its emergence is marked by a growing sense of urgency and deepening awareness that the changes must go to the roots of what has led to the current threat of catastrophe.

In June 2015, the 10th Whitehead International Conference was held in Claremont, CA. Called "Seizing an Alternative: Toward an Ecological Civilization," it claimed an organic, relational, integrated, nondual, and processive conceptuality is needed, and that Alfred North Whitehead provides this in a remarkably comprehensive and rigorous way. We proposed that he could be "the philosopher of ecological civilization." With the help of those who have come to an ecological vision in other ways, the conference explored this Whiteheadian alternative, showing how it can provide the shared vision so urgently needed.

The judgment underlying this effort is that contemporary research and scholarship is still enthralled by the 17th century view of nature articulated by Descartes and reinforced by Kant. Without freeing our minds of this objectifying and reductive understanding of the world, we are not likely to direct our actions wisely in response to the crisis to which this tradition has led us. Given the ambitious goal of replacing now dominant patterns of thought with one that would redirect us toward ecological civilization, clearly more is needed than a single conference. Fortunately, a larger platform is developing that includes the conference and looks beyond it. It is named Pando Populus (pandopopulus.com)in honor of the world's largest and oldest organism, an aspen grove.

As a continuation of the conference, and in support of the larger initiative of Pando Populus, we are publishing this series, appropriately named "Toward Ecological Civilization."

~John B. Cobb, Jr.

OTHER BOOKS IN THIS SERIES

An Axiological Process Ethics, Rem B. Edwards
Panentheism and Scientific Naturalism, David Ray Griffin
Organic Marxism, Philip Clayton and Justin Heinzekehr
Theological Reminiscences, John B. Cobb, Jr.
Integrative Process, Margaret Stout and Jeannine M. Love
Replanting Ourselves in Beauty, Jay McDaniel and Patricia Adams Farmer, eds.
For Our Common Home, John B. Cobb, Jr., and Ignacio Castuera, eds.
Whitehead Word Book, John B. Cobb, Jr.
The Vindication of Radical Empiricism, Michel Weber
Intuition in Mathematics and Physics, Ronny Desmet, ed.
Reforming Higher Education in an Era of Ecological Crisis and Growing Digital Insecurity, Chet Bowers
Protecting Our Common, Sacred Home, David Ray Griffin
Educating for an Ecological Civilization, Marcus Ford and Stephen Rowe, eds.
Socialism in Process, Justin Heinzekehr and Philip Clayton, eds.
Putting Philosophy to Work, John B. Cobb, Jr., and Wm. Andrew Schwartz, eds.
Two Americas: Liberal Education & the Crisis of Democracy, Stephen C. Rowe

INTRODUCTION:

WHAT TO DO IN THE CURRENT ECOLOGICAL CRISIS

John Culp

A GROWING AWARENESS OF ECOLOGICAL ISSUES has developed over the past 10 years in spite of the efforts of climate change deniers and other special interests who benefit from current practices causing the degradation of the environment. Although the environmental movement has a long history, popular culture gradually has begun to recognize the importance of the environment for existence on the planet.

Many believe that a technological solution to the continuing environmental destruction can be found. However, finding ways to improve existence on the planet, or even to continue the present type of existence, requires more. Natural science research is directed at finding the causes of our present ecological destruction, as well as alternative ways to live that will avoid the destruction; nevertheless, more than natural science is needed. In fact, scientific research requires direction for its practices, and funding to make those practices possible. Values must be identified to help guide which technologies to develop. Private enterprise is important, but funding needs will require more than the interest of wealthy individuals.

Furthermore, discoveries of more efficient machinery, alternative sources of energy, or chemical ways to reverse global warming will still need to be implemented, and for that, cooperative action is required. Individuals working from limited personal resources will not be able reverse the course of ecological disaster. Even groups of individuals contributing significant financial resources will fail to halt the increasing destruction of the environment because they will still be limited in terms of their capabilities and their understanding of what is needed. A concerted, collaborative effort is needed.

Thinking about collaboration between individuals calls to mind the many ways in which people organize and relate to other individuals and groups. These political structures and actions enable the natural sciences to have an impact beyond the immediate situation. In other words, it is politics and political science that make it possible for the work of the natural sciences to impact the coming environmental disaster. Only broadly supported movements offer any hope for areas devastated by strip mining practices. Fracking will not be stopped simply by studies showing its negative impact upon the environment. Even demonstrations against the planned construction of a large coal shipping terminal can at best stop the construction of that one terminal. What is needed is collaboration and communal action. But consciousness of ways that political structures make collaboration possible is not always present, and when it is present, political consciousness may be narrowly limited to such organizational entities as political parties, or to specific theories such as socialism or democracy, nationalism or internationalism.

For many people today, the acceptable political structure is democracy. Democracy encourages the participation of many people in the governance of a group. This allows for 1) diversity, in that many options can be considered, and 2) inclusiveness, which elicits cooperation and coordination of actions. Democracy is often assumed to be the political order best suited to respond to the current situation and to work toward the continuation of society. However, a variety of threats to democracy have arisen in the past century.

The increased power of international corporations, which are not limited to particular nations, or even geographical locations, has given rise to centers of power that exclude many people. Similarly, the creation and control of money significantly impacts contemporary political organization in ways that limit the input of many people and their concerns. The connections among individuals that are based on location, ethnicity, language, commonality of interest, or some combination of these factors, are breaking down with the centralization of power in international organizations and corporations, or specific nations. It is important that the development and role of these centers of power be understood. Even though these threats to democracy counter efforts to work for the well-being of the environment, recognizing the loss of contributions from the many may provide an opening for future developments that will contribute to the development of a healthy response to the ecological crisis.

John B. Cobb, Jr. has worked for years to increase peoples' awareness of the destruction of the environment, to analyze the factors leading to this destruction, and to offer insight into ways to respond. In the late 1960s, as a leading theologian in the development of process theology, Cobb began to think and write about the impending ecological crisis.[1] In the 1980s, Cobb emphasized the importance of economic theory for public policy about the environment and challenged dominant economic concepts.[2] Throughout these years of warning, he continued to emphasize the importance of hope.

Cobb bases his thinking about the environment on his theological development of Alfred North Whitehead's philosophy. This theoretical foundation of his work can be seen in his emphasis upon the relational nature of all reality, including God and the world. Both God and the world are constituted by their relationship with each other. God's creative activity presents possibilities to the world. The world then makes possible the actualization of values in the biosphere, the complexity of which emerges through the process of evolution. This presentation of possibilities enables the world to transcend the determination of the past. The world, in turn, makes actual the possibilities that God has made available. Without the actualization provided by the world, there would be no newness coming out of the past. The goal of God's creativity is a just, participatory, and sustainable world that upholds the value of all creation. That goal cannot be actualized without the involvement of the world. Further, God's presence in both the natural and human realms challenges the many dualisms, such as the dualism of nature and humanity, that have contributed to the ecological crisis. Humans have the responsibility to bring about a world that affirms the value of God's creative activities.

God's saving activity provides the basis for hope that the world can accomplish the goal of a world that upholds the value of all creation. God's saving activity both preserves value that has been accomplished, and redeems what is lost due to the rejection of the divine possibilities offered to bring about the values of justice, participation, and sustainability. Hope in God enables people to actualize the possibilities for salvation that God offers to the earth. Belief in the Spirit as the giver of life and love provides the ground for hope that makes it possible to do something about the disastrous situation confronting the planet.

In an effort to develop and demonstrate a carefully thought out collaborative response to the present ecological collapse, Cobb provided the inspiration and work to bring about the international conference, "Seizing an Alternative: Toward an Ecological Civilization." This conference brought together people from around the world to think about how to respond to the ecological crisis. The conference was a practical expression of his theological commitments and his encouragement of others to make their own unique, and hopeful, contributions. The conference was held in Claremont, California, June 4–7, 2015. It sought both to facilitate awareness of the issues facing the environment and to propose responses to the increasing ecological destruction. More than 1,000 presenters from 80 fields of specialty offered an international transdisciplinary approach to ecology. The conference was organized into different sections, each with its own tracks, dealing with specific aspects of the ecological disaster. Plenary sessions sought to bring together a variety of topics, locations, and responses.[3] The breadth of the conference included topics such as "The Threatening Catastrophe: Responding Now," "Reenvisioning Nature; Reenvisioning Science," and "The Transformative Power of Art." Within the section on "The Threatening Catastrophe: Responding Now" a specific track entitled "Political Collapse" was organized by Cobb, who personally invited many of the participants to examine political structures that have led to our current ecological issues and to suggest possible alternatives.

This book grew out of the desire to make the presentations and discussions in the "Political Collapse" track available to a broader audience. Following the general structure of the track, the first essay sets out the background of our current political situation. The next section of essays considers specific international issues and responses in three different nations. The focus narrows to the U.S. in the next section, recognizing both the significance of the role of the U.S. in the ecological collapse, and the need to increase the depth of analysis and the creativity of responses. This section analyzes specific aspects of political life in the United States and asserts that understanding our current political situation requires consideration of financial structures. After the analysis of political problems hindering U.S. action, responses to the ecological crisis, nationally, locally, and individually are presented. This last section of essays gives examples of specific actions being taken in order to respond to ecological problems.

A brief summary of the individual essays indicates the nature of these analyses and responses. Cobb, in "The Collapse of Democratic Nation States," provides a brief history of the current political order, acknowledging that its decay makes the future appear bleak. However, this decay offers possibilities and thus hope for change.

Although many societies have contributed to our present circumstances, this cultural diversity also offers a rich array of responses. Accordingly, the next group of essays considers the problems and possibilities from Japan, Brazil, and Greece. In

"Progress toward an Ecological Civilization: Ecological Footprint Success and Fukushima Nuclear Disaster," Yoshihiko Wada and Katsunori Iha first describe a way to measure the unsustainable impact of human culture on the environment, then warn how nuclear energy disasters, such as the Fukushima catastrophe, limit efforts to bring change. The Japanese response to Fukushima, as well as governmental responses to Chernobyl and Three Rivers, provides an example of the economic and political forces that make responsible ecological civilization so difficult to accomplish. Lília Marianno, in "Brazilian Contributions to Rebuilding: Brazilian Cases of Socio-political and Economic Resistance," contributes an historical review that describes how colonialism, militarism, and slavery have shaped political struggles in Brazil today. In spite of the current problems, several examples of alternatives offered by communities at the base of society provide hope for social development and practical skills that can transform the reality of many people. Thomas Greco's essay on the Greek debt crisis, "Greece and the Global Debt Crisis," shows how that crisis threatens the stability of the global financial infrastructure and Western democratic civilization. He proposes a different form of globalization based on local self-determination.

Essays focusing on conditions in the U.S. that have brought about ecological collapse begin with Carl Herman's "Integrity for the Whole Truth, and Nothing but the Truth." Herman uses the metaphor of the emperor's new clothes in his analysis of the U.S. economic empire. He challenges the lies that have been told to justify U.S. wars, the creation of unpayable debt by the banking system, and the media's covering of these crimes. Joseph Hough, in "Chris Hedges on the Corruption of Democracy and the Collapse of Hope in National Politics," then considers Chris Hedges' prophetic writings about climate change, the spread of major military conflicts, the displacement of huge populations, and the globalization of free market capitalism. While Hough agrees with Hedges' critique of the dependency of the major political parties upon donations from the richest one percent, the history of third-party movements demonstrates the ineffectiveness of Hedge's call for such a movement. Social justice is more likely to occur through support for a major party candidate whose positions recognize the importance of equal justice. Sheila Collins, in "The "Revolution" We Need," examines the successes and failures of past social movements. She concludes that a successful revolution will be both electoral and extra-electoral, and it will draw upon international law to establish its legitimacy. Ellen Brown, in "How America Became an Oligarchy," explains the capture of democracy by big money as the culmination of the globalization of transnational corporations. She proposes that one way for governments to regain their sovereign powers is by creating money themselves rather than allowing money to be created by banks making loans. Thomas Greco, in "How Private Currencies and Credit Clearing Exchanges Can Help Save Civilization," explains that local communities can take back their power by allocating credit directly amongst themselves. He cites examples of the work of currencies and credit clearing circles that bypass corporate banking and political elites.

Identifying ways to respond — to analyses of the problem and proposals for action — moves the discussion beyond the general to the specific. Governmental reform, volunteer organizations, and technological advances offer possibilities for change. Gayle McLaughlin, in "Richmond, California: A Local Community Defines Its Destiny," tells how she and others organized to elect leadership that successfully challenged control of a multinational billion-dollar industry in a metropolitan area. The Richmond Progressive Alliance addressed economic, social, and environmental issues facing the city of Richmond, CA. Chevron's contamination of land, sea, and air along with its political power contributed to many of these issues. In the continuing reform efforts of the alliance and the city, Richmond offers both a model and challenge to others. Voluntary organizations at the international level and in local units provide another way to work to bring about a better ecological structure. Tina Clarke, in "Local Responses to Crisis and Collapse," stresses the importance of local resiliency in the face of ecological collapse. She shows how the Transition Towns Network assists local organizations in bringing about change in their communities. James Long, Ashley Mazanec, and Michael Brackney collaborated in "SanDiego350 Activism" to give the brief history of a local organization affiliated with 350.org International. They describe its mission, organizing structure, day-to-day operations, membership building, action teams, and activities. In so doing, they provide specifics about how their local organization has worked effectively to bring about improvements that lessen this one locality's impact on the climate. Finally, David Stone, in "Rebuilding the Foundation: The Critical Role of Materials for a Sustainable World," recognizes the environmental cost of materials used to construct energy-efficient buildings and vehicles. Materials used in construction and manufacturing also contribute to the ongoing ecological collapse. Stone describes an innovative technology using waste materials that provides a cleaner and greener alternative to Portland cement. This new material was then used to adapt the homeland of the Tohono O'odham Native Americans to a predicted mega-drought.

This collection of essays would not have been possible without the inspiration and encouragement of John B. Cobb, Jr. The participants in the political collapse track and the authors represented herein greatly facilitated the process of collecting these essays. They not only made the collection possible, but their cooperation and hard work modeled the type of effort that is needed if we are to avert an even greater ecological catastrophe.

ENDNOTES

1   Cobb's major book on the environment is *Is It Too Late? A Theology of Ecology* (Beverly Hills: Bruce, 1972). For essays published on ecology see "The Meaning of Salvation," *Mid-Stream*, Vol. 9:4 (1970), 127–63; "Christian Theism and the Ecological Crisis," *Religious Education*, Vol. 66:1 (1971), 31–35; "Process Theology and Environmental Issues," *The Journal of Religion*, Vol. 60:4 (1980), 440–58; "Process Theology and an Ecological Model," in Philip N. Joranson and Ken Butigan (eds.), *Cry of the Environment: Rebuilding the Christian Creation Tradition* (Santa Fe, NM: Bear & Company, 1984), 329–36;

"The Resurrection of the Soul," *Harvard Theological Review*, Vol. 80:2 (1987), 213–27; "Ecology, Science, and Religion: Toward a Postmodern Worldview," in David Ray Griffin (ed.), *The Reenchantment of Science: Postmodern Proposals* (Albany, NY: State University of New York Press, 1988), 99–113; "Befriending an Amoral Nature," *Zygon*, Vol. 23:4 (1988), 431–36; and "Postmodern Christianity in Quest of Eco-Justice," in D. T. Hessel (ed.), *After Nature's Revolt. Eco-Justice and Theology* (Philadelphia: Fortress Press, 1992), 21–39.

2   For Cobb's books on the impact of economics on the environment, see, with Charles Birch, *The Liberation of life: From the Cell to the Community* (Cambridge: Cambridge University Press, 1981); with Herman Daly and Cliff Cobb, *For the Common Good: Redirecting the Economy Toward Community, The Environment, and a Sustainable Future* (Boston: Beacon, 1989); *Sustainability: Economics, Ecology, and Justice* (Maryknoll: Orbis, 1992); and *Sustaining the Common Good: A Christian Perspective on the Global Economy* (Cleveland: Pilgrim, 1994).

3   For the complete schedule, see http://www.pandopopulus.com/conference/.

Part One
The Challenge

❧ 1 ❧

THE COLLAPSE OF DEMOCRATIC

NATION STATES

John B. Cobb, Jr.

ABSTRACT: *A brief history of the current political order may be bleak, but it also allows for more positive developments—some of which are appearing in parts of the world not controlled by the American economic empire. Other positive indications can be seen in popular movements, state banks, local money creation, food production, and sustainable construction methods.*

RESPONDING TO THE POLITICAL ELEMENTS of the present ecological crisis involves a double purpose. First, a description of the gestalt of political order and what can be projected in the near future is needed. Without such a gestalt, any attempt to rebuild risks irrelevance and futility. This will be bleak. However, the decay of current forms of political order may leave space for something that will, in at least some respects, be better. Second, it is crucial to give some indication of positive developments and new possibilities that can direct more fruitful efforts. Without hope, motivation for action will be lacking. In this opening essay, I will chiefly consider in very broad strokes where we are, how we got here, and what we can hope for.

Political order has always been part of human life. However, for hundreds of thousands of years the political was not distinct from the cultural and social. In tribal life these are all one. With the rise of cities, some distinctions began to emerge. Governance had a some-what distinct structure. City states sometimes conquered others and established empires in which governance was further developed as a distinguishable part of the social and cultural situation.

I will follow the European development. When the centralized top-down government of imperial Rome collapsed in the West, a feudal order arose. Higher levels (often kings) competed for power with lower level nobility. These political structures existed alongside the better organized church, and political authorities typically sought legitimation from the church. The use of Latin by the church gave that language a status and use that was associated with superior authority. It was the language of education.

In this context people identified themselves by religion on the one side, and local feudal lords, on the other. Ethnic identity was secondary. It was typically associated with a spoken language. The diverse languages gradually gained importance with the growth of literature and increased use in education. National feeling expressed itself in the desire for one's mother tongue to be given equal status with Latin. Of course, a common language is typically connected with shared culture. The emergence of literature in the several languages standardized these languages and increased national feeling. Because of the central importance of Christianity, translation of the Bible into multiple languages was a major step in the rise of nationalism. More and more people began to identify themselves by their nationality.

The move from feudal structures to the state system was furthered by urbanization and trade. The feudal order is quite natural for agricultural societies. Power is in the hands of those who control the peasants and appropriate their surplus. Some local lords subordinate others, and a hierarchy of power and wealth is established. But the rise of towns and trade generates separate centers of wealth and thus of power. These developed networks were not bound by proximity. They preferred to deal directly with governments ruling over larger areas.

This development of nations around a common language led to demands for national independence and the formation of nation states. These could have diverse forms of government, but because popular feeling brought these states into being, governments generally sought legitimacy by representing that feeling. There was a tendency for more and more people to want a voice in national government. Voting for representatives with some political power became common. Thus there was an internal push in nation states toward democracy. By the end of World War I, the democratic nation state was the accepted norm.

Europeans were not the only creators of nation states. Japan and China were also important examples. Until their contact with the West, they were better understood as empires with feudal structures culminating in emperors. But their contact with the West rather quickly led to the growth of democratic ideals.

On the other hand, much of the rest of the world was politically organized for the convenience and profit of empires, chiefly European ones. After World War I, some previous empires were broken up into independent states. After World War II most colonies were given or attained formal independence. They were then expected to become states like the nation states even though, in many cases, their boundaries were little informed by cultural and linguistic distinctions. Accordingly, they were assigned an almost impossible task: they were invited to be democratic even though there was no national feeling to support their unity.

Democracy is possible only where the great majority of people consent to be ruled by a particular government. If the boundaries of a state contain several national communities, each of which feels its connection with members of their nationality living in other states, such consent is difficult to achieve. To take a clear example, many Kurds have strong national feeling as Kurds, whether they live in

Turkey or Iraq or Syria or Iran. A "nation state" of Kurdistan would receive from them the sort of loyalty that the French have to France. But many of them will never give to the states in which they reside that sort of allegiance. If the states whose boundaries contain them do not wish to surrender territory, they will not be able to give to their citizens the degree of freedom and participation in government that France can give to its citizens. A state not supported by national feeling must inherently be authoritarian to a considerable degree.

Of course, it is not impossible to generate national feelings around a state that is multi-ethnic. Shared historical experience can substitute for ethnic connections. Switzerland has done this without suppressing ethnic distinctions. The United States has been remarkably successful in this regard by requiring all ethnic groups to learn the same language and assimilate the same history. Canada has gained the loyalty of two linguistically defined communities by treating both as equal. But if Great Britain and France began to fight each other, probably Canada's unity and ability to function as a democracy would be badly strained. The most remarkable success story may be India, which, despite the many languages and cultures of its people, has achieved a state-wide identity that enables it to be remarkably democratic. Perhaps the great number of divisions reduces the intensity of any one of them.

The point here is only that many of the new countries have an inherently difficult task in creating loyalty to the state from people whose tribal or national feelings conflict with this loyalty. In many cases, the unity of such states can be maintained only by authoritarian government. Genuine democracy is not possible.

The situation in the Near East is worsened by Israel's preference for weak neighbors. Since relatively strong Arab states ruled by authoritarian governments contain large groups that are disenfranchised, outsiders who desire to weaken these states can support the aspirations of these excluded groups in the name of democracy. However, the result of overthrowing strong rulers is not democracy but weakness. In a world dominated by American imperialism, interventions are the norm, and, even apart from external meddling, some artificially created states in Africa are unlikely to succeed.

But the recently created non-national states are not the only ones that fail. The long-established democratic nation states are also in crisis. American empire threatens them as well. National governments anywhere are obviously weakened by the hegemony of a foreign nation. The European nations for the most part have accepted American hegemony to such an extent that it is difficult to consider their foreign policies as those of independent nation states. They are often the instruments through which American goals are supported by the United Nations.

The attempt to rebuild from the present political situation will have to deal with the threat of American imperialism to the health of other states around the world. However, the major current threat to the healthy survival of national democracies in Europe is economic and specifically financial. This is not unrelated to American hegemony, but it needs consideration in its own terms.

The tension between economic and political concerns is far from new. In any nation in which the wealth is in the hands of the political rulers, as in an ancient monarchy or a feudal system, there is little tension. But where manufacture and commerce by private citizens flourish, centers of wealth arise that are not proportionally represented in official government circles. In this situation, individuals with political power, even kings, are subject to influence by those who are in position to reward them economically and thus influence national policies. Actually, this influence has often been very great. When governments have needed to borrow money, as for military purposes, those in position to supply it have often been able to dictate the terms.

The influence of money was greatly enhanced by the emergence of private banking. The banks are able to create money and so to lend amounts far in excess of their actual wealth. This control of money-creation has been immensely important in the past. Now, in much of the world, it has given banks overwhelming control over human affairs. In the United States, Wall Street makes most of the truly important decisions that are directly attributed to Washington. We saw recently that the government of Greece was powerless to prevent control of Greece by external financial institutions.

So-called democracies long limited the separation of wealth and power by restricting participation in governance to the propertied class. When these restrictions were removed, wealth could still largely control elections. First, running for office became expensive, so that those who seek office require wealthy sponsors to whom they are then beholden. Second, the great majority of voters have little independent knowledge of those for whom they vote or of the issues to be dealt with. Their judgments are, accordingly, dependent on what they learn from the mass media. These media, in turn, are controlled by moneyed interests.

A third way in which the primacy of the market works against democracy is less direct. The market inherently grows in size because of economies of scale and the desire of producers to expand their markets. The result is urbanization and mobility of the population. Democracy is a fragile plant that needs watering. A large segment of the population needs some experience in participation in decision-making. In a stable population, living in small towns, there are many opportunities for this. In many cases citizens could participate in the governance of the town or its schools. In the United States in the nineteenth century, churches provided opportunity for many to participate in some kind of institutional leadership. Labor unions were another important opportunity for participation in making and implementing decisions. In the great urban centers now dominating the country, opportunities of this sort are scarce. Without a citizenry experienced in democratic practice, democracy is reduced to occasional opportunities to vote. Most voters are poorly informed and easily manipulated.

In the United States the franchise was widely extended from the early days of the country's history until recently, and on some issues popular opinion has played a large role. Giving black men and later women the right to vote was a major step in this direction. Labor organizations gained considerable power and were able to influence the media and to finance successful candidates for office. When the wealthy feared Communism they allowed American labor to flourish. For several decades the nation had two parties that actually represented distinct classes. However, as the threat of Communism faded, the power of labor was destroyed, and, in order to survive, the two parties had to serve the interests of the same economic class. The extent of control by wealth over elections and elected officials now renders the notion of "democracy" almost meaningless.

When most concentrations of wealth were within a single nation, the power of money that distorts and destroys democracy did not weaken the state. The state was an essential instrument of the wealthy classes. Typically, given democratic structures, these classes also needed the support of large sections of public opinion and accordingly made some concessions to the well-being of all citizens. However, today's global economy is fully transnational. The money power is not much interested in boundaries between states and generally works to reduce their influence on markets and investments. It meets some resistance because national feeling continues strong. But overall, the global market trumps national interests. Thus transnational corporations inherently work to undermine nation states, whether they are democratic or not.

Whereas attention must be paid to the weakening of countries around the world, the collapse of democracy and even of states brings a focus on how imperial power controlled by financial interests destroys democracy within the imperial power itself. This expresses itself not only in the political and economic realms but also in law, education, culture, and society.

Glimmers of hope exist for the rebuilding of a healthy political order. However, we will not try to describe the kind of political order for which we ultimately hope. Looking at global developments suggests that the growth of American empire may be ending, and that it is already being forced to retreat. Positive developments in those parts of the world that are not controlled by the empire and have relative freedom from the transnational corporations can be recognized. Typically these countries have retained some control over money-creation and can therefore deal with their problems without hopeless indebtedness to private financial institutions. There are plenty of problems everywhere, but Russia, China, and India may be charting better courses than those permitted within the American empire. South America is an especially interesting case study. For a decade it seemed to be gaining independence of the United States. But now it seems that the United States is regaining control. Argentina has been brought back in line, and the experiment in independence in Venezuela is collapsing. As I write, it seems that Brazil is being brought to heel. Still it is not clear that this is a long-term defeat of the independence movements in South America or a temporary setback. It is interesting that the instrument of control in South America as in Greece is largely financial.

Further, positive developments are possible within the governments of the United States and its imperial allies and protégés. Even in these unlikely places there are those in position of power in governments and in corporations who recognize the destructiveness of current trends and seriously seek alternatives. Rather than simply giving up on the powers that be, we need to identify and support those who work within the established order to preserve and establish programs and policies that make possible some remnants of participatory governance. Popular movements (such as the struggle for rights for Blacks and women) have succeeded in affecting government policies. Evaluating the environmental movement (with special attention to 350.org) can offer additional insights in how to retain remnants of participatory governance.

A test case of the struggle between democracy and corpocracy in the United States is the response to the Transpacific Partnership (TPP). It was known by the corporate world from the beginning that this would not have the support of the American people; so it was negotiated in secret and the corporate-controlled press did not inform the public. When those of us who were somewhat aware of what was happening talked about it, we were typically dismissed as "conspiracy theorists." Most supposedly well-informed people do not believe anything until it is reported in the *New York Times.*

Since most Republicans support Wall Street and the oil interests, and since the TPP was negotiated by a progressive Democratic president, I expected little opposition in Congress. However, democracy was not as dead as I had feared. The opposition was more articulate and better led than I had expected, although it was overcome and "fast-track" was awarded the agreement. In the past this has meant that when the agreement is brought back for an up-or-down vote with no amendments considered, it easily passes.

My expectations would probably have been fulfilled had it not been for a remarkable 2016 primary season. The opposition of the American people to TPP was such that no candidate for nomination to president was prepared to defend it. Although Hilary Clinton had been an active participant in negotiating the agreement and is the candidate of the corporations and banks that demand it, she stated that she was opposed. This makes clear that no one supposes that the American people favor this "trade agreement." But by Clinton's denying her support, it was removed from the debate, giving it a better chance of passage.

Obama understood that congresspersons cannot vote for TPP right now, but he remains confident that when the election is over, they will enact it.* Most will do the bidding of those whose largess has enabled them to be elected. It will be surprising if the expectations of the establishment are not fulfilled. But the people have surprised the decision makers in the primary, and they may surprise us all again! Perhaps, just perhaps, the democrats are not as fully controlled by the oligarchs as I had come to believe.

Further, as it becomes obvious that the economies of countries that are not so fully controlled by global capitalism are surpassing those that are so controlled, important issues may so divide the current elite as to open the door to significant political change. For example, the establishment of state banks is not impossible. The proposal to

---

Editor's note: President Obama signed the TPP agreement in February 2016. President Trump later withdrew the U.S. from the agreement.

develop a system of postal savings might be seriously discussed at the national level. Some capitalists may recognize that the destruction of the middle class also weakens the market for the goods they want to sell.

Judgment about our current task is affected also by the possibility, even probability, of a collapse of the global capitalist system. We cannot ignore these possibilities in responding to the collapse of democratic processes and the state system. Especially if the economic collapse is not too abrupt, it may open the door to a change of leadership and basic direction without a full political collapse.

Despite the importance of continuing work at the national level, there are strong indications that our primary focus should be local. Even changes at the national level are likely to be possible only if bottom up movements bring great pressure on institutional leadership.

Climate change is increasingly being recognized as likely to lead to a collapse of global structures of all kinds including national governments. When it becomes clear that our present global system of food production and distribution has collapsed, the question will be who can survive on regional and even local production. Regional and local institutions are likely to supersede national and global ones in actual importance and power. Creating democratic communities now at these levels, outside the present system of government, may be the most hopeful direction for our efforts.

Examples of local communities that can survive and flourish even if national and global structures collapse are appearing. We believe that this local withdrawal from the empire and the global market will be helpful even before collapse. Of crucial importance is meeting our basic necessities without reliance on the national or global system of production and consumption. This will also have to be in ways that can depend on local sources in a time when climate is likely to be much less favorable. At this point the differences between economics and politics will not have much importance.

Experiments and developments that merit consideration and evaluation are already happening in various places. One important topic is local money-creation. Another is urban gardening, learning to produce food with very little water, and changing eating habits. Another is the construction of shelter with local materials in sustainable ways. Authentic communities of mutual care will be essential in responding to severe challenges, and working together now can help to create these. There are also movements that involve whole towns in taking those relevant steps that are now possible. We will need to think together about what are the most important current developments to evaluate. Envisioning a hopeful future that we can now anticipate in our actions may be our most important task.

Part Two
Global Issues and Possibilities

2

PROGRESS TOWARD AN ECOLOGICAL CIVILIZATION

Ecological Footprint Success and the Fukushima Nuclear Disaster

Yoshihiko Wada and Katsunori Iha

ABSTRACT: *The Ecological Footprint, which measures how much area is needed to support an economy, provides a reliable and user-friendly indicator of progress towards an ecological civilization. Calculations show that 1.6 Earths are necessary to support our current level of global consumption. The Ecological Footprint has been adopted by many mainstream organizations throughout the world. However, Japan's experience with the Fukushima nuclear disaster and its aftermath threaten progress toward an ecological civilization. This threat arises from the power of domestic and global forces promoting nuclear power and nuclear weapons. These powers have hindered Japan in dealing openly and honestly with the Fukushima disaster and can hinder global progress toward an ecological civilization.*

THE CONCEPT OF ECOLOGICAL FOOTPRINT (EF) ANALYSIS

We are pleased that Pope Francis released an encyclical in June 2015 and that he emphasized the importance of transforming our civilization to "integral ecology," which is consistent with the concept of "ecological civilization." It is necessary to have a reliable and user-friendly indicator to monitor the progress of our civilization toward this direction. The Ecological Footprint (EF) analysis is one of the most trusted and successful sustainability indicators that can assess this progress.

Ecological Footprint measures how much area of bio-productive land and water is necessary to support our economy or our lifestyle, and compares the results with the supply side, i.e., how much area of bio-productive land and water is available to our economy.[1] The former represents the economy's demand for ecosystem services (such as production of renewable resources that we consume, and absorption of wastes that we generate). The latter represents the supply capacity of the ecosystems. The former is called Ecological Footprint and the latter is called Biocapacity (BC).[2] If EF, the demand side, is greater than the BC, the supply side, then that means the economy is faced with "ecological deficit." Such an economy is ecologically not sustainable. This scientific tool, which assesses the balance between EF and BC, is simply called Ecological Footprint indicator/analysis. In other words, EF is a tool to analyze whether human economy is being managed "within the means of nature."

Ecological Footprint calculation results show that in order to sustain the human economy as a whole, 1.6 "Earths" are necessary (data year: 2012). This figure was derived through dividing humanity's total Ecological Footprint (20.1 billion global hectare, gha) by the planet's total Biocapacity (12.2 billion global hectare, gha).[3] This result suggests that the human economy as a whole has already exceeded the planet's Biocapacity and is running into "ecological deficit." Further growth induces more problems than benefits.

Another EF calculation shows that based on the Japanese average consumption rate, some 2.9 Earth-like planets are required. This figure was derived from comparing the Japanese per capita EF figure (5.0 gha in 2012) with the globally available BC per capita (1.7 gha in 2012).[4] This means that Japanese dwellers should cut their consumption by more than half.

ACCEPTANCE OF ECOLOGICAL FOOTPRINT BY CIVIL
SOCIETY AND MAINSTREAM ORGANIZATIONS

The EF results seem to have had some impact on overall Japanese awareness of the problem.[5] World Wildlife Fund for Nature Japan (WWF Japan) and Ecological Footprint Japan (EFJ) have been active in promoting the EF concept and conveying the calculation results and its implications, using the phrase, "One Planet Living" or "One Planet Economy."

William Rees (Professor Emeritus of the University of British Columbia, Canada) and Mathis Wackernagel (President, Global Footprint Network, USA) are co-developers of Ecological Footprint. They started to develop this indicator in the early 1990s in Vancouver, Canada. In the ensuing 25 years, this sustainability indicator has gained recognition in many parts of the world. Scientific communities such as the Global Footprint Network (GFN) and Stockholm Environment Institute (SEI) as well as civil society organizations, such as WWF and Best Foot Forward have been working tirelessly, pressuring mainstream organizations, local and national governments, international organizations such as the United Nations, and the European Union to adopt this sustainability indicator.[6] A number of scholars in many parts of the world have become involved in Ecological Footprint work. These include, to name only a few, researchers from the University of Sydney in Australia, Cardiff University in the United Kingdom, and many Chinese universities and research institutes such as Shanxi University of Finance and Economics.

Many local governments in Europe and North America have undertaken studies of their own Ecological Footprint. In the United Kingdom, in particular, more than 100 local authorities have calculated their own EF by utilizing user-friendly computer software such as the Footprint Tool for Local Authorities (FLAT), and the Resources and Energy Analysis for Planning (REAP) (Paul, et al. 2010). In Japan, Tokyo, Tsuda City, Sano City, Nara City, and Kyoto City have conducted studies on their Ecological Footprint.

So far, thirteen national governments have adopted the Ecological Footprint as one of their official national sustainability indictors, namely, Switzerland, Japan, United Arab Emeritus (UAE), Ecuador, Finland, Latvia, Luxembourg, Scotland, Wales, Argentina, Costa Rica, Indonesia, and the Philippines.

In recent years, Asian countries have shown strong interest in utilizing EF figures. The Philippines, for example, is particularly active in promoting the use of EF on both national and local levels. *A Measure for Resilience: A 2012 Report on the Ecological Footprint of the Philippines* was published by Global Footprint Network (2012), which worked closely with Philippines' Climate Change Commissioner Nadarev "Yeb" Saño, and with funding from the French Agency for Development. Providing the Philippines with a new framework to measure resilience, the report was endorsed by President Benigno Aquino III* with a forward in the report, and formally adopted by the Cabinet Cluster on Climate Change Adaptation and Mitigation.

Indonesia's Ministry of Public Works completed a report on the country's Ecological Footprint in 2010 as a basis for informing policy to guide the country on a development path that does not compromise its rich natural capital. The report notes that Indonesia has a wealth of Biocapacity, but in some places—particularly Java—high population threatens that surplus.

Japan has been actively accumulating Ecological Footprint data at the government, business, and research levels since the late 1990s. In 1996, the Ministry of the Environment first introduced the concept of the EF in the State of the Environment Report. In 2003, the Ministry of Land, Infrastructure, Transport and Tourism calculated the EF of Japan and that of each prefecture. In 2006 the Japanese government adopted the EF as part of Japan's Basic Environmental Plan. In 2012 Japan's Asahi Glass Foundation awarded the prestigious Blue Planet Prize to Drs. William Rees and Mathis Wackernagel for developing the EF concept. In the same year, the Kao Corporation presented a report on the EF analysis of their products at a meeting

Editor's note: Populist candidate Rodrigo Duterte became president in 2016. A controversial leader, he nevertheless signed the Paris Agreement and supports climate action. The Phillippines is especially vulnerable to climate change.

of the Institute of Life Cycle Assessment, Japan. In 2014 Fujitsu and WWF Japan has developed teaching material to be used on tablet computers in school classrooms. Teaching staff equipped with tablet computers are dispatched free of charge to elementary and junior high schools so that students can learn about the EF concept and calculation. The Ministry of Internal Affairs and Communications is providing funding for this project of environmental education.[7]

Although voters rejected the referendum, it is nontheless encouraging that Switzerland put its national Footprint goal on the ballot in 2016. The initiative proposed that Switzerland live on a Footprint that could be replicated worldwide by 2050.[8]

Internationally, the European Union and the Association of Southeast Asian Nations (ASEAN) have been proactive in conducting studies on how the EF can benefit their member countries. GFN and the Keidanren Conservation Nature Fund based in Japan jointly conducted a Footprint study of the ASEAN in 2014.[9] A similar research project was carried out in the Mediterranean region, called the Mediterranean Ecological Footprint Initiative. This study was conducted by the GFN's European Office with supports from UNESCO, the MAVA Foundation and other organizations.[10]

The United Nations Environment Program (UNEP)'s Financial Initiative, in partnership with 14 leading financial institutions, and the Global Footprint Network have studied how to integrate environmental risks and resource constraints into country risk analysis. Ecological Footprint plays a central role in this study.[11]

In order to transform our current destructive civilization into an ecological one, it is necessary for us to make sure that our economy is being managed "within the means of nature." The Ecological Footprint has been adopted in many mainstream organizations and educational institutions throughout the world and has been instrumental in visualizing whether an economy is ecologically sustainable or not. This positive and hopeful trend will definitely facilitate the goal of achieving ecological civilization in near future.

RADIOACTIVE CONTAMINATION OF LAND AND WATER
CAUSING DAMAGE TO HUMAN BODIES OF THE MOST
VULNERABLE IN FUKUSHIMA AND BEYOND

While a remarkably encouraging trend of the adoption of Ecological Footprint has occurred in many parts of the world, there is an extremely worrisome situation challenging progress toward an ecological civilization: the Fukushima nuclear disaster and its aftermath. The Fukushima Dai-ichi nuclear reactors of Tokyo Electric Power Company (**TEPCO**) continue to emit highly toxic radioactive water into the ocean.[12] The soils in Fukushima and surrounding regions are being contaminated by highly radioactive fallout substances such as cesium and strontium.

Tree leaves and barks have been contaminated by these toxic radioactive substances. As time goes by, these contaminated leaves and barks have become sources of contamination for forest streams, rivers, and rice fields. Even the decontaminated land areas are being re-polluted by the cyclical flow of falling contaminated leaves and barks. Rainfalls have been contaminated with radiation. The rainfalls pollute our homeland far away from Fukushima. The situation is hopeless and miserable.

During the 2020 Olympic and Paralympic site selection process, the Japanese Prime Minister Mr. Shinzo Abe assured the world that "everything is under control." However, that was absolutely wrong. The contaminated land and water have already damaged the health of Fukushima's children aged 18 or younger, the most vulnerable population. For example, by March 2016, approximately 380,000 youths living in Fukushima had been examined. Among them, 172 youths were diagnosed with thyroid cancer or with the high possibility of contracting the disease.[13] The occurrence rate of thyroid cancer is somewhere between 20–50 times higher than the rate observed between 2003 and 2009.[14] The Japanese government and Fukushima Prefectural government have admitted the increased rate. They have never, however, admitted the causal relationship between the Fukushima nuclear disaster and the higher observed rate of occurrence of the disease. But there is no rational explanation if this causal relationship is rejected.

That laws are being violated in Fukushima and beyond, and that human rights and dignity being infringed upon can be seen in terms of radiation exposure. The Japanese legal system clearly prohibits the general public from living in areas where radiation exposure is expected to be more than one milli Sievert (Sv) per annum. After the Fukushima nuclear accident of March 2011, however, the Japanese government revised this standard upward for Fukushima Prefecture and surrounding prefectures, allowing residents to live in areas where the expectation of radiation exposure is less than 20 milli Sv per annum. Even infants and small children are put into this dangerous and unlawful situation. This standard is significantly higher than the 5.2 milli Sv per annum that is applied to workers at nuclear reactors and medical radioactive facilities.

In 2017 the Japanese government decided that the evacuation would be lifted if these areas have been decontaminated and the annual radiation level is expected to be less than 20 milli Sv per annum. All voluntary evacuees from these areas were told they would no longer receive official assistance, such as housing subsidies, after April 2017, because the government had determined that this contamination level is not hazardous to human health. Thus, voluntary evacuees have no right to receive assistance for living away from their hometown, which is now supposed to be safe to live in, according to the Japanese government. Many local governments, such as Kyoto City and Osaka City, had their own assistance plans for voluntary evacuees from Fukushima. The Japanese government officers ordered local governments to refrain from providing assistance to the evacuees as of April 2017.[15]

Why does the Japanese government have double standards for radiation exposure? The Japanese residents living outside Fukushima are not allowed to be exposed to radiation of more than one milli Sv per annum. But Fukushima residents are forced to be exposed to radiation exposure as high as 20 milli Sv per annum. Injustice prevails in Japan.

The current Japanese government is trying to resume operating nuclear reactors in Japan, even though the causes of the Fukushima nuclear incident have not been fully identified and determined. They have installed new sets of nuclear regulations under a newly established governmental body, the Nuclear Regulatory Authority (NRA). The regulations are supposed to have incorporated the precious lessons derived from the Fukushima disaster. However, these regulations have severe defects, including: 1) failing to consider risks from eruptions of volcanoes and airplane crashes, 2) failing to consider simultaneous failures of devices, 3) excluding appraisal procedures in terms of adequacy of evacuation plans, and, 4) using an inadequate calculation method for estimating "basic earthquake ground motion." The currently employed Irikura-Miyake method would lead to underestimation of basic earthquake ground motion of nuclear reactor sites.[16]

THE EXISTENCE OF A POWERFUL NUCLEAR CONGLOMERATE IN JAPAN AND A GLOBAL LOBBYING GROUP TO PROMOTE NUCLEAR ENERGY AND NUCLEAR WEAPONS

Even if all of us, including our national governments, committed now to working toward ecological civilization, we know that we would still face many disasters. How we face them will determine our chances of realizing the world toward which Pope Francis has called us. Japan has faced a disaster, but it has not dealt with it openly and honestly. Accordingly, the Japanese people are paying a high price. The reason for Japan's failure appears to be the power of domestic and international forces that promote nuclear power and nuclear weapons. Perhaps the world can learn from Japan's failure and prepare to overcome, or at least counter, the opposition of those who profit from silence and misrepresentation.

The Japanese nuclear conglomerate consists of nine major electric companies, megabanks, heavy industries, major trading companies (for importing nuclear fuels and reactors), general contractors and subsidiaries, the transportation industry, as well as the commercial mass media.[17] The Yomiuri newspaper, especially, has acted as propaganda media for disseminating nuclear safety myths in Japan. The Japanese government, especially the Ministry of Economy, Trade and Industry (**METI**) sits in the center of this circle. A number of conservative politicians are also part of this group. Academic circles from the departments of nuclear engineering and nuclear physics in the universities play significant roles in expanding this knowledge base, advancing technologies, and educating students. Finally, we believe that some "yakuzas," Japanese underground mafia, are part of this. They recruit workers from slum areas in such large metropolises as Osaka and Tokyo. The workers are dispatched to nuclear power plants, given high-risk repair and monitoring jobs, and exposed to high-level radiation. They are often fired just before they contract fatal diseases such as leukemia and cancer. They frequently are forced to write a letter saying they will not sue the company for health damages in exchange of small amount of retirement allowances.

Nobody from this group, not even **TEPCO** managers and **METI** officers, have been charged or punished for causing the Fukushima nuclear disaster. It seems to us that they committed a crime of "willful negligence."

The nuclear conglomerate openly and strongly urges the Japanese government to allow reoperation of many existing nuclear reactors. This obsession, stubbornness, and irrationality remind us of the Japanese imperial militarism and fascism which prevailed before the end of WWII.

The International Atomic Energy Agency (**IAEA**) and the International Commission on Radiological Protection (**ICRP**) work closely together to back this up. They try to justify the "peaceful" use of nuclear technology, by inflating the benefits of nuclear energy and intentionally underestimating the risks and damages associated with nuclear energy use, including uranium mining activities.[18] They work to prohibit the military use of nuclear science and technology, except for the five acknowledged nuclear weapon-possessing nations, namely, the United States, the United Kingdom, Russia, France, and China. This symbolizes the hypocritical character of these organizations.

CONCLUSIONS

In conclusion, we thank Pope Francis for highlighting the urgent need for us to transform our economy and civilization as a whole into an "ecological civilization." The increasing recognition of the Ecological Footprint indicator in many parts of the world shows that we are moving in that direction. At the same time, however, we need to listen to the silenced voices of the victims of nuclear disasters — not only in Fukushima, but also Chernobyl and Three Mile Island, as well as such contaminated places as uranium mine sites in the Navajo Nation in the U.S., rare-earth refineries in China and Malaysia, and nuclear weapons test sites in various parts of the world.

ENDNOTES

1   W. E. Rees, "Revisiting Carrying Capacity: Area-based Indicators of Sustainability," *Population and Environment: A Journal of Interdisciplinary Studies*, Vol. 17:3 (1996): 195–215; M. Wackernagel and W. E. Rees, *Our Ecological Footprint: Reducing Human Impact on the Earth* (Gabriola Island, B.C., Canada: New Society Publishers, 1996).

2   B. Ewing, D. Moore, S. Goldfinger, A. Oursler, A. Reed, M. Wackernagel, *Ecological Footprint Atlas* (Oakland, CA: Global Footprint Network, 2010), online: http://www.footprintnetwork.org /images/ uploads/ Ecological_Footprint_Atlas_2010.pdf (accessed 15 August 2016); M. Borucke, D. Moore, G. Cranstonb, K. Graceya, K. Iha, J. Larsona, E. Lazarus, J. C. Morales, M. Wackernagel, and A. Galli, "Accounting for Demand and Supply of the Biosphere's Regenerative Capacity: The National Footprint Accounts' Underlying Methodology and Framework," *Ecological Indicators*, Vol. 24 (2013): 518–33; D. Lin, L. Hanscom, J. Martindill, M. Borucke, L. Cohen, A. Galli, E. Lazarus, G. Zokai, K. Iha, D. Eaton, M. Wackernagel, *Working Guidebook to the National Footprint Accounts: 2016 Edition* (Oakland:

Global Footprint Network, 2016), online: http://www.footprint-network.org/documents/National_Footprint_Accounts_2016_Guideook.pdf (accessed 25 August 2016.

3   Global Footprint Network, "National Footprint Account: Public Data Package (an Excel sheet)," 2016.

4   Global Footprint Network, 2016.

5   Y. Wada, "Cikyu Ikko bun no Keizai Tasse Jyokyou wo Kashikasuru Ekorojikaru Futtopurinto Shihyo (Ecological Footprint as an Indi-cator for Visualizing the Progress Toward 'One Planet Economy')," *Kankyo Kenkyu (Environmental Research)*, Vol. 152 (2009): 14–24 (in Japanese).

6   For an example, see J. Kitzes, A. Galli, M. Bagliani, J. Barrett, G. Dige, S. Ede, K.-H. Erb, S. Giljum, H. Haberl, C. Hails, S. Jung-wirth, M. Lenzen, K. Lewis, J. Loh, N. Marchettini, H. Messinger, K. Milne, R. Moles, C. Monfreda, D. Moran, K. Nakano, A. Pyhälä, W. Rees, C. Simmons, M. Wackernagel, Y. Wada, C. Walsh, T. Wiedmann, "A Research Agenda for Improving National Ecolog-ical Footprint Accounts," *Ecological Economics*, Vol. 68:7 (2009): 1991–2007; and WWF and Global Footprint Network, et al., *Living Planet Report 2014: Species and Spaces, People and Places* (Gland, Swit-zerland: WWF International 2014. https://www.wwf.or.jp/activities/lib/lpr/WWF_LPR_2014.pdf (accessed on August 10, 2016).

7   WWF Japan and Global Footprint Network. *Nihon no Ekorojikaru Futtopurinto 2015 (The Ecological Footprint for Sustainable Living in Japan).* (2015) (in Japanese and English), http://www.footprintnet-work.org/images/article_uploads/Japan_Brochure_2015_LoRes.pdf (accessed 11 August 2016.

8   A. Mombelli, "Reducing Switzerland's Carbon Footprint by 2050," SWI swiss info.ch website, posted on 11 August 2016, online: http://www.swissinfo.ch/eng/xxxxxxxxxxxxxxxxxxxxxxx_copy-of-un-economia-verde-per-salvare-il-pianeta-terra/42337308 (accessed 18 August 2016.

9   K. Iha, P. Poblete, D. Panda, S. Winkler, "A Footprint Analysis of ASEAN: Ensuring Sustainable Development in an Increasingly Resource Constrained World," *Asian Biotechnology and Development Review*, Vol. 17 (2015): 57–67.

10 Global Footprint Network and Mediterranean Ecological Footprint

Initiative, *How Can Mediterranean Societies Thrive in an Era of Decreasing Resources?* (2015), http://www.footprintnetwork.org/documents/MED_2015_English.pdf (accessed 15 August 2016.

11   UNPE-Financial Initiative and Global Footprint Network, *A New Angle on Sovereign Credit Risk E-RISC: Environmental Risk Integration in Sovereign Credit Analysis* (2012), http://www.unepfi.org/fileadmin/documents/ERISC_Phase_1.pdf.

12   H. Koide and H. Takano, *Auto obu Kontororu: Fukushima Gempatu Jiko no Amarini Kakoku na Genjitu (Out of Control: Harsh and Severe Reality of Fukushima Nuclear Accident)* (Kadensha, 2014), in Japanese.

13   H. Shiraishi, "Kajoshindan-Ron no Haigode Naniga Okite Irunoka? (What is happening behind the overdiagnosis hypothesis?)," *Kagaku (Science)*, Vol. 86:8 (2016): 783–89 (in Japanese).

14   T. Tsuda, "Kojosen Gan Deta no Bunseki Kekka (Results of Data Analysis of Thyroid Cancer)," *Kagaku (Science)*, Vol. 86:8 (2016), 797–805 (in Japanese).

15   M. Kowata, "Fukushima de Okotteiru Genjitu: Fukusihma-ken, Ookuma-machi Choukai Giin no Shogen (Reality of What is Happening in Fukushima: A Testimony of a Township Council Member of Ookuma Town, Fukushima)," an oral presentation during the annual meeting of No Nukes Asia Forum (NNAF) held in Iwaki City, Fukushima, on 24 March 2016 (in Japanese).

16   H. Nagasawa, "Irikura-Miyake Shiki Mondai to Shin Reshipi: Naze Juyo Nanoka? (Problem of Irikura-Miyake Method and an Alternative New Recipe: Why is This Important?)," an oral presentation during the Meeting for Preventing Nuclear Reactor Earthquake Disaster: Warning from Dr. Kunihiko Shimazaki, Former Vice-Chair Person of the Nuclear Regulation Authority, held at Doshisha University, Kyoto on 31 July 2016 (in Japanese).

17   K. Kobayashi, *Kokusai Genshiryoku Robi no Hanzai (Crimes of International Nuclear Robby Group)*, (Ibun-sha, 2013) (in Japanese).

18   Y. Nakagawa, *Houshasen Hibaku no Rekishi (History of Exposure to Radioactivity)*, Expanded Version (Akashi Shoten, 2011).

3

BRAZILIAN CONTRIBUTIONS TO REBUILDING

Brazilian Cases of Socio-Political and Economic Resistance

Lília Dias Marianno

ABSTRACT: *This essay contributes to the discussion of political collapse in democratic nations by offering a Brazilian perspective. It includes a historical review of Brazil's sense of itself as a nation, with its inheritance of militarism and slavery, and it presents some alternatives found by engineering students and professors.*

WHEN WE WERE CHALLENGED by John B. Cobb, Jr. in 2013 to respond to the global ecological crisis by participating in the 2015 "Seizing an Alternative" conference, we Brazilians never could have imagined how many changes in political and economic order we would experience in the following years. At the time of this writing, we are facing our worst democratic crises as an independent nation (claimed in 1822). Dr. Cobb's provocative reflection, "The Collapse of Democratic Nation States," has had the double effect of providing a gestalt of our current status and giving us some indications of positive developments and new possibilities.

I found in his speech some points that have strong applications to Brazil's case, and, in turn, some examples from our context that can enlighten this discussion. Of course, dozens of political events have happened in our country since June 2015, and we cannot predict where we are going as a nation. Right now, Brazil is, regrettably, an excellent example of a nation in democratic collapse. This chapter is thus a testimony from somebody who is in the eye of a hurricane.

The heuristic chosen[1] to take part in this colloquium has the following structure: 1) detach the "heart" of Cobb's purpose, identifying specific points where Brazilian life can contribute, 2) offer a brief historical review of Brazilian life as a nation that provides context for Brazilian insights, and 3) describe some creative ways Brazilians have found to offer some light at the "end of the tunnel." Testimony from some students and professors engaged in strategic engineering and social development offer helpful ways that political structures can contribute creative responses to the ecological crisis.

SOME OF DR. COBB'S REFLECTIONS

The *ethos* and the *pathos* of the colloquium,[2] as described by Dr. Cobb, fit the Brazilian case perfectly. What follows is a paraphrase of Cobb's opening essay to this volume.

Cobb claims, "the decay of current forms of political order may leave space for something that will, in at least some respects, be better."[3] Our conversations must lead us to the better alternatives.

Political order is a part of human life. For hundreds of thousands of years, political order was not distinct from the cultural and social orders. For a long time, political order was legitimated by the church through the imposition of the Latin language as a way to rule education. This "sovereignty" was exercised over people who identified themselves by religion and not by ethnicity. A common tongue is an expression of national feeling; it connects people to their own culture. The effort to translate the Bible into many languages made the construction of nationalism easy.

The feudal order, so natural for agricultural societies, was challenged by urbanization and trade, with the rise of towns generating centers of power. People preferred government control over larger areas, and Western civilizations formed nation-states with people participating in public decisions and pushing for democracy. The democratic nation state was an accepted norm by the end of WWI. Japan and China are also good examples of this route.

After World Wars I and II, when places still under colonial control progressively gained their independence, they faced a stark reality: the fragile linguistic distinctions and boundaries that had been imposed on them by their colonial masters made impossible the task of becoming democratic. These new nations lacked the sense of nation, of unity, that makes democracy possible.

When this national feeling is impossible, for such reasons as people of different ethnicities and languages living in the same geographic boundaries, conflicts happen and authoritarianism in government is a natural consequence. Also, in a world where American imperialism still dominates, interventions are the norm.

Even long-established democratic nations, along with the more recently formed states, may be in crisis. They are both threatened by American empire and debilitated internally by their internal leaders. U.S. goals are supported by the United Nations, and this affects the democratic health of states around the world.

The tension between economic and political agendas leads nations to borrow money for military purposes and dictatorial control. This led to the emergence of private banking, because private banks are able to create money and consequently financial dependence. This dependence significantly and directly affects the control of elections.

As the great majority of voters have little independent knowledge of those for whom they vote, they are dependent on what they learn from the mass media, which is controlled by moneyed interests. Democracy is a "fragile plant" because a large segment of the population has no experience in decision-making and also lives in small cities, on the margin of big-city power centers. Their democratic citizenry is reduced to opportunities to vote.

Transnational corporations work to undermine nation states, whether they are democratic or not. How did these concentrations of wealth with the accompanying power come into being and, especially, what was the role of money-creation in this process? The imperial power controlled by financial interests destroys democracy in the political and economic realms, law, education, culture, and society.

Global developments suggest that the growth of American empire may be ending, and that it is being forced to retreat. One can identify positive developments in those parts of the world that are not controlled by the empire and that have relative freedom from the transnational corporations. Typically, these countries have retained some control over money-creation and can therefore deal with their problems without hopeless indebtedness to private financial institutions. There are plenty of problems everywhere but, on the whole, Latin American countries, including Brazil, are displaying encouraging signs of health.

Turning now from Cobb, I examine Brazilian history, from colonialism to democratic-state, to help outsiders understand our national identity, since our reputation is sometimes reduced to the "country of football and carnival joy." Then I will end with the objective of this chapter.

THE HISTORICAL CONTEXT OF BRAZILIAN UNIQUENESS

The histories of the United States and Brazil differ at many points. The entire development of the economic perspective of both countries is very engaged with their historical identities. Brazilian history is divided in three phases: colonialism, empire, and republic.

Colonialism: the beginning of Brazilian nation life (1500)

Brazil was discovered in 1500 but "invented" as a nation just after 1808 when the king of Portugal's noble family came to live in our lands. Since 1500, we were considered a "big farm" for Portugal's exploitation. There was no development as a nation, no roads, no commerce, no significant buildings. Almost nothing was done for the progress of this big colony in its first centuries. It was a time was characterized only by exhaustive and abusive exploitation. For 300 years, we were in a stationary position of feeding our colonizer's exploitive needs.

One little known aspect about our Amerindian nations is their response to the Portuguese colonization. The Amerindians, especially the Guarani culture (the southern), were friendly with the visitors. Because the Counter-Reformation of European Catholics brought the Jesuit order to Brazil, the Brazilian Amerindians had been evangelized since 1500. As a result of this evangelization, the Amerindians believed they were offering a very good service to God by helping the king of Portugal become richer. They helped to fill European ships peacefully, without fights or resistance, almost saying "thank you for the opportunity to full your ship with my gold." In the north, the Tupi nations were less passive, and, because most of our aboriginal population is centered in the north of our country, the southern Amerindians lost their identity. It should be noted, however, that the profile of the Atlantic South Amerindian Nations is totally opposite from the Pacific South Amerindian nations. The "Pacific" struggled unto death against Spanish dominion, defending their lands, families, and indigenous sovereignty. But the Atlantic indigenous nations were assimilated, acquiescing to the invaders. In a few centuries, they were extinguished by the diseases of the white colonizers and the hard slave-work the Europeans imposed on them. Although most of the indigenous nations in Brazil were extinguished, some thousands of Amerindians remain.

When Amerindians' physical condition was found to be "too weak for the hard-job," the natives were progressively replaced by imported African slaves. The slavery in our country is a shame of our history. It persisted legally until 1889, making Brazil the last country in the world to free its slaves. That legacy is reflected in our history of jobs and economic progress. We are still struggling to achieve justice in the case of the slavery of black people in Brazil.

The only country in Americas called capital of an Empire (1808)

From our beginnings as a new country, a culture of passive spirit in the face of imperialist oppression developed as part of the Brazilian people's identity. Our people did not work hard for our own economic development, but to enrich the pockets of the richest. Portugal's king only paid attention to Brazil because his country became weak through dependence on natural resources from, and commerce with, Africa and India. When the French Revolution forced him to escape from Napoleon's power, another chapter in our history started. At this time Brazil was acclaimed an "Empire" (without being a true empire).

It was a unique experience in South America. No other country in all the Latin continent experienced the coming of a royal family to their land, transforming it into the capital of empire and changing the aesthetic of places and people. When we visit other countries in Latin America, we generally see the signs of European colonization in the architecture: big old buildings where the religious style is visible. In Brazil, besides the presence of old religious constructions, we see many signs of a royal habitation, too. Brazil was not developed economically into an empire; it was a colony that was called an empire. This masquerade accentuated the non-equal distribution of wealth. Although the empire had only had a short life (empire in 1808, independent country in 1822 and republic in 1889), it still affected the mental state of some segments in our society. This was in contrast to the U.S., which achieved success and national prosperity with its continuing "Protestant ethic and the spirit of capitalism,"[4] and to the changed thinking about jobs, employment, and worker's rights brought about by European Marxists.

This mental model of empire turned Brazil into the last country to sign an abolitionary letter. Our government kept slavery, with its immoral, nonhumanitarian practices even after the prohibition of slave commerce in the rest of the world.[5] Our people work hard, but in their social imaginary, they are working for anyone but themselves.

Advent of Republic (1889): trampled and
followed by quick political changes[6]

The establishment of a constitutional system in Brazil reveals how much change we faced in our political and economic order in a short period of time. When the leaders of our country became aware of how much the country needed to grow, and how delayed we were with our national development compared to a much younger country like the United States, the initiatives undertaken to compensate for lost time promoted too many changes and were accompanied by an immature social mind about nationality, nationalism, and economic development.

Throughout the 18th century, traditional schemes of public domain at the political, philosophical, and juridical levels were severely questioned and new forms, or ordinations, and foundations for political power were raised. These developments were a reflection of important victories in the law systems of developed countries. (In 1787, the U.S. Constitution started a new age, Constitutionalism, followed by the Universal Declaration of Human Rights in 1789 and the French Constitution in 1791).

The first constitutional letter was an imperial initiative. The young Emperor Pedro I, not interested in returning to Portugal, declared Brazilian independence on September 7th of 1822. He nominated himself as the eternal defender of Brazil. The first Brazilian Constitutional Letter sustained the monarchy as constitutional and hereditary. Legislative power was instituted with a General Assembly, Chamber of Deputies, senators, and indirect elections with representation according to provincial territories.

In 1889 the monarchy was overthrown and a transitional provisory government established by the military. Two years later the First Constitution of the Federative Republic of Brazil was validated. This document established the presidential system, the Federal State, the popular representation in the Congress, the permanent union of provinces, and a laic state.

This Constitution worked until 1930, when we had a Civil Revolution. A drastic economic breakdown and the growth of the bourgeoisie brought big changes in our system of government. Getúlio Vargas (1930–45) was installed by the military as president in 1932, and in 1934 a new Constitution was adopted, but with a strong accent of racist segregation. This constitution privileged fascist paradigms, and eugenics programs were also incentivized. While the constitution promoted some advances such as women voting (!), it also started Brazil's financial dependence upon developed countries and international banks.

Black people, who a few decades earlier were still slaves, had no autonomous social and economic life. They were restricted to the social margins, and only in the last 30 years have they had more access to superior education. The National Alliance for Freedom, a movement with strong Socialist, Communist, and Syndicalist principles, grew but was repressed and closed in 1935. All presidents with socialist principles were repressed until a new dictatorial system was installed, again with military interference. Fundamental rights were not fulfilled, and political parties were dissolved. Freedom of thought was severely repressed and censored. Strikes, torture, and many conditions of civil war grew. But, simultaneously, the biggest state companies were created to exploit oil, minerals, iron, and other natural resources.

Even with all the ascendant fascist tendencies in Brazil, in an historical paradox, our soldiers struggled admirably during WWII against Germany and Italy. In 1945 Getúlio Vargas began an attempt to meet people's needs and made many improvements. Some progress was made in favor of the nation. But then he was impeached by the military and one of them became president. After five years, the people demanded Getulio Vargas back as president (1951–54). He stood for the peoples' desires, but the military pressed and pushed him so much that he committed suicide in 1954.[7]

Some years later, politicians with socialist ideals tried to gain power with popular legitimacy, but before they succeeded, the military again took power, this time with U.S. military and financial support. (The U.S. was shaken by the possibility of Brazil becoming another "Cuba" on the Latin continent). The military coup d'état of 1963/1964[8] marks the beginning of another 30 years of dictatorial power in our country.[9] Brazil was never so dependent on American empire as during the early part of these years. I was born the next year (1965), and I would not know a Brazil relatively free of military control until I was almost 20 years old. I remember those military years as a hard time, a time of poverty and scarce resources, a time of only "national development" with no progress reflected in families' lives. Freedom of expression was censored.

Only in 1989 did Brazil begin the walk towards a real democracy. The popular movement called "Diretas Já" (direct elections for president, right now!) is a beautiful and emotionally stirring part of our history. The people, especially the poorest segments in our society, were struggling and demanding, "we want to elect our president." However, we still waited eight more years to have a real peoples' representative in the presidential chair.

The first candidate to appear who declared an intention to oppose the military and its wealthy supporters was elected, but impeached some years later. During this time, we were governed by someone who was weak and accorded power by the "right." The next president was somebody put in power who did not represent the popular segment. Finally, in the following elections, someone representing the poor people, the rustic president Lula, was elected. And he really represented the poorest in our society, around 80% of population.[10]

Lula's presidential platform for governance became famous in the whole world for improvements by means of social projects, an inclusion policy, and true goals for improving the quality of life for the poorest. He came from that segment and understood, better than others, the life of a poor person. During his governance, the level of poverty fell, and wealth grew to 50–64% for the whole population.[11]

I will not discuss current concrete growth or decline because right now we are almost in a civil war in Brazil. People have 10,000 different opinions about true social and economic development. This is reflected in violence and never-ending debates, with contributions through massive social networking on Facebook, etc. that offer a superficial and nonhistorical analysis of the true situation.

JOINING COBB'S REFLECTION WITH OUR HISTORY

1. In Brazil, the political order is not distinct from the cultural and social orders, even though we are in a postmodern age. We are a young nation compared with many other, older nations. We can only begin to understand the results of the last presidential elections (November 2014), if we realize that cultural and social aspects still definitively influence the way our people respond to politics. The devastation of our indigenous tribes, and the 400 years of slavery, literally dominate our culture and society for most of our 515 years of existence as a country. This sad part of our history affects and sometimes defines almost everything about our process of becoming one nation. These elements also affect the way Brazilians think about work, jobs, and employment relations.

2. In our case, we still do not have a "national feeling" to support a national unity. We are taking the first steps in developing a national sense about what is good and bad for us as a country. We are divided into 27 states, including our capitol. But the political division of states has small influence on the way we are constructing a "national feeling." The conception of governmental autonomy in our states is relatively poor. Social construction, especially the economic stratification of the population, has a strong influence.

The ethnic roots mixed in our veins are African, Indigenous, and Western European. But this ethnic diversity is not the same problem as seen in the U.S. and other countries with histories of strong racial conflicts. We do coexist. Cross-ethnic marriages have been normal in our history since its beginning. We don't have ethnic ghettos or closed ethnic communities in big proportions that affect the national order. Miscegenation is the best definition for who we ethnically are, and we are totally open ethnically. This strongly rooted miscegenation many times confounds us about who we really are as a nation. Miscegenation results in loose ethnic identity. While we have problems with racism, it works in different ways and with different motivation behind the scenes.

We are a nation with hundreds of aboriginal languages that are still active, but they do not represent the major Brazilian linguistic context. The great majority of our more than 193 million Brazilians,[12] despite our enormous geographical area (8.515.767 km),[13] speak Portuguese (not Spanish as many people think). Brazilian Portuguese is different from the Portuguese of Portugal due to the great number of indigenous words, different accents, and regional words, and conceptions in our vernacular practice. Our geographic area can be compared to a continent.

3. In our country we have dozens of parties, of every political inclination that can be imagined. Society is auspiciously divided into two main segments. While the minority segments have the opportunity for political representation, the power of the media carries the majority for these two main segments. The small parties could be more representative, but it is almost impossible, with this diversity, to gain representation in public opinion. We don't have one "right" side. The "right" is composed of dozens of parties. Also, we do not have a "left" side representing socialist tendencies. We have dozens of "left" parties. "Public opinion," in general, represents the opinions of owners of mass media, such communications vehicles as TV, radio, newspapers, and magazines, as Cobb claims.

4. Voting, howerver, is not a free option. Every Brazilian is obligated to vote after the age of 18 years. Brazilians cannot drive a car before age 18, but, if they want, they can vote at age 16. If a Brazilian does not vote, many aspects of his/her social life (public or private employment, a license to drive a car, social security, a passport, etc.) will be blocked. The non-exercise of our "right to vote" blocks almost everything we do as a citizen. This is almost a mockery of the true sense of liberty, but it is our reality. Many people don't like this obligation because it was created by the dictatorial military system. It has been present during our last 150 years as a republic, ever since we began to understand Brazil as a country.

5. For the last 15 months, I have observed my own people like a satellite, orbiting slowly around the nation, distancing myself from the

problem and seeking a more accurate/provocative perspective. I was trying to get a perspective less involved with the political conflicts we are facing now, when factions from the right are fighting to impeach the elected president, rather than allowing her to continue to govern.*

I cannot say the big corporations have total control of our economy. Our economy does not work as it does in the U.S. Maybe we abused Keynes' theory when we proposed a regulatory role for the state. In Brazil, the state has too much control over regulatory aspects of our economy. We have two federal banks (Banco do Brasil and Caixa Econômica Federal) for normal use by the people. In the past we had state banks, too. Each State of the Federation had its own public bank, but this system is not working anymore.

Banco do Brasil is a normal trade bank that controls exchange/cambial policy and interest taxes. Caixa Econômica Federal also works as a regulatory agency, but is focused on housing finance policies, hypothecation, and housing development.

We also have BNDS—National Bank of Social Developing, which works to finance agriculture and private entrepreneurs. All of these examples are public banks. They rule the behavior of the private banks.

One example: five years ago, when Dilma Roussef wanted to rule the economy with a stronger hand, she ordered the public banks to lower interest taxes. All private banks had to lower their taxes, too, because people were running to close their accounts in private banks to gain the benefit from the public banks. As result, every bank lowered interest taxes, and people in debt ran to the banks to pay off their debts (of course, we were not in a large economic crisis).

The biggest corporations that affect our economic balance are the

*NOTE: In 2018, the opposition prevailed by impeaching Dilma Rousseff. She was removed from the presidency. Also, ex-President Lula is actually in jail in order to prevent him from running for president. He has more than 50% of the intentions to vote. To understand the political coup and the context watch the President Dilma Roussef conference on Berkeley University, California, USA on April 17, 2018 with English subtitles available: https://www.youtube.com/watch?v=Q6o3PakCOg4&t=233s, or https://www.youtube.com/watch?v=Q6o3PakCOg4&t=495s.

originally state companies like Petrobras (our producer of oil and gas), Vale do Rio Doce (our mine producer), or Furnas (our producer of electric and nuclear energy), and those companies contracted by them.

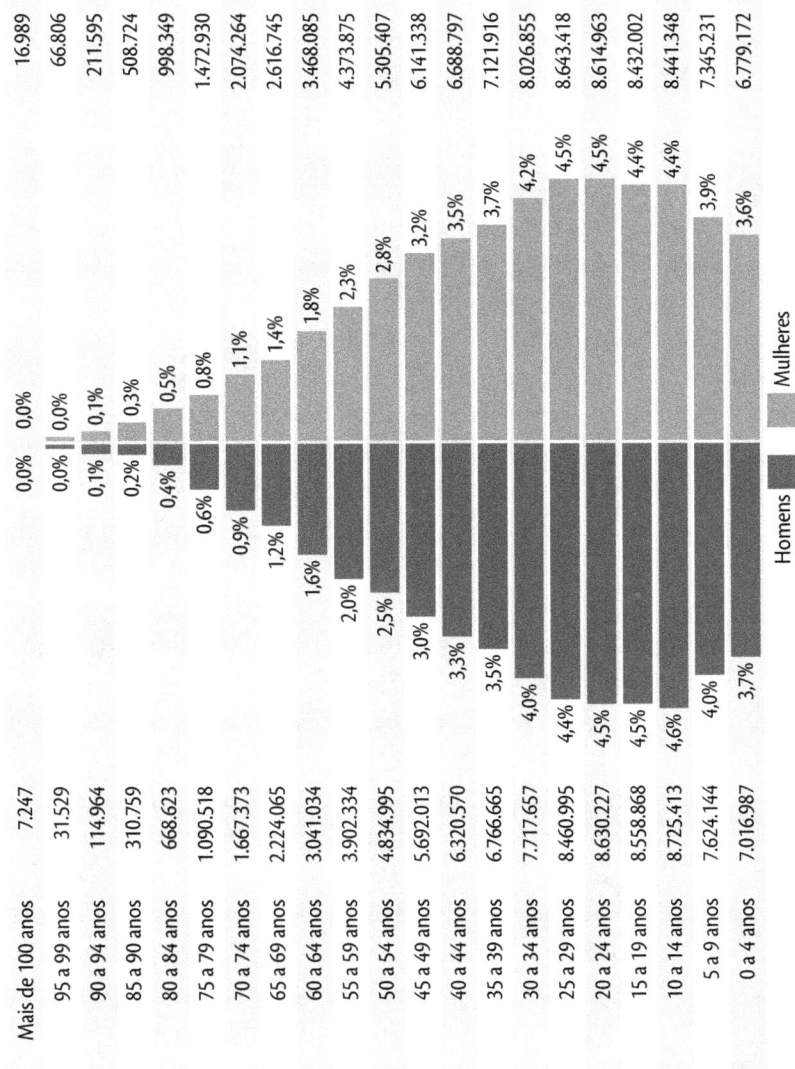

Figure 1: Percentage of economy contributed by men (homens) and women (mulheres), by age (anos). Sinopse dos resultados do censo de 2010, Instituto Brasileiro de Geografia e Estatística.

This can be illustrated by the presidential decision to increase taxes on the electric energy supply. Since the levels of water reserves for generating electricity were low, the president ordered a "red flag,"—a sizeable tax increase on an energy supply that was already taxed. In one month, we were paying 100% more than the month before. When the Brazilian government regulates, the population generally feels abused because, unlike the previous example, the government typically adds taxes to already-established taxes. So, if the big corporations don't dominate our economy, but the public administration controls everything in this area, in whose hands is the power of our economy?

6. A significant part of our economy comes from youth and women entrepreneurs (Figure 1).[14] Research into the evolution of entrepreneurship in Brazil by Global Entrepreneurship Monitor (GEM), with the participation of the London Business School and Babson College, shows this. The number of small companies with less than three months of activity grew 97% from 2008 to 2012. In 2008, just 2.93% of the adult population were owners of their own enterprises. Fifty-two percent of these new entrepreneurs in 2012 were between the ages of 18 and 34.[15] These changes have much to do with the age of our active population. In Brazil the life expectancy is ascending, but we still are dominated by a youth population and by the zeitgeist that rules their behavior. Our economic and political maturity is significantly affected by the age of the majority of our citizens.[16]

7. Right now, public opinion and participation play important roles in Brazil. We are in the midst of the most representative, democratic age in our history and also in our worst crisis. We did not come from a feudal constitution like most Western nation states, but from a colonial constitution. In fact, we are in a postcolonial era, and our significant jump from colonialism to postcolonialism happened without any transitional period of empire; it just happened in the title of the country.

The Brazilian government and the whole nation have never had the intention of being a country with political or economic power over other nations. Perhaps our long history as a colony has interfered with any possibility of gaining power over other nations. When we make an economic decision to help another country, the decision is shaped by identification, partnership, and cooperation rather than by domination. We were dominated by another nation and that is too hard a condition for any nation.

The United States has never been politically controlled by other countries. I suspect this is one aspect contributing to the passivity of a significant number of American people in accepting the imperialistic decisions about other countries made by the U.S. government. But I am not sure that the U.S. will never be dominated by another economic world power. Only history will tell us.

INTERLUDE: SOME BRIEF REFLECTIONS

President Dilma Roussef was re-elected by the people in 2014 to continue developing the country. She belongs to the same party as President Lula, and many Brazilian supposed she could accomplish the same "social improvement" of the country. But her actions as president have been affected by the economic scandals involving state companies, and by members of her party involved in these scandals. In fact, it is a hard time. It is very difficult to diagnose what is true in this moment.

Brazil is in crisis. The social-political and economic order has collapsed. The Internal National Production in recent years is more negative than it has ever been. We are exporting less than importing. We faced absurd levels of inflation during the military government (1964–89). We have almost returned to that status. If people try to compensate by buying fewer expensive products from other countries, the monetary exchange overtaxes each coin spent in foreign countries, especially in the United States. This decision on exchange policy was an attempt to balance trade. But in this crazy economy, big corporations, which provide employment for hundreds of thousands of civilians, are leaving our country. My job is in the capital, in oil and gas production, and the financial crises in that city are bigger than in any other city of the country. A true, good democratic government needs to equilibrate all aspects involved. Social projects are important and necessary, but without money being generated by the productive sectors, who can feed the poor or those without jobs? The economy is not working well in our country right now.

The exercise of a satisfactory democracy, which our people hoped would happen when the military was no longer in power, is affected by the immaturity of an young country that still has not learned how to self-manage. Young nations suffer a lot, trying to free themselves from the moral-social-economic and political inheritance of colonization, slavery, and military autocracy. The legacy is too big. Only countries that have lived under colonialism can understand the problem of the "national body" that I am talking about. This situation leads us to question the meaning of democracy for a country that still has not learned the deepest implications of this practice for human life.

What follows is a list of some aspects that I find crucial if a nation is to truly "seize" the alternative offered by this conference.

s an exercise; it is a learning. Nations need time to learn it. As Cobb has said, democracy is a fragile plant. It needs to be nourished, especially in those countries dominated by big empires in the colonial system of the past. The United States and several other world economic powers never experienced so great a degree of domination.

2. Democracy also requires more time to be learned in countries that existed under military dictatorships for a long time. People who were repressed every time they tried to lift their voices need time for learning to walk with autonomy and making the right political decisions. We faced both: colonialism and military dictatorships. We are learning! And I am proud of my people because we are learning it very quickly. We are compensating for hundreds of years of colonization and military dictatorships with a growing autonomy.

3. Brazil is famous for football (soccer) and carnival. We have an expression about soccer games, and also in samba, called *gingado*. The *ginga* is a movement of the body that people do that looks like a

type of dance inspired by African and Indigenous peoples, our biggest ethnic groups. *Ginga* is very typical in Capoeira (Brazilian martial art) and in our native dances. We are descendents of Indians and Africans. For us, *ginga* is survival. Many people criticize Brazilians because we always try to do things our own way, by breaking the rules. But rule-breaking became our survival. There is no other way to resist military dictators. It was our resistance. It is not a way developed with the objective of taking advantage of others, as some people think. All our cultural statements have a long historical construction behind them. Our *ginga*, our ability to be creative, to make new realities from catastrophe; our resilience, our persistence, our way to believe that some better day without evil is coming, and that we just need to survive until then — that is our inheritance from our Guaranis nations.[17]

4. *Ginga* pushed us to do for our people things the governors never did. We never waited for governors to start social initiatives and projects such as environmental projects. These initiatives came from the grass roots in Brazil. In fact, governors in Brazil learned to work with the margins of our society because it was the churches and hundreds of nonprofit organizations (NGOs) that started projects and achieved very good results.

5. In 1992 the United Nations conference called Eco-92 was hosted in our country, in my city of Rio de Janeiro. Twenty years later we got a followup of that conference (Rio +20). Since 1992, Brazil has started to change minds about environmental questions. Many people have no idea how much Brazil has been seizing alternatives through thousands of nonprofit organizations responding to questions of social responsibility (based on ISO 26000) and environmental topics (based in ISO 9000 series).[18]

CREATIVE ALTERNATIVES MADE IN BRAZIL

To prepare this paper, I spoke with dozens of people for a year and a half. I listened to them, seeking to understand their vision, questioning obscure aspects, and asking for good alternatives that would exemplify what Brazil can contribute to rebuilding after ecological collapse. Among several alternatives, I found some that I would like to share. All of these alternatives came from poor people. They are the *"ginga"* in action, in its purest significance and color.

1. When public education does not teach children how
to be inclusive, the children invent alternatives and
involve big corporations in those alternatives.

A project where I am particularly involved is in the field of robotics, which is promoted by FLL (FIRST Lego League). FIRST means *For Inspiration and Recognition of Science and Technology*. This is a non-profit program for youths from 9 to 14 years . It is available in many countries including Brazil, as well as in the U.S. and Canada. The objective of this project is to celebrate the sciences and technology among youth, using real social needs arising from their contexts and backgrounds. A theme, related to the sciences and the international community, is proposed by FIRST, then an international competition is promoted with those themes. The themes of 2014 and 2015 were, respectively, education and trash track (reverse logistic and residual recycling).[19]

In the competition, children are challenged to use the principles of engineering to create a robot out of materials developed by Massachusetts Institute of Technology, in partnership with LEGO Mindstorms. The challenge is to develop several tasks inside the chosen theme for that year. The youth are challenged to innovate with ideas and solutions for the problems from their own contexts using the ludic as a resource of learning and innovation.

This project has been given the name *Robotic in the Schools #inovareaprender* for public schools on Macaé County, Rio de Janeiro State, Brazil. The city places enormous demands on environmental and social request topics. It is an important scene for global production of oil and gas, and powerful corporations in subsea oil exploitation are based there. The city is called the Brazilian Capital of Oil, and it hosts one of the biggest expositions of the world (Brazil Offshore).[20]

The corporations have a great power to transform reality around them when they take seriously their social responsibility.

For the 2014 FIRST Championship, ten of Macaé's public schools (public schools in Brazil are education for the poorest children) sent teams, and four of them received prizes. The theme that year was education, and one winning robotic project was created by a 9-year-old child concerned with the problems of two of his classmates. Because they were poor, their families had no money to send these boys with dyslexia to a special school. They had to enroll in normal classes, causing a lot of difficulties in learning. Their classmates, concerned about their needs, developed a robotic project (the size of glove) with special light sensors to help people with dyslexia, and also the blind, to read. Another winner in this competition was a child who, using robotics, created a prototype for a special wheelchair for a girl with a pathogenic disease named Lobstein Disease (imperfect osteogenesis) or Crystal Bones Disease. It is important to note that both ideas came from poor children in public schools, from a rural zone of a city recognized as the main producer of oil and gas. Who motivated these children to create things to make life easier for their student colleagues? In the another competition, they won the national championship again! One of the students also created a selective collector of trash for recyclables in poor communities. This is *ginga*.

2. When the banks are a problem, we create new money.

A city in the northwest part of the country, very far from cosmopolitan resources, faced a serious problem in trading its agricultural produce. They had no banks in the city, so there was not enough money in circulation to pay for them. In the poorest parts of our country, there are more than 5,000 cities with no banks, no automated sources of cash, and no other organization where they can get money. In this situation, even receiving a monthly salary is a problem. Here's what the city's residents did. First, they created a city council to support the common economy. This council was formed by ordinary citizens. Then they created their own money! They called this alternative money "Cocal."[21] This solved the problem of inadequate distribution of money, it supported their economy, and it also served to develop social projects and social benefits for those who needed more.

Cocal is not the only example. A similar solution was adopted by the citizens of Maricá County. They developed a community bank and a new money called Mumbuca.[22] The names Maricá, Cocal, and Mumbuca are indigenous names. These and other indigenous terms were assimilated into the Brazilian Portuguese vocabulary, and are not present in Portuguese dictionaries. Such terms are the fruit of Guarani influence in our lives. Five years ago there were just 51 communitarian banks in the whole country. As of December 2014, there were 104. People create their own bank and their own money. This is *ginga!*

3. When big corporations do not respect the people who live around them, we stop their operations.

Since the Seizing an Alternative conference in June 2015, a big ecological catastrophe happened in Brazil in Minas Gerais, one of our inner states. In November 2015, two dikes built by Samarco, a mining company, collapsed and spilled over the whole city of Mariana. The water was contaminated with heavy metal, mud, and solid residues. This and all the rest of the mining trash flowed into the Gualaxo river. More than 100 houses were destroyed and more than one dozen people died. The damage from all that water, including metals, bricks, and mud, covered more than 60 km and destroyed the water supply for six cities. The waste ran for more than 10 thousand square km, crossing two states.

In the first city, Mariana, a small city, the damage was comparable to a hurricane and estimated at about 100 million Brazilian reais. Samarco was justly punished with a fine. Their directors said, "there is nothing toxic in the water," but 62 million cubic meters of iron mine waste were delivered with the mud. The company that manages the sewage system said that the index of iron in the water was 1.366.666 percent, which is one million and three hundred thousand percent over the highest level of tolerance. Manganese exceeded the tolerance level by 118.000 percent, and aluminum exceeded tolerance by 645.000 percent. It is impossible to make the water safe for Mariana's citizens to drink.

The cities will never recover, and some scientists say the environment will take centuries to be rid of all of contaminants. The mud spread through the states of Minas Gerais and Espírito Santo and flowed into the ocean. Animals dependent on the water died from asphyxia.[23]

The tragedy is bigger. Samarco is not a privately held company. Fifty percent of the of the bank share is owned by the State Minery Vale do Rio Doce, associated with BHP Billiton. Vale do Rio Doce, already identified as a public company, belongs to Brazilian Public System of corporations. A state company!

Who is doing the "*ginga*" in this case? The rest of our aboriginal people! Those who are almost extinguished. They are the storytellers of "The Death of the Sweet River." The Krenak tribe put cement and concrete on the railway to stop the mining activity. They cry for the death of the river.[24] Only the aboriginal people can feel how serious their loss is and how it affects their culture, their story, and their lives.[25] The Krenak are demanding responsibility for this ecological catastrophe in their own way. This is *ginga*.[26]

These examples provide alternatives to the ecological crisis. These solutions did not come from powerful people, or even from scientists. They came from the community, from the society, from the base, from families, children, and Indians. This is *ginga*.

Sergio Sismondo says,

> A society that has accepted modern technology finds itself on a path of increasing scientists and engineers who are always members of communities, trained into the practices of those communities and necessarily working with them. These communities set standards for inquiry and evaluate knowledge claims. There is no abstract and logical scientific method apart from evolving community norms. . . . claims about the

social construction of knowledge leave no role for the material world to play in the making of knowledge about it.[27]

In my job we used to say, "engineering is trial and fail." The most perfect engineering project is not excused from failures. The most ideal solutions are not exempt from risk or surprises on the way. As a nation, we are engineering for our future, and we are also learning to be democratic and take responsibility for our votes. True development is what contributes to the common good and to the common wealth. My hope is for *ginga* to teach us, and to teach any nation open to learning it, to hear the ways of the ancestors in the preservation of life. The ancestors inspire our engineering, and they inspire our nation.

ENDNOTES

1   I borrow heuristic as an engineering concept, as a method to solve engineering problems, because I am convinced we are reinventing ourselves as a nation. This method is proposed by Billy Koen, *Discussion of The Method: Conduction the Engineer's Approach to Problem Solving* (New York: Oxford, 2003).

2   Referencing Mortimer Adler's structure in his *How To Speak, How To Listen* (New York: MacMillan, London: Collier, 1983).

3   For this and following references to Dr. Cobb, see the introductory essay in this collection.

4   This is the Portuguese title of Max Weber's book. His approach to jobs, economical development, and religion was contrary to the understanding of work proposed by Karl Marx.

5   This historical context has contemporary significance. Organizational management researchers in Brazil are busy seeking to understand how this scar in our history affects everything related to work and how much of Brazilian worker behavior on the job is affected by it. These studies are recognizing that Brazilians were obligated to work too hard all the time. Workers compare their situation to slave labor, working for anybody other than themselves and with punishment by their "owners." The slaves worked hard! And they never could progress in their life even by working hard. Since organizational psychologists (joined by sociologists and anthropologists) discovered

this important collective imaginary about work in our culture, they have considered alternative methods for motivation, conflict-management, lifestyle/personal improvement, and class mobility. This symbolism of work in our culture also explains why Marxist ideas were never successful in Brazil, and why they still struggle to be accepted. In my classes for industrial engineering students, I face the problem daily. A better discussion about this perspective was established by Lívia de Oliveira Borges and Oswaldo H. Yamamoto, *Construção histórica e desafios contemporâneos,* in José Carlos Zanelli, et al., *Psicologia, Organizações e Trabalho no Brasil,* 2nd ed. (Porto Alegre: Artmed, 2014), 25–73. Also see Edgard Decca, *O nascimento das fábricas* (São Paulo: Brasiliense, [n.d.]).

6   This summary of constitutional development in Brazil was done in dialogue with Pedro Lenza, *Direito Constitucional Esquematizado,* 16th ed. Revista, atualizada e ampliada (São Paulo: Saraiva, 2012), 100–31.

7   A full documentary about Era Vargas, "Getúlio (Vargas) do Brasil: vida e obra política" is available at https://www.youtube.com/watch?v=Ekj-zmB7sY8.

8   For a documentary about the dictatorial revolution of 1964 and United States interference, see Flavio Tavares, "O dia que durou 21 anos" at https://www.youtube.com/watch?v=U9igtFREBY0. Some parts are in English.

9   Regarding that time, see my introductory text: Lília Marianno, "Apresentação ao texto de Milton Schwantes, Igreja como povo: 'Meu Povo em Miquéias'" in *Milton Schwantes: escritos de história e paixão,* ed. Nancy Cardoso Pereira (São Leopoldo: CEBI, 2012), 65–69.

10   Some statistics say the line of poverty in Brazil 20 years ago extended over 90% of population.

11   For this information see http://politica.estadao.com.br/noticias/geral,indice-de-pobreza-no-brasil-cai-50-em-oito-anos,714372. The public organization Fundação Getulio Vargas controls the economic index in our country.

12   Brazilian population in 2012, http://g1.globo.com/politica/noticia/2013/08/populacao-brasileira-ultrapassa-200-milhoes-de-habitantes-diz-ibge.html.

13 Brazilian Geographic Area(Brazilian Institute of Geography and Statistic), http://www.ibge.gov.br/home/geociencias/cartografia/default_territ_area.shtm.

14 Sinopse dos resultados do censo de 2010. Brasília: Instituto Brasileiro de Geografia e Estatística — Federal Report, http://vamoscontar.ibge.gov.br/atividades/ensino-fundamental-6-ao-9/49-piramide-e-taria. Acessed 31/05/2016. In the graph, the left side represents the men and the right side represents the women. The numbers on the left represent the age of population, and on the right side, how much of the population is counted in that percent.

15 See the complete report at http://www.sebrae.com.br/Sebrae/Portal%20Sebrae/Anexos/GEM%20Nacional%20-%20web.pdf.

16 Pirâmide etária do Brasil, http://populationpyramid.net/pt/brasil/2015/ accessed June 2015.

17 See the presentation by Dr. Claudio Carvalhaes, "The ritual of World's End of Guaranis Nations," presented in Section VII, Track 6: The contributions of indigenous wisdom, in the 10th International Whitehead Conference: Seizing an Alternative: Toward an ecological civilization.

18 Wonderful examples were presented at the Seizing an Alternative conference by Dr. Lourdes Brazil Argueta, "Building Paths for Sustainability in the Conleste Region: Children's Contributions," in Section V, Track 6: Birth-pangs of Ecological Civilization.

19 For further details about FIRST LEGO LEAGUE, see https://pt.wikipedia.org/wiki/First_Lego_League.

20 County of Macaé (https://pt.wikipedia.org/wiki/Maca%C3%A9) is a city in the north of the state of Rio de Janeiro surrounded by oil production. With 200,000 inhabitants, the original population is very poor and faces astronomic environmental demands. Processes of public management in Macaé have been transformed by sustainable politics, procedures, actions, and rules. Odebrecht Ambiental was hired to build the sustainable sewage system for the whole city, a project for the next 30 years covering the whole extended area of 1,215,904 square km. Until now only 1/5 part has been completed. The project, titled "Trash Track," is in a city where the most important rivers still catch the trash of houses without sewage systems. It is really too big to be put in

practice by children of the same poor families of the city. The story about Macaé's children taking part in the FIRST Championship is available at http://www.macae.rj.gov.br/noticias/leitura/noticia/ projeto-de-iniciacao-a-robotica-contara-com-espaco-especifico.

21 See: "Alternative Money in São João do Arraial. Communitary agency creates their own money" at http://g1.globo.com/pi/piaui/ noticia/2014/02/sem-agencia-bancaria-cidade-do-piaui-cria-banco-local-e-moeda-propria.html.

22 See: http://g1.globo.com/rj/regiao-dos-lagos/noticia/2014/04/para-diminuir-pobreza-marica-no-rj-cria-1-moeda-social-eletronica-do-pais.html.

23 Some reports about this accident can be found at Belo Monte Dossier, https://www.socioambiental.org/pt-br and http://meexplica. com/2015/11/entenda-a-tragedia-de-mariana-em-minas-gerais/.

24 https://noticias.uol.com.br/cotidiano/ultimas-noticias/2015/11/19/ indios-lamentam-tragedia-em-mg-o-rio-doce-sabia-que-ia-ser-morto.htm. See also https://www.youtube.com/watch?v=RVnf3Ap-7guQ; or the same documentary divided in 3 episodes (playlist) https://www.youtube.com/watch?v=IKkjWR6nuLE&list=PL23Phn-nJ3sbGfLzqt1D5PliRxo62180ef.

25 For the way Krenak life was affected by the Mariana tragedy, see https://www.youtube.com/watch?v=hU2EBsefgMo.

26 Federal statistics have registered that the Brazilian aboriginal nations are growing in the last decades. In 1991 they were estimated at 200,000 people. In 2001 they were registered at 734,000 people. The public administration considers this to be the result of public policy for race and gender implemented by the federal government in the last decades. (We call it the "Identity Affirmation Policy.") The policy is causing more Indian descendants to identify themselves as such in urban spheres. In Brazil, different from the U.S., Indians are not only "protected people" by public policy, but they are privileged citizens. They have privilege with quotas for study in universities; they are also owners of their protected lands. They can demand a tribute from each Brazilian who wants to travel through their lands, if they choose. See special studies in O Brazil Indígena. (Brazilian Institute for Geography and Statistic) http://indigenas. ibge.gov.br/estudos-especiais-3/o-brasil-indigena.

27 Sergio Sismondo, *An Introduction to Science and Technology Studies*, 2nd ed. (Blackwell: Malden, MA, 2010), 11.

4

GREECE AND THE GLOBAL DEBT CRISIS

Thomas H. Greco, Jr.

ABSTRACT: *The Greek debt crisis is emblematic of a more general, decades-long pattern of economic exploitation and reactionary politics that threatens not only the European Union but the stability of the global financial infrastructure and Western democratic civilization. The situation calls for a different form of globalization, not one that is dominated by transnational banks and corporations, but one that is built upon local self-determination and self-reliance, and based on local and domestic control of money, credit, and finance. Greece (and other debtor countries) can recover a measure of sovereignty and rebuild its economy by combining "debt triage" with public and private actions for creating domestic liquidity.*

IN THE SUMMER OF 1977, I first ventured abroad from North America on a journey to explore ancient civilizations, cultures, and religions, and to experience contemporary life in Egypt, Israel, and Greece. During my six-week odyssey, I was able to visit the Pyramids, amble over the Holy Land, and visit the temple ruins of Athens and Delphi.

65

At one point while in Cairo I came upon a scene that greatly troubled me. There was a small burro hitched to an enormous cart that was laden to the hilt with onions. I felt nauseous as I watched the poor animal lying on its side being flogged by a man in a vain effort to rouse it to the task of moving what seemed to be an impossible load. As a stranger in a strange land, I felt helpless to intervene and quickly moved away. I often wonder what might have been the ultimate outcome, but in my imagination I see the man with the whip standing over the lifeless body of that animal lying in the street, and weeping in worry and frustration.

THE GREEK PREDICAMENT

Now, when I contemplate Greece's current predicament, that image comes to mind. I see Greece as that beaten and dying animal, overburdened with debt that is beyond its capacity to service, and being flogged by its creditors in a vain attempt to get it to pay up. In my mind's eye I see a future in which the dead carcass of Greece is being carved up and distributed amongst the creditor institutions. In actuality, Greece will survive, but under new (foreign) management, as she is forced to sell off her assets at fire-sale prices.

In the eyes of the Germans and other creditors, represented by the so-called "troika" institutions (the European Commission, the European Central Bank, and the International Monetary Fund), the Greek people are lazy freeloaders who have been living "high on the hog" at their expense, and who now balk at repaying what they borrowed. But there is another side to the story that paints a different picture, and, even if there is a bit of truth in that characterization, what is there to be gained by creditors insisting upon their "pound of flesh"? As civilization has advanced, debtor prisons have been eliminated and bankruptcy laws have been instituted to protect people and companies from creditors who insist upon collecting more than debtors, for whatever reason, are able to pay. Why can't nations be afforded the same considerations?

First of all, it was not the Greek people who did the borrowing, it was a series of Greek governments that were either corrupted, coerced, or seduced into taking on a series of debts that were increasingly burdensome. Greece was lured into the debt trap from which it seems impossible to escape. Ellen Brown has summarized in her article, *The Greek Coup: Liquidity as a Weapon of Coercion*, some of the many moves that were made to ensnare the Greek government, and by extension, the Greek people.[1]

- The 2001 Goldman Sachs derivatives scheme, which doubled the nation's debt by 2005.

- The 2008 bank-induced credit crisis; in which the Greek government was forced by the ECB to bail out its insolvent private banks.

- The 2009 intentional criminal overstatement of Greece's debt by a Eurostat, which triggered the first bailout and accompanying austerity measures.

- The Greek prime minister replaced with an unelected technocrat, former governor of the Bank of Greece and later vice president of the ECB, who refused a debt restructuring and oversaw a second massive bailout (90% of which went to the banks) plus further austerity measures.

- December 2014, Goldman Sachs warns that central bank liquidity could be cut off if the Syriza Party were elected.

- When it was elected in January, the ECB made good on the threat, cutting bank liquidity to a trickle.

- When Prime Minister Tsipras called a public referendum in July at which the voters rejected the brutal austerity being imposed on them, the ECB shuttered the banks.

- The new bailout agreement being worked out forces the Greek government to surrender its public assets to the same private interests that caused the crisis.

And where has all the bailout money gone? A recent academic study from the European School of Management and Technology highlights the utter futility of the bailout programs in pulling Greece

out of the quagmire of debt bondage and economic depression. The
report concludes:

> This paper provides a descriptive analysis of where the Greek
> bailout money went since 2010 and finds that, contrary to
> widely held beliefs, less than €10 billion or a fraction of less
> than 5% of the overall programme went to the Greek fiscal
> budget. In contrast, the vast majority of the money went to
> existing creditors in the form of debt repayments and interest
> payments. The resulting risk transfer from the private to the
> public sector and the subsequent risk transfer within the
> public sector from international organizations such as the
> ECB and the IMF to European rescue mechanisms such as
> the ESM still constitute the most important challenge for
> the goal to achieve a sustainable fiscal situation in Greece.[2]

Much of the early Goldman Sachs involvement was aimed at
helping Greece to appear qualified, when it was not, to enter the Euro
currency union. Strong eurocentric sentiments and frustration over
inflation of the drachma made adoption of the euro currency popular
amongst the Greek people. But investigative reporter Greg Palast,
with Michael Nevradakis, has made some compelling arguments that,
"the euro itself . . . is the virus responsible for Greece's economic ills,"
and that "The imposition of the euro had one true goal: to end the
European welfare state."[3]

If that be the case, then it is not Greece alone that has been a
target. Palast and Nevradakis continue, pointing out, "Each Eurozone
nation, unable to control neither the value of its own currency, nor
its own budget, nor its own fiscal policy, could only compete for
business by slashing regulations and taxes."

Whether that was the intention or not, Greece's participation in
the euro currency union makes it almost impossible for it to correct
its trade deficits vis-à-vis the other countries in the eurozone. It can
be argued that, in real terms, Germany and other eurozone countries
have been able to buy Greek goods and services at bargain prices,
while selling their own products to Greeks at a premium.

But the crisis in Greece is only a symptom of a far more pervasive illness, one that is global and affects every nation and every individual in the world. We are presently experiencing a contest for sovereignty between the advocates of "government by the people" on one side, and on the other the elite global cabal that has for a long time been driving the world toward a neo-feudal "new world order," a cabal whose power is based on their control of the machinery of money, banking, and finance (Figure 1). They have created an interest-based, debt-money system in which debts will always increase faster than the supply of money that is available to pay them. This *debt-growth imperative* puts debtors collectively in an impossible situation. This system is therefore illegitimate, immoral, and illegal.

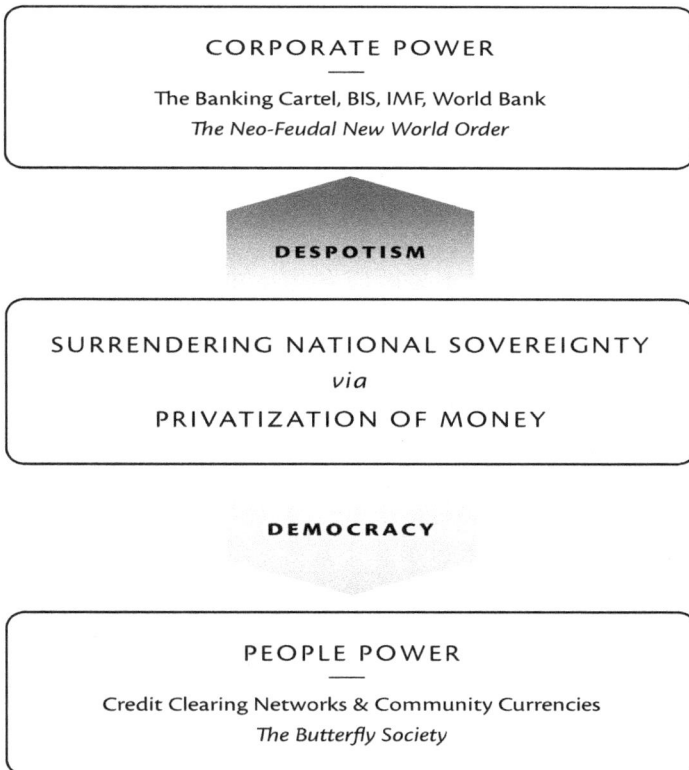

CORPORATE POWER
––
The Banking Cartel, BIS, IMF, World Bank
The Neo-Feudal New World Order

DESPOTISM

SURRENDERING NATIONAL SOVEREIGNTY
via
PRIVATIZATION OF MONEY

DEMOCRACY

PEOPLE POWER
––
Credit Clearing Networks & Community Currencies
The Butterfly Society

Figure 1: Surrendering National Sovereignty via Privatization of Money, Thomas H. Greco

Their control over the creation of money and the allocation of credit has enabled those few at the top of the banking/corporate pyramid to control politics worldwide and to push through a succession of tax cuts and treaties that, in the name of economic growth and "free trade," have caused governments to cede ever more power into the hands of this banking and corporate elite. In light of that, it is clear that democratic government is in grave danger, not only in Greece, but everywhere in the world.

In sum, the dimensions of the current predicament of Greece (and other debtor countries) include a staggering debt burden, declining economic output, high unemployment, an adverse balance of trade, imposed austerity, and loss of sovereignty. Greece has, in effect, with the help of the IMF, become an internal colony of the European Commission and banking establishment.

THE GREEK MILIEU

Over the past few years I have visited Greece several times, worked with some innovative grassroots initiatives, and consulted a number of different authors in an effort to understand not only the genesis and dimensions of the Greek debt crisis, but also the Greek culture and mentality. As is usually the case, the views of different authors often conflict. The best I can do is to list some of their assertions and advise the reader to draw their own conclusions. A comprehensive SWOT[4] analysis is beyond the scope of the chapter, but I will highlight a few of the factors that appear to be significant.

According to Aristos Doxiadis,[5] Greeks tend to be individualistic or *familistic*, "neither obedient nor cooperative, possess a zero-sum mentality, and have a sense of entitlement." He argues that rebuilding the Greek economy will require creative interaction with the underlying realities of Greek society: the family, the small business, and the habits of rentocracy and of low-trust opportunism.

Nikos Tsafos, who according to some of my Greek friends is overly critical and not up to date, lists the following as problems in his book, *Beyond Debt.*[6]

- An inefficient civil service
- Pension inequities
- Corruption and cronyism
- Tax evasion
- Inhospitable business environment
- Over-regulation of small business sector
- Inflexible employment
- Lack of competitiveness
- Unreliable statistics

But it seems to me that some of what these authors see as disadvantages are actually strengths. The Greeks have a number of advantages that make them resilient and will enable them to resist exploitation and eventually reclaim their sovereignty. Here are some of them:

- Small, family-owned business is still the mode in Greece.
- Small-scale, dispersed ownership of land and business, especially in agriculture and tourism.
- 57% of employed Greeks are either self-employed or employed in firms of under 10 workers.
- Self-employment, micro-employment, and family business are stable and fundamental institutions that provide multiple sources of income and a fallback occupation even for highly educated Greeks.
- Family solidarity provides for income sharing.
- Families invest heavily in real estate and education.
- There has been a low level of foreign investment, which means that absentee ownership has been minimal. (Unfortunately this is changing as the government is forced to sell off its assets to

satisfy the conditions of the bailout, and banks restrict the flow
of credit to small enterprises).

PRESCRIPTIONS FOR GREECE AND OTHER DEBTOR COUNTRIES

Now that we recognize the elite agenda and the true nature of the
political currencies that are being used to beat governments and peoples into submission, it is clear that we must find ways to:

1. disencumber ourselves of obligations that have been fraud-
    ulently imposed on us,

2. reduce our dependence on those systems and structures that
    disempower and exploit us, and

3. build functional alternatives that serve the common good.

Here are the steps that will eventually need to be taken by Greece
and others that find themselves in a similar predicament.

1. *Respite*

Delay debt repayment and freeze the amount owed (no
further accrual of interest).

2. *Reduction*

Renegotiate the amount to be paid to creditors. Select which
creditors to be paid in full and which to be paid in part or
not at all.

3. *Recovery and Restructuring*

Develop a long-term strategy for rebuilding the local and
domestic economies and democratic governments.

Greece and its creditors need to recognize the fact that *the
Greek government is insolvent* and needs to be relieved of its crushing
debt burden, while at the same time the Greek leadership needs to
develop a long-range plan for rebuilding the Greek economy and

stabilizing and balancing its budget in a way that assures it will not again fall into the same morass of problems. What might that plan look like?

First, the Greek government must push its creditors to relieve it of a big portion of its debt burden to stabilize the situation and give the Greek economy a chance to recover; second, the economy must be rebuilt from the bottom up in a way that will make it more robust, sustainable, and even "anti-fragile."[7] That means reducing dependence upon foreign capital and export markets, and increasing reliance upon internal resources.

Such a plan must be worked out with input and participation from the widest possible range of interests, including municipal governments, small and medium sized businesses, labor organizations, and the nonprofit sector, as well as corporate business, but the national government should make a commitment to do the following:

1. Eliminate impediments to self-help initiatives and local community self-reliance, giving municipalities greater autonomy.

2. Support entrepreneurship and small business. This may take the form of small business incubators and co-working spaces, plus reducing or eliminating burdensome regulations and taxes.

3. Encourage investment in domestic enterprises and infrastructure.

4. And most importantly, support the emergence of supplemental sources of home-grown liquidity, i.e., credit clearing exchanges and private and community currencies that are spent into circulation by trusted domestic producers of goods and services that are in everyday demand.

DEBT TRIAGE

With regard to its debts, the government needs to find respite and relief. As in a corporate bankruptcy, all debts must be frozen with no further accrual of interest until its finances can be restructured, then, decisions must be made about which obligations will be honored and which will be repudiated. Government obligations should be divided into three categories.

1. Obligations to pension funds, municipalities, schools, employees, and contractors. Except in cases where there was fraud or corruption, these must be fully honored.

2. Obligations to banks that have loaned money that they created "out of thin air," and obligations to supra-bank entities like the **IMF**, World Bank, **ECB**, etc. Much of this debt should be repudiated as illegitimate, immoral, and even illegal.

3. Legitimate obligations to non-bank corporations and certain other entities should be honored but the period of repayment should be stretched out with annual repayments being capped at a reasonable percentage of total output (**GDP**) so as not to impede capital formation or impose undue hardship on the people.

In all cases, any interest that has been paid on loans in the past should be considered as principal repayment.

CREATE DOMESTIC LIQUIDITY

The fundamental need of any developed economy is for a means of payment (liquidity) to facilitate exchange of real goods and services. As described above, the **ECB** cannot be relied upon to provide an adequate supply of euro currency, nor is the euro a "friendly" instrument for enabling domestic trade. The provision of domestic liquidity, in turn, enables higher levels of domestic trade and fosters domestic economic development. Initiatives can originate from the government, from communities, or the business sector. Here are some examples:

• Tax Anticipation Warrants

   Tax revenues provide a solid foundation for the issuance of a government currency. There is plenty of historical precedent for Tax Anticipation Warrants or notes, and many contemporary writers have put forth proposals of that kind for Greece. But there are limits to everything, and if this Greek currency is to be both interest-free and inflation-free, the government must, along with balancing its budget, limit the amount of warrants it issues to some reasonable proportion of its annual revenues. They also must not be favored with legal tender status beyond the government's own promise to receive them back, at face value, in payment for taxes and dues. But, tax anticipation notes will not provide enough liquidity for the economy to thrive as it should. So what else needs to happen?

• Reemployment Notes

There is also precedent for "development loans" to be made by government agencies to support domestic business and industry and thus get the wheels of commerce turning again and put unemployed people back to work. The government should therefore establish a national Development Bank to allocate, especially to small and medium-sized domestic businesses, what might be called *Reemployment notes* (or *credits*). These should be interest-free and repayable within a relatively short period of time, say one or two years, but they should be issued in a steady stream to maintain liquidity at an optimal level. These loans should go first to businesses that have a ready supply of goods and services that can immediately be sold. As the Reemployment notes are used to pay employees and suppliers, they begin to circulate throughout the domestic economy enabling numerous transactions to occur prior to their repayment. By the simultaneous injection of currency and goods into the market, inflation and debasement of this currency will be avoided.

• Private Currencies and Credit Clearing Exchanges

A further step should be to encourage and support the emergence of non-governmental payment media. Private and community currencies have a long history and they have again been popping up around the world over the past 30 years. Most of these have had very little impact, but if properly done, such currencies have enormous potential for revitalizing local economies and promoting resilience and self-reliance. Private currencies that are spent into circulation by trusted producers of desired goods and services can provide "home grown liquidity" that is readily available and interest-free. By monetizing the value of goods and services that are already in the market and waiting to be bought, private currencies can also be inflation-free. Like tax anticipation warrants, these too have the power to put people back to work and connect unmet needs with available supplies. Railway notes that were issued during the 19th century are one example of how valued services can be monetized to provide a sound circulating medium of exchange.[8]

An even better way of achieving the same results is by organizing *Mutual Credit Clearing associations* to enable reciprocity amongst businesses that exchange goods and services with one another. The 80-year-old Swiss WIR cooperative business circle is a good example of the successful application of the clearing process, as are the scores of commercial trade exchanges (sometimes called "barter exchanges") that have been operating successfully for the past several decades all over the world. One such successful exchange that I recently visited, called Sardex, has for the past five years been providing domestic liquidity on the island of Sardinia through the credit clearing services it provides for its 3,000 business members.

Meanwhile, at the grassroots level, systems like LETS[9], and the Greek version called TEM, are struggling to find the proper procedures needed to achieve effective scale and scope of operation. They, too, have enormous potential benefits, especially if ways can be found to harmonize their structures and operations with those of the commercial trade exchanges.

• Solidarity Loans

> We are all together in this battle for freedom, sovereignty, and a humane world order. People everywhere need to stand in solidarity with the people on the front lines, and right now the front lines are in Greece. It has been suggested that supporters might help cash-starved small businesses operating in places like Greece by making small euro loans to them through crowdfunding or crowdsourcing campaigns. Such a program might help some businesses to hang on a bit longer, but liquidity added to the Greek economy in this way would only provide a small amount of short-term relief because the euro currency will quickly be drained away from the domestic economy as payments are made on external debts, or to pay for imports, or as people hoard physical cash. However, there is a way that euro loans can provide longer term liquidity that will not leak out of the country or be hoarded.

The government can provide "home grown liquidity" (payment media) by issuing its own national currency that could circulate alongside the euro, but that must be done in ways that are non-inflationary and maintain parity with the euro. Any currency issued by the government therefore must not be forced to circulate by making it a general legal tender. Only the government should be required to accept its own currencies as payment of taxes and other dues; everyone else should be free to refuse it or discount it. However, when issued in proper proportion to its anticipated revenues, government-issued currencies will be acceptable in the marketplace at par with the euro.

HOW DOES IT WORK?

Crowdfunders or peer-to-peer lenders can provide euros or other political currencies to a nonprofit entity that would act as trustee that would then make loans to selected businesses, not in euros but in the form of Solidarity Notes (**SOL**). Each **SOL** note would be

100% backed by euro or other currency deposits like Swiss francs, or, better yet, by real assets that will hold their value despite bank failures, deposit confiscation, or debasement of political currencies by the monetary authorities.

SOL currency can then be used by the selected businesses to pay their employees and suppliers who can, in turn, use them to make purchases from shops or other providers of desired goods and services. SOL currency will change hands many times prior to repayment of the loans, circulating throughout the Greek economy, in parallel with euro currency for the duration of the loan, which might be two or three years, or even longer. As the business borrowers earn back the SOL, they will repay their loans at maturity. The trustee will then return to the original lenders the political currency that they provided as backing for the SOL. Whatever income is derived from the political currency investments can be used to cover the costs incurred by the trustee organization in administering the program, and any residual income might be paid out as dividends to the people who provided the capital.

The key to success of this program is to provide the SOL loans to established businesses that have desired goods and services that are already available and waiting for buyers. The goods and services could be food, medicines, clothing, housewares, building supplies, energy, or any other necessities, plus essential services like transport and medical care. In each case SOL provides the payment media needed to connect available supplies with unmet needs.

In summary, this is the process:

- Supporters provide a trustee organization with deposits of euros, dollars, pounds, or other political currency that the trustee invests in various financial and real assets (just as retirement funds do).

- Using those assets as backing, the trustee then issues a private currency, called SOL, by making interest-free, short-term loans to qualified domestic producers and sellers of essential consumer goods and services.

- This enables the reemployment of idle workers and the sale of available goods and excess capacity,
- while at the same time satisfying basic needs, without inflation.
- **SOL** loans are then repaid to the trustee and that amount of **SOL** is extinguished.
- The assets that backed that amount of **SOL** are liquidated and deposits are returned to the original donors.
- The process is continuous as new deposits enable new **SOL** loans to be made.

Although we have been speaking about issuing domestic currencies in the form of printed notes, they might also be issued in digital form as account balances that are accessed by means of credit or debit cards or transferred using the newer mobile phone technologies. Each of these forms of manifestation has its own particular advantages and disadvantages, so the choice must be tailored to the local situation.

This approach to *sanitizing and domesticating* political currencies can also be applied to improve the performance of the many community currencies that are sold into circulation, such as Bristol and Brixton Pounds in the U.K., Toronto and Salt Sprig Island Dollars in Canada, and Berkshares in the U.S.

Besides the actions outlined above, the Greek government must also take bold action to correct the internal errors and imbalances that have plagued it for a long time. Corruption, cronyism, tax evasion, and over-regulation of small business are but a few of the problems that need to be addressed. And finally, the Greek people must embrace the spirit of solidarity and cooperation if they are to reclaim their dignity, survive as a nation, and maintain the quality of life that so many visitors flock to Greece to experience. If all that can be achieved, then Greece, the historical "cradle of democracy" can blaze a trail for others to follow toward a new *convivial* world order of peace, freedom, and a dignified life for all.

ADDITIONAL RESOURCES

Yannis Palaiologos, *The Thirteenth Labour of Hercules* (London: Portobello Books, 2014). The author is a reporter for Kathimerini newspaper. This book provides his views about the Greek crisis. See also Yannis Palaiologos @yanpal7.

Michael Lewis, *Boomerang: Travels in the New Third World* (New York: W. W. Norton & Company, 2011).

Yanis Varoufakis, "A New Deal for Greece — a Project Syndicate Op-Ed" at https://www.project-syndicate.org/commentary/greece-debt-deal-by-yanis-varoufakis-2015-04?barrier=true; blog: http://yanisvaroufakis.eu/.

TEDxAcademy, "A Modest Proposal for Transforming Europe," http://youtu.be/CRRWaEPRlb4.

ENDNOTES

1   http://www.commondreams.org/views/2015/07/31/greek-coup-li-quidity-weapon-coercion. Accessed 11 April, 2016.

2   J. Rocholl and A. Stahmer, "Where did the Greek bailout money go?" ESMT White Paper No. WP–16–02, http://static.esmt.org/publications/whitepapers/WP-16-02.pdf.

3   http://www.opednews.com/articles/GREECE-D-We-Voted-No-to-by-Greg-Palast-Austerity_Euro_European-Union_Europe-an-Union-150706-62.html, accessed 8 July 2015.

4   SWOT stands for strengths, weaknesses, opportunities, and threats.

5   Aristos Doxiadis, "The real Greek economy: owners, rentiers and opportunists," https://www.opendemocracy.net/aristos-doxiadis/owners-rentiers-opportunists, accessed 4 April 2015.

6   Nikos Tsafos, *Beyond Debt: The Greek Crisis in Context* (North Charleston, SC: CreateSpace, 2013).

7   The idea of anti-fragile has best been articulated by Nassim Nicholas Taleb in his book, *Antifragile: Things That Gain from Disorder* (New York: Random House, 2012).

8   See, for example ,Walter Zander, *Railway Money and Unemployment*, 1933; available at http://www.walterzander.info/acrobat/Railway%20 Money.pdf.

9   **LETS** (Local Exchange Trading System) is a credit clearing circle process that was originated in 1983 by Micheal Linton and has since spread around the world. For more information see https://en.wiki-pedia.org/wiki/Local_exchange_trading_system.

Part Three
U.S. Issues and
Possibilities

INTEGRITY FOR THE WHOLE TRUTH

AND NOTHING BUT THE TRUTH

Carl Herman

ABSTRACT: *Historical oligarchs typically control government, what is used for money, and media. 21ˢᵗ century humans are awakening to the obvious facts of the Emperor's New Clothes in three areas. 1) Current US/ UK/Israel wars are not even close to lawful, and the "reasons" for those wars are now officially disclosed as lies that were known to be lies as they were told. 2) The US does not create money, but its Orwellian opposite: debt, created by banks. This system causes unpayable debt. Identifying "debt" as "money" and pretending the escalation of public debt is somehow "good" is massive and fundamental fraud. 3) Corporate media "covers" these crimes to hide the obvious— the Emperor's New Clothes—from public discovery. Our world in 2015 features a dramatic contest between these factors of political collapse versus an awakening public demanding obvious solutions for peace, debt-free money, and comprehensive factual reporting. The outcome depends on the overall integrity of humanity to address obvious facts of our condition and to demand solutions.*

THE EMPEROR'S NEW CLOTHES AS THE STORY OF TODAY

The analogy of *The Emperor's New Clothes*[1] applies to 21ˢᵗ century humans in three areas that reveal the oligarchs of present-day Earth.

First, U.S./U.K./Israel wars are not even close to lawful, and the "reasons" given for those wars have been officially disclosed as lies that were known to be lies as they were told. Second, the U.S. does not create money but its Orwellian opposite: debt, created by banks. This system functions like adding negative numbers forever, causing unpayable debt. Calling "debt" "money" and pretending the escalation of public debt is somehow "good" is massive and fundamental fraud. Third, corporate media "covers" these crimes to hide the obvious truths of the *Emperor's New Clothes* from public discovery.

These factors of political collapse dramatically counter an awakening public demand for peace, debt-free money, and comprehensive factual reporting. Seizing an alternative for ecological civilization depends on the overall integrity of humanity in addressing obvious facts of our condition and demanding solutions. Connecting all three elements in our world will contribute to our awakening and realization of obvious solutions.

Our analogy of *The Emperor's New Clothes* has government officials, messengers (corporate media), and many in the public who claim that political leadership is "covered" by the noblest appearances, and those who fail to perceive this are either "unfit for their posiitons" or "hopelessly stupid," to cite the original text from Hans Christian Andersen. The game-changing central fact, of course, is that the emperor *is* naked. These naked facts are easy to explain, to objectively observe, and to prove for anyone caring to look. Indeed, a child points it all out irrefutably and with easy confidence, proving that the "official story" has zero credibility for any objective observer. As some in the crowd find the courage to speak, the emperor at first continues the pretense along with his "officials." However, the illusion is shattered within moments as the "whole town" begins pointing and speaking up.

Unlawful wars in Iraq and Afghanistan

> No treaty, however much it may be to the advantage
> of all, however tightly it may be worded, can provide

absolute security against the risks of deception and evasion.[2]
~President Kennedy, June 10, 1963

Wars exercise a destructive impact on the ecology. Official deceit-
fulness and support for wars enable the ecological destructiveness.
The U.S./U.K./Israel "official story"[3] is that current wars are lawful
because they are "self-defense." The element of The *Emperor's New
Clothes* here is that "self-defense" means something quite narrow
and specific in war law. U.S./U.K./Israel armed attacks on so many
nations in current and past wars do not even come close to the definition of "self-defense." Simple variations of one method characterize
these three nations and their several wars: 1) ignore war law, 2) blame
the victim and claim "self-defense," and 3) ensure that "officials" and
corporate media never state the simple and obvious facts of war law
and war lies. By broadening the scope, we see the same elements
in several cases, which proves that certain wars were unlawful and
involved massive deception.

A nation can use military, police, and civilians in self-defense for
any attack upon the nation. This is similar to the legal definition of
"self-defense" for you or me walking down the street: we cannot attack
anyone unless we are either under attack or imminent threat. And if
we are under attack, we can use any reasonable force in self-defense,
including lethal force.

International Treaties

Two world wars begat two treaties to end nations' armed attacks
forever. These two treaties are the Kellogg-Briand Pact (the official
title is "General treaty for renunciation of war as an instrument of
national policy") and the United Nations Charter.[4]

Article Six of the U.S. Constitution,[5] which defines a treaty as U.S.
"supreme Law of the Land," makes the importance of these treaties
clear. U.S. policy may only complement an active treaty, and never
violate it. This is important because all of us with oaths to the U.S.
Constitution[6] are sworn to honorably refuse all unlawful war orders,

and military officers are sworn to arrest those who issue such orders. Indeed, we suffer criminal dishonor if we obey orders for armed attack when they are not "self-defense," and family dishonor if we so easily reject the legal victory won from all our families' sacrifices through two world wars.

The Kellogg-Briand General treaty for renunciation of war, as an instrument of national policy, uses the legal term "renounce;"[7] meaning to surrender access, that is, to remove that which is renounced as lawful option. This active treaty[8] contains two crucial articles:

ARTICLE I

The High Contracting Parties solemnly declare in the names of their respective peoples that they condemn recourse to war for the solution of international controversies, and renounce it, as an instrument of national policy in their relations with one another.

ARTICLE II

The High Contracting Parties agree that the settlement or solution of all disputes or conflicts of whatever nature or of whatever origin they may be, which may arise among them, shall never be sought except by pacific means.

The United Nations Charter is a global agreement to end wars of choice outside of a very narrow legal definition of national self-defense against another nation's armed attack. The only area of legal authority of the U.N. is the use of force for security. All other areas are advice for consideration by an individual nation's legislature. The U.N. is not global government. The Preamble of the United Nations[9] states that to

save succeeding generations from the scourge of war. . . . to establish conditions under which justice and respect for the obligations arising from treaties and other sources of international law can be maintained, and. . . to ensure, by the acceptance of principles and the institution of methods, that armed force shall not be used.

The U.N. purpose[10] includes:

> To maintain international peace and security, and to that end: to take effective collective measures for the prevention and removal of threats to the peace, and for the suppression of acts of aggression or other breaches of the peace, and to bring about by peaceful means, and in conformity with the principles of justice and international law, adjustment or settlement of international disputes or situations which might lead to a breach of the peace.

Various articles provide specific directions for nations. Chapter I, Article 2, includes these details:

> (3.) All Members shall settle their international disputes by peaceful means in such a manner that international peace and security, and justice, are not endangered.

> (4.) All Members shall refrain in their international relations from the threat or use of force against the territorial integrity or political independence of any state, or in any other manner inconsistent with the Purposes of the United Nations.

> (5.) All Members shall give the United Nations every assistance in any action it takes in accordance with the present Charter.

Chapter V, Articles 24 and 25 state, respectively:

> In order to ensure prompt and effective action by the United Nations, its Members confer on the Security Council primary responsibility for the maintenance of international peace and security, and agree that in carrying out its duties under this responsibility the Security Council acts on their behalf.[11]

> The Members of the United Nations agree to accept and carry out the decisions of the Security Council in accordance with the present Charter.

Also in Chapter V, Article 33 includes these additional details:

(1.) The parties to any dispute, the continuance of which is likely to endanger the maintenance of international peace and security, shall, first of all, seek a solution by negotiation, enquiry, mediation, conciliation, arbitration, judicial settlement, resort to regional agencies or arrangements, or other peaceful means of their own choice.

(2.) The Security Council shall, when it deems necessary, call upon the parties to settle their dispute by such means.

This is followed by Chapter VI, Article 37:

Should the parties to a dispute of the nature referred to in Article 33 fail to settle it by the means indicated in that Article, they shall refer it to the Security Council.

And from Chapter VII, articles 39, 40, and 51, respectively:

The Security Council shall determine the existence of any threat to the peace, breach of the peace, or act of aggression and shall make recommendations, or decide what measures shall be taken in accordance with Articles 41 and 42, to maintain or restore international peace and security.

In order to prevent an aggravation of the situation, the Security Council may, before making the recommendations or deciding upon the measures provided for in Article 39, call upon the parties concerned to comply with such provisional measures as it deems necessary or desirable.

Nothing in the present Charter shall impair the inherent right of individual or collective self-defense if an armed attack occurs against a Member of the United Nations, until the Security Council has taken measures necessary to maintain international peace and security.

The U.S. war in Afghanistan fails to live up to these treaties. It fails first of all because there was no armed attack by another nation's government. The International Court of Justice (ICJ) is the judicial branch of the U.N. Their definition of "armed attack"[13] is by a nation's government. Because the leadership of the CIA and FBI both reported[14] that they had no evidence the Afghan government had any role in the 9/11 terrorism, the U.S. is unable to claim Article 51 protection for military action in Afghanistan or numerous other countries.[15] The legal classification of what happened on 9/11 is an act of terrorism, a criminal act, not an armed attack by another nation's government.

The U.S. war in Afghanistan also fails as an exercise in self-defense. American Daniel Webster helped create the legal definition of national self-defense[16] in the Caroline Affair as "necessity of that self-defense is instant, overwhelming, and leaving no choice of means, and no moment for deliberation." Article 51 only allows self-defense until the Security Council takes action, which they did in two Resolutions beginning the day after 9/11 (1368[17] and 1373[18]) claiming jurisdiction in the matter. The U.S. attack on Afghanistan came nearly a month after the 9/11 terrorism. The U.S. use of force overseas could be a legal application of Article 51 if, and only if, the U.S. could meet the burden of proof of an imminent threat that was not being responded to by the Security Council. To date, the U.S. has not made such an argument.

In conclusion, unless a nation can justify its military use as self-defense from armed attack from a nation's government that is "instant, overwhelming, and leaving no choice of means, and no moment for deliberation," all other acts of war are unlawful. The legal definition of "self-defense" ends when the attack terminates. In general legal definition,[19] no party is allowed use of force under the justification of "self-defense" if the law can be applied for redress and remedy.

Self-defense justification for attack on Afghanistan

The U.S. 1973 War Powers Act[20] (**WPA**), in response to the Vietnam War, reframes the Founders' intent of keeping the power of war in the hands of Congress. It also expressly limits the president to act within U.S. treaty obligations. The principle treaty applying to the use of war is the U.N. Charter. This means that presidential authority as commander-in-chief must always remain within the limitations of the U.N. Charter to be lawfully issued orders. It's not enough for

Congress to authorize use of force. That force must always and only be within the narrow legal definition of self-defense clearly explained in the U.N. Charter. Of course, if a government wanted to engage in unlawful war today, it could construct its propaganda to sell the war as "defensive." The future of humanity to be safe from the scourge of war is therefore dependent upon our collective ability to discern lawful defensive wars from unlawful wars of aggression.[21] The authorization by Congress of U.S. presidential discretion for military action in Afghanistan[22] and Iraq[23] referenced WPA.

Governments have been vicious killers over the last 100 years using "self-defense" to justify their wars.[24] The U.S. itself has started 201 foreign armed attacks[25] since WWII, causing the world's peoples to conclude in polling that the U.S. is the nation most threatening to world peace.[26] U.S.-started armed attacks have killed nearly 30 million people.[27] Ninety percent of these deaths are innocent[28] children, the elderly, and ordinary civilian women and men. These U.S. armed attacks have resulted in more war dead than Hitler's Nazis,[29] and they continue a long history of U.S. wars of aggression that have been initiated by lies. The most decorated U.S. Marine general in his day warned all Americans of this fact, namely, that lies initiate wars.[30]

The attack on Afghanistan on October 7, 2001, continues this history of unlawful war because the attack was not a response to an attack that was "instant, overwhelming, leaving no choice of means, and no moment for deliberation." In order to justify self-defense, the U.S. would have the burden of proof to show an imminent threat of another attack. U.S. Ambassador to the U.N. John Negroponte, in his letter to the U.N. Security Council (UNSC)[31] invoking Article 51 for the attack upon Afghanistan mentions only "ongoing threat"; which does not satisfy this burden of proof.

Furthermore, Article 51 requires that a self-defensive war be responding to an attack by a nation's government. The CIA and FBI refute that the Afghan government was responsible for the terrorism on 9/11. Also, self-defense ends when the attack ends. The U.S. war began four weeks after 9/11 ended, making the U.S. war one of choice and not defense. Finally, Article 51 ends self-defense claims when the U.N. Security Council acts. Resolution 1373 provides clear language of international cooperation and justice under the law, with no authorization of force. The spirit of the U.N. Charter rejected war as a policy option and requires nations to cooperate for justice under that law. The U.S. has instead embraced and still embraces war, with its outcomes of death, misery, poverty, and fear being expressly against the wishes of humanity and the majority of Americans. These acts are clearly unlawful and should be refused and stopped by all men and women in military, government, and law enforcement.

Some argue that the U.N. Security Council Resolution 687[32] from 1991 authorizes resumption of force from the previous Gulf War. This resolution declared a formal cease-fire, which means exactly what it says: stop the use of force. The resolution was declared by UNSC, and no individual nation has authority to supersede UNSC's power to continue or change the status of the cease-fire. The categories of crime for armed attacks outside U.S. treaty limits of law are 1.) Wars of Aggression[33] (the worst crime a nation can commit), and 2.) treason[34] for lying to U.S. military, ordering unlawful attack and invasion of foreign lands, and causing thousands of U.S. military deaths.

Arguments that the Iraq war was unlawful

All of the lawyers in the U.K. Foreign Affairs Department concluded the U.S./U.K. invasion of Iraq was an unlawful War of Aggression.[35] This stunning information was disclosed at the UK Chilcot inquiry by the testimony of Foreign Affairs leading legal advisor, Sir Michael Wood. Wood added that Prime Minister Tony Blair's office chastised his legal department's professional work for putting their unanimous legal opinion in writing.[36] Wood also testified that Foreign Secretary Jack Straw preferred to take the legal position that the laws governing war were vague and open to broad interpretation. "He took the view that I was being very dogmatic and that international law was pretty vague and that he wasn't used to people taking such a firm position."[37]

Moreover, the U.S. and U.K. "legal argument" further contradicts their U.N. Ambassadors' statements that 1441[38] did not authorize any use of force. John Negroponte, U.S. Ambassador to the U.N. said,

> [T]his resolution contains no "hidden triggers" and no "automaticity" with respect to the use of force. If there is a further Iraqi breach, reported to the Council by UNMOVIC, the IAEA or a Member State, the matter will return to the Council for discussions as required in paragraph 12.[39]

Negroponte's letter does invoke a legal Charter Article of self-defense by pointing to the loss of over 3,000 lives on 9/11. The letter portends legal evidence of al-Qaeda's "central role" in the attacks and claims military response is appropriate because of al-Qaeda's ongoing threat and continued training of terrorists. This reasoning argues for a reinterpretation of self-defense to include pre-emptive attack while lying by omitting that such an argument would not be necessary if the current action were not outside the law. Sir Jeremy Greenstock, U.K. Ambassador to the U.N. said,

> We heard loud and clear during the negotiations the concerns about "automaticity" and "hidden triggers"—the concern that on a decision so crucial we should not rush into military action; that on a decision so crucial any Iraqi violations should be discussed by the Council. Let me be equally clear in response. . . . There is no "automaticity" in this resolution. If there is a further Iraqi breach of its disarmament obligations, the matter will return to the Council for discussion as required in paragraph 12.[40]

West Point Grads Against the War have further legal arguments[41] regarding violations of war treaties, based on further analysis of the U.N. Charter and expert supporting testimony. The U.S. Army's official law handbook[42] provides an excellent historical and legal summary of when wars are lawful self-defense and when they are unlawful. Importantly, after accurately defining "self-defense" in war, Judge Advocate General authors/attorneys explicitly state that war is illegal unless a nation is under attack from another nation's government, or can provide evidence of imminent threat of such attack,

> Anticipatory self-defense, whether labeled anticipatory or preemptive, must be distinguished from preventive self-defense. Preventive self-defense — employed to counter non-imminent threats — is illegal under international law.[43]

However, despite the accurate disclosure of the legal meaning of "self-defense" in war in the law handbook of the U.S. Army, leaders then ignore this meaning to claim "self-defense" as a lawful reason for U.S. wars without further explanation. Young Abraham Lincoln wrote eloquently to defend the U.S. Constitution from unlawful tyrants within our own government.[44] In Congress, he spoke powerfully and truthfully that the president's claims for armed attack and invasion by a foreign country were lies. Although warmongers slurred Lincoln's name at the time, history proved him correct in asserting the president of the U.S. was a warmongering liar,

> I carefully examined the President's messages, to ascertain what he himself had said and proved upon the point. The result of this examination was to make the impression, that taking for true, all the President states as facts, he falls far short of proving his justification; and that the President would have gone farther with his proof, if it had not been for the small matter, that the truth would not permit him. . . . Now I propose to try to show, that the whole of this, — issue and evidence — is, from beginning to end, the sheerest deception.[45]

Lincoln also wrote that "pre-emptive" wars were lies, and "war at pleasure."[46]

David Swanson's *War is a Crime* provides another resource for documentation and analysis. Ironically, Americans would never allow a favorite sport such as baseball or football to be similarly destroyed by such *Emperor's New Clothes* lies about those rules/laws.[47]

Known lies used to start Iraq/Afghanistan war

Evidence disclosed by the U.S. government shows that claims justifying the U.S. war against Iraq and Afghanistan were known to be lies as they were told to the American public and were not "mistaken" intelligence. Four basic fact claims were presented by U.S. political leaders to justify the invasion of Iraq:

1. Iraq had Weapons of Mass Destruction (WMD), a general name for specific chemical and biological weapons.

2. The U.S. intercepted aluminum tubes that could only be used to refine nuclear material; it was claimed this was irrefutable evidence that Iraq had restarted a nuclear weapons program.

3. The U.S. claimed that Saddam's attempt to purchase enriched uranium from Niger provided more evidence that Iraq had reconstituted nuclear weapons development.

4. The U.S. claimed that Saddam had links to Al Qaeda, the alleged terrorists who attacked the US on 9/11.

Evidence challenges each of these claims

1. George Tenet, Director of the CIA, acknowledged that all U.S. intelligence agency reports, "never said there was an imminent threat."[48] The rejection of any immanent threat was based on a long history of intelligence reports[49] showing that the chemical and biological weapons under consideration were relatively weak without a delivery system, and that Iraq was highly motivated not to use them against the U.S. given their understanding that such use would provoke war with the world's most powerful military. Although all 16 U.S. intelligence agencies stated in writing in their official National Intelligence Estimate report that there was no evidence of any imminent threat, U.S. leaders used an argument of WMD as a reason for war.

2. The Bush administration's claim[50] about aluminum tubes that could only be used as centrifuges to refine fissionable material for nuclear weapons was directly refuted by the U.S. Department of

Energy and the International atomic Energy Agency.[51] It was their conclusion that the tubes in question were too small in diameter and too thick; that using aluminum as the material would be "a huge step backwards"; and the anodized surface made it impossible for them to serve this purpose. They also found that the tubes were easily explained for conventional use, since the specifications perfectly matched tubing for other purposes.[52] The Senate Committee on Intelligence[53] agreed that this claim had no basis from any available evidence.

3. The "Niger documents"[54] were cited by President Bush in the 2003 State of the Union Address. These papers were written in grammatically poor French, had a "childlike" forgery of the Niger president's signature, and had a document signed by a foreign minister who had been out of office for 14 years prior to the date on the document. The document showed up shortly after the Niger embassy in Rome was robbed,[55] with the only missing items being stationery and Niger government stamps. The same stationery and stamps were used for the forged documents. The CIA warned President Bush[56] on at least three occasions to not make the claim due to the ridiculous evidence. In addition, if Saddam really were making an illegal uranium purchase, it's likely that both Saddam and the Niger government officials would insist on not having a written record that would document the crime. Republican U.S. Ambassador to Niger, Joseph Wilson, confirmed these problems about the information and reported it in detail to Vice President Cheney's office and the CIA.[57]

4. All U.S. intelligence agencies reported that no relationship between Saddam Hussein and Al Qaeda existed.[58] Vice President Cheney made an unsubstantiated reason for war while all 16 U.S. intelligence agencies officially reported no such evidence existed and compelling evidence existed to refute the claim.

As noted earlier, some justified the Iraq war by arguing that U.N. Security Council Resolution 687 from 1991 authorized resumption of force from the previous Gulf War. But this resolution declared a formal cease-fire stopping the use of force. The resolution was declared by UNSC and held in their jurisdiction, which meant that no individual nation had the authority to supersede UNSC's power to continue or change the status of the cease-fire.[59]

The U.S. acknowledges the Afghanistan government had nothing to do with 9/11. The U.N. Security Council issued two Resolutions after 9/11 (1368[60] and 1373[61]) calling for international cooperation for factual discovery, arrests, and prosecutions of the 9/11 criminals. The Afghan government said it would arrest any suspect upon presentation of evidence of criminal involvement. The U.S. rejected these resolutions and violated the letter and intent of the U.N. Charter by armed attack and invasion of Afghanistan.

The U.S. government requested the cooperation of the Afghanistan government for extradition of Osama bid Laden to be charged with the 9/11 attacks. The Afghan government agreed, as per usual cooperative international law, as soon as the U.S. government provided evidence of bin Laden's involvement.[62] The U.S. government refused to provide any evidence. The Afghan government refused to allow U.S. troops to enter the country until evidence was provided; moreover, the government made its argument to the world press that the rule of law apply to the U.S. extradition request. The U.S. invaded Afghanistan without providing evidence and without UN Security Council approval. President Bush stated, "There's no need to discuss evidence of innocence or guilt. We know he's guilty." [63] The Afghani government did not attack the U.S., and there was no evidence of imminent threat. The U.S. violated the U.N. Security Council's legal authority.

MONEY AS A MOTIVATION FOR WAR

In addition to demonstrating that unlawful wars, justified by lies, are vital for understanding our political situation, the motivation for these wars must be identified. Because resources and money motivate war, knowing what we use for money is also crucial to our understanding of political collapse.

Recognition of the monetary debt system

Our monetary system is a debt system, impossible to ever decrease or repay. People have recognized that debt is the basis for our monetary system.

> That is to say, under the old way any time we wish to add to the national wealth we are compelled to add to the national debt. Now, that is what Henry Ford wants to prevent. He thinks it is stupid, and so do I, that for the loan of $30,000,000 of their own money the people of the United States should be compelled to pay $66,000,000— that is what it amounts to, with interest. . . . But here is the point: If our nation can issue a dollar bond, it can issue a dollar bill. . . . It is absurd to say that our country can issue $30,000,000 in bonds and not $30,000,000 in currency. Both are promises to pay; but one promise fattens the usurer, and the other helps the people. ~Thomas Edison and Henry Ford.[64]

> When our Federal Government, that has the exclusive power to create money, creates that money and then goes into the open market and borrows it and pays interest for the use of its own money, it occurs to me that that is going too far. I have never yet had anyone who could, through the use of logic and reason, justify the Federal Government borrowing the use of its own money. . . . The Constitution of the United States does not give the banks the power to create money. The Constitution says that Congress shall have the power to create money, but now, under our system, we will sell bonds to commercial banks and obtain credit from those banks. I believe the time will come when people will demand that this be changed. I believe the time will come in this country when they will actually blame you and me and everyone else connected with this Congress for sitting idly by and permitting such an idiotic system to continue. I make that statement after years of study. ~Wright Patman, excerpts from September 29, 1941, as reported in the Congressional Record of the House of Representatives, 7582–83) [65]

The Guardian,[66] a U.K. newspaper that is the world's third most-read online newspaper, posted a revealing article, "The truth is out, money is just an IOU, and the banks are rolling in it." In this article the author explains that the Bank of England[67] and U.S. Federal Reserve admit that what we use for money is created as debt by private banks.[68]

Our situation

This system is like adding negative numbers forever. The aggregate debt only gets larger and will never be repaid, because this is what we use for money. Also, as we see today, the interest and debt total becomes tragic-comic since we can't get close to affording to pay. Since the 1913 legislation of the Federal Reserve, the U.S. has had a national "debt system," the Orwellian opposite of a monetary system. What we use for money is created as a debt, with the consequence of unpayable and increasing aggregate debt. That is, private banks and the Federal Reserve (their privately owned pinnacle bank, by their own admission)[69] create credit/debt that we use as money.[70] The result is an escalating and unpayable national debt[71] and a real-inflation rate more than double the stated rate.[72] This becomes the literal mother of all conflicts of interest. An honest Fed would at least ask for independent professional cost-benefit analyses to determine if government-created debt-free money and public credit would do better than their ever-increasing and unpayable aggregate debt.

Obvious solutions: monetary and credit reform

Monetary reform creates debt-free money as a public service for the direct payment of public goods and services. This would replace the existing system of creating what we use for money out of debt. Monetary reform nationalizes the Federal Reserve (this name is deceptive because it is not a government entity) and retains its use for bank administrative functions. Fractional reserve lending by private banks would also be made illegal, with the U.S. Treasury having sole legal authority to issue new money that would benefit the American public rather than the banking industry. About 30% of the national debt is intra-governmental holdings[73] with about 16% held by the Fed.[74] This debt would be cancelled, as it becomes a bookkeeping entry with nationalization. Of the publicly held debt of various parties holding U.S. Securities, the U.S. Treasury would monetize (pay) the debt in proportion to fractional reserves being replaced with full reserves over a period of one to two years to monitor money supply and avoid inflation. This means the U.S. government would create debt-free money to pay the debt as it is due, exactly to the extent that a private bank's ability to create credit is reduced. The purpose of this is to avoid inflation. In contrast, today we only pay the interest in the national debt, similar to a household paying only the interest of a credit card debt as the total owed only and always increases under these mechanics.

The American Monetary Institute has a proposal called the American Monetary Act to carry out this reform.[75] Economist Milton Friedman has endorsed its proposal.[76] The governmental cost of this reform is negligible because it simply authorizes Congress to enter money into its own account to directly pay for public goods and services. In fact, Americans would save money from decreased reliance on taxes.

The benefits are astounding: the American public would no longer pay over $400 billion every year for national debt interest payments[77] (because almost 50% of the debt is intra-governmental transfers, this is a savings of over $200 billion/year). If lending is run at a nonprofit rate or at nominal interest returned to the American public (for infrastructure, schools, fire, and police protection, etc.) rather than profiting the banks, the savings to the U.S. public is conservatively $2 trillion. Of $60 trillion total debt,[78] a conservative current interest cost of 5% is $3 trillion every year. Two trillion dollars of savings, if the profits are transferred to the American public rather than to the banking industry, is probably low. If the U.S. Federal government increased the money supply by 3% a year to keep up with population increases and economic growth, we could spend an additional $500 billion yearly on public programs, or refund it as a public dividend. This savings would allow us to simplify or eliminate the income tax (of the U.S.

federal government's @$4 trillion annual budget, about $1.7 trillion is received from income tax[79]). The estimated savings of eliminating the income tax, with all its complexity, loopholes, and evasion, is $250 billion/year.[80] The total benefits for monetary reform are conservatively over three trillion dollars every year to the American public. Three trillion is $3,000,000,000,000. This saves the @100 million U.S. households an average of $30,000 every year. Another way to calculate the savings is to figure those amounts per $50,000 annual household income (for example, if your household earns $100,000/year, you save @$60,000 every year with these reforms).

Closely related is credit reform that replaces private bank credit with public credit. Public credit transfers interest payments from private profits to public service. Trial and error will inform total money supply, with an option of removing money from the supply through some form of simple taxation. For example, if public credit issues mortgages and credit cards at @5%, this form of taxation can pay for public goods and services with the ability to raise or lower the interest rate.

The astounding benefits of public banking can be seen in that state-issued mortgages and a credit card at 5% interest would replace all current state taxes while abundantly funding all current state public goods and services. It also releases CAFR funds, worth trillions, back to the public.[81] The benefits include paying the national debt, ending a national debt forever, issuing money and credit for full employment, and optimal infrastructure. Government can become the employer of last resort for hard and soft infrastructure investment. This provides triple benefits for employment, the best infrastructure we can imagine, and falling overall prices to the extent infrastructure investment contributes more economic output relative to costs of inputs. Infrastructure investment reduces overall prices in the current debt-funded model that typically adds @50% of the projects' nominal cost to its total cost.[82] Monetary reform with infrastructure means the cost of debt funding disappears, making this employment even more attractive. Additional potential benefits are reductions of crime and other social costs related to human despair as people see and participate in creating a brighter future for all.

According to our current *Emperor's New Clothes* farce, the statutory purposes of the Fed are stable prices, maximum employment, and moderate interest rates.[83] Checking the data on prices confirms that the dollar has lost over 95% of its value since the Fed went to work for "stable prices." Further, the official measurements for inflation were redefined in 1980 and 1990 and that lowers today's inflation rate by @8%.[84] Examining the cumulative effect of accelerating prices shows that prices are 30 times more expensive since the Fed began in 1913.[85]

Considering employment, the official definition of "unemployment" is also a lie of omission. If someone works just one hour a week, they are considered "employed." If adults want work and are not currently applying for jobs because they have found their efforts to be in vain, they are not counted as "unemployed." If we counted unemployment the same way we did in the Great Depression, the U.S. has had that same level of unemployment since 2009, between 20% and 25%.[86] We have unemployed people in this country, resources to put to work, and infrastructure to improve. Unemployment only occurs because money is debt in our current system. If the government restored the constitutional power to issue money directly, we would not have the problem of unemployment. The only way to achieve full employment is for government to be the employer of last resort. When free-market capitalism cannot employ, we either put people to work on infrastructure/public service jobs, or we don't achieve our goal of full employment. If the public jobs provided to the unemployed and funded by government-created money provide greater economic benefit than their cost, then inflation will actually decrease from creating those jobs. Minimizing unemployment provides another advantage. An important and connected statistic: the U.S. Government Interagency Council on Homelessness has compiled studies on the cost-benefits of housing the homeless and providing food, medical care, and job-employment services versus just leaving them on the streets. In every case study the costs for their care are less.

LYING CORPORATE MEDIA: PROPAGANDA
TRYING TO HIDE NAKED EMPIRE

Evidence of governmental and corporate control of media

Three weeks before W. Bush's election for a second term in 2004, his Senior Advisor and Deputy Chief of Staff, Karl Rove, chided Pulitzer-winning journalist, Ron Suskind. Rove said that guys like [Suskind] were "In what we call the reality-based community," which he defined as people who "believe that solutions emerge from your judicious study of discernible reality." "That's not the way the world really works anymore," he continued.

> We're an empire now, and when we act, we create our own reality. And while you're studying that reality — judiciously, as you will — we'll act again, creating other new realities, which you can study too, and that's how things will sort out. We're history's actors. . . . and you, all of you, will be left to just study what we do.[87]

In the 1975 Church Senate Committee hearings, CIA Director William Colby's testimony made the stunning disclosure that over 400 CIA operatives were controlling US corporate media reporting on specific issues of national interest in Operation Mockingbird.[88] This game-changing testimony was confirmed by the research of Pulitzer Prize-winning reporter Carl Bernstein. When corporate media refused to publish Bernstein's article, it became a cover story for *Rolling Stone*. Bernstein provided additional information about CIA control from the senate report and subsequent corporate media "reporting."

> Pages 191 to 201 were entitled "Covert Relationships with the United States Media." "It hardly reflects what we found," stated Senator Gary Hart. 'There was a prolonged and elaborate negotiation [with the CIA] over what would be said." Obscuring the facts was relatively simple. No mention was made of the 400 summaries or what they showed. Instead

the report noted blandly that some fifty recent contacts with journalists had been studied by the committee staff, thus the impression that the Agency's dealings with the press had been limited to those instances. The Agency files, the report noted, contained little evidence that the editorial content of American news reports had been affected by the CIA's dealings with journalists. Colby's misleading public statements about the use of journalists were repeated without serious contradiction or elaboration. The role of cooperating news executives was given short shrift. The fact that the Agency had concentrated its relationships in the most prominent sectors of the press went unmentioned. That the CIA continued to regard the press as up for grabs was not even suggested.[89]

Importantly, U.S. corporate media today is heavily concentrated in just six corporations, making the message much easier to control. The official government rhetoric for war on Iran provides a specific case of corporate media collusion. As U.S. leaders threatened more unlawful war on Iran, three points give evidence that the ongoing "reasons" to war-murder Iranians were known lies, even as they were being told. First, President Obama lied to Israeli media a week before his March 2013 visit: "We think it would take over a year or so for Iran to actually develop a nuclear weapon."[90] This repeated claim is a lie because it counters reports of no Iranian efforts to develop a nuclear weapon in the last 10 years by all 16 U.S. intelligence agencies' most current official National Intelligence Estimate. These estimates are updated when intelligence suggests status change.[91] All IAEA official reports are based their full-time monitoring of all Iran's nuclear material and plants. Also, several definitive official U.S. reports state the same.[92] Second, U.S. leaders in government and corporate media continuously lie with the claim that Iran's president threatened to "wipe Israel off the map."[93] This claim is easily proven to be a criminal lie by simply reading the October 2005 speech in question. The speech's text is crystal clear in context and content: if Israel continues to suppress Palestinian rights, then Israel's government will go down the path of Iran under the Shah and Iraq under Saddam. Third, the US overthrew Iran's democracy from 1953 to 1979 and then used Iraq to attack, invade, and attempt to re-conquer Iran from 1980 to 1988.[94]

Furthermore, U.S. corporate media lie to allow torture, a war crime, by dropping reporting of waterboarding as torture. "Torture at Times: Waterboarding in the Media" published by Harvard's Kennedy School of Government reviewed the four most-read newspapers in the U.S. The report found that from the 1930s to 2004, *The New York Times* reported waterboarding as torture 82% of the time, and *The Los Angeles Times* did so 96% of the time. After stories broke that the U.S. was waterboarding "detainees," the papers' reporting of waterboarding as torture dropped to 1% and 5%, respectively.[95] In addition, after the U.S. admitted to waterboarding, *The Wall Street Journal* called it torture in just 1 of 63 articles (2%) and *USA Today* never called it torture.

The genesis of oligarchic control of American major media was reported in the U.S. Congressional Record in 1917.[96] U.S. Congressperson Oscar Callaway claimed evidence that J.P. Morgan had purchased editorial control over 25 of the nation's most influential publications in order to create public support for U.S. entry into World War I and for his new banking legislative victory, creation of the Federal Reserve system. Mr. Callaway's colleagues voted down an official investigation.

Polling proves the 99.99% are waking to U.S. corporate media lies. Corporate media won't report the following polling data, but the American public have noticed something is very wrong with their "news," both as reported by government and regular media. According to a 2007 poll by the Pew Research Center, the majority of the American public sees the U.S. major media news organizations as politically biased, inaccurate, and uncaring. Among those who use the Internet, two-thirds report that major media news do not care about the people they report on, 59% say the news is inaccurate, 64% see bias, and 53% summarize their view on major media news as "failing to stand up for America."[97] In their 2009 poll, "just 29% of

Americans say that news organizations generally get the facts straight, while 63% say that news stories are often inaccurate."[98] Gallup's 2014 poll recorded the lowest ever U.S. public confidence in accurate news reporting from corporate media's television news: 18%.[99]

Growing awareness and resistance to control

The public will defeat the official lies through trial and error, as Dr. King and Gandhi discovered. What they learned is that destructive lies can be overcome by broad public and political communication of the facts, while simultaneously making formal policy requests to honor the law. This process has been summarized as "First they ignore you. Then they laugh at you. Then they fight you. And then you win."

> One thing we have endeavored to observe most scrupulously, namely, never to depart from the strictest facts and, in dealing with the difficult questions that have arisen during the year, we hope that we have used the utmost moderation possible under the circumstances. Our duty is very simple and plain. We want to serve the community, and in our own humble way to serve the Empire. We believe in the righteousness of the cause, which it is our privilege to espouse. We have an abiding faith in the mercy of the Almighty God, and we have firm faith in the British Constitution. That being so, we should fail in our duty if we wrote anything with a view to hurt. Facts we would always place before our readers, whether they are palatable or not, and it is by placing them constantly before the public in their nakedness that the misunderstanding . . . can be removed. *-Mohandas K. Gandhi, Indian Opinion* (1 October 1903)

> 'A time comes when silence is betrayal.' That time has come for us. . . . The truth of these words is beyond doubt but the mission to which they call us is a most difficult one. Even when pressed by the demands of inner truth, men do not easily assume the task of opposing their government's policy, especially in time of war. Nor does the human spirit move

without great difficulty against all the apathy of conformist thought within one's own bosom and in the surrounding world. ~Dr. Martin Luther King, "Beyond Vietnam: A Time to Break Silence."[100]

Readers and writers in alternative media can explain, document, and prove that much of these "created realities" are not even close to the foundational principle of "limited government" within the U.S. Constitution.

The problems we face are due to a lack of integrity. The solution can come from the following:

1. Empower people with the facts so they can be actively engaged in shattering the collective deceptions depicted in such stories as *The Emperor's New Clothes*. The general public will never consent to what is being done to them if they are empowered with accurate, comprehensive information on their condition. The informed will be motivated to reject thoughtless obedience to authorities in government, religion, and a .01% privileged class connected to government.

2. Educate everyone enough so they can consider and discuss factual evidence in full freedom.

3. Empower everyone with voice and vote to relate facts to policies in order to continuously optimize the unalienable rights of life, liberty, and pursuit of happiness.

When enough people are willing to apply their education to seek accurate information and to exercise their integrity in stating simple facts, humanity will be in position to seize the alternative of a brighter future for all Earth's inhabitants. This alternative will bring:

1. Peace, as the 99.99% realize they've been lied to and led into unlawful wars by the same nations who colonized every part of the planet, then engaged in two world wars among themselves.

2. Prosperity, as what we use for money is created debt-free for direct payment of public goods and services, and as at-cost credit to allow good-faith, transparent experimentation to optimize public benefits rather than the oligarchic .01% looting in the tens of trillions.

3. Truth, as media work to report on good-faith exploration of what's possible for all the inhabitants of our beautiful and currently viciously dominated planet Earth.

ENDNOTES

1   See https://en.wikipedia.org/wiki/The_Emperor%27s_New_Clothes.

2   J. Kennedy, Towards a Strategy of Peace. 10 June 1963, https://www.npr.org/documents/2006/oct/american_speeches/kennedy.pdf.

3   http://www.washingtonsblog.com/2014/05/us-military-legal -argument-current-wars-self-defense-whatever-say.html.

4   Both are listed in the US State Department's annual publication, *Treaties in Force* (2013 edition pages 466 and 493).

5   https://en.wikipedia.org/wiki/Article_Six_of_the_United_States _Constitution.

6   http://www.washingtonsblog.com/2013/09/us-military-no-lawful -orders-exist-for-unlawful-wars-arrest-those-who-issue-them.html.

7   http://legal-dictionary.thefreedictionary.com/renounce.

8   Among many sources for treaty text: http://avalon.law.yale.edu/ 20th_century/kbpact.asp.

9   http://www.un.org/en/sections/un-charter/preamble/index.html.

10 http://www.un.org/en/sections/un-charter/chapter-i/index.html.

11 http://www.un.org/en/sections/un-charter/chapter-v/index.html.

12 http://www.un.org/en/sections/un-charter/chapter-vi/index.html.

13. K. Zemanek, Armed Attack, Oxford Public International Law, October 2013, http://opil.ouplaw.com/view/10.1093/law:epil/9780199231690 /law-9780199231690-e241.

14 https://www.counterpunch.org/2002/09/17/the-illegalities-of -bush-s-war-on-afghanistan/.

15 See https://www.globalresearch.ca/uk-chilcot-inquiry-the-iraq-war-was-an-unlawful-unanimous-legal-opinion-of-foreign-office-lawyers/5317696;

http://www.washingtonsblog.com/2013/08/cheat-sheet-on-syria.html;

on Ukraine: http://www.washingtonsblog.com/2014/04/iraq-war-propagandists-push-lies-urkaine-drum-confrontation-russia.html;

on Iran: http://www.washingtonsblog.com/2015/03/iran-wipe-israel-map-read-600-words-confirm-usisrael-criminal-war-lies.html;

http://www.washingtonsblog.com/2015/03/usukisrael-unlawful-wars-aggression-iraq-iran-gangster-business-analogy.html;

http://www.washingtonsblog.com/2015/03/usisrael-01-lie-unlawful-war-aggression-iran-99-99-must-choose-arrests-global-nuclear-war.html;

on Russia: http://www.washingtonsblog.com/2014/08/u-s-targeted-nuclear-armed-russia-regime-change.html;

on ISIS: http://www.washingtonsblog.com/2014/09/isis-common-maos-red-guards-khmer-rouge-muslim-empires-antiquity.html;

on Korasans: http://www.washingtonsblog.com/2014/09/khorasans-fake-kardashians.html.

16 Among many to explain the "Caroline test," see: A.M. Hayes, Cameron and the Caroline: are UK drone strikes on ISIS "self defense"? *North Carolina Journal of International Law* (23 Sept 2015), http://blogs.law.unc.edu/ncilj/2015/09/23/cameron-and-the-caroline-are-uk-drone-strikes-on-isis-selfdefense.

17 http://www.un.org/press/en/2001/SC7143.doc.htm.

18 http://www.un.org/press/en/2001/sc7158.doc.htm.

19 http://www.lectlaw.com/def/d030.htm.

20 http://avalon.law.yale.edu/20th_century/warpower.asp.

21 In general legal definition, no party is allowed use of force under the justification of "self-defense" if the law can be applied for redress and remedy, Defense, self-defense, The 'letric law library, https://www.lectlaw.com/def/d030.htm (among many with this uncontested and universally accepted legal principle).

22 https://www.gpo.gov/fdsys/pkg/PLAW-107publ40/html/PLAW-107publ40.htm.

23 https://www.gpo.gov/fdsys/pkg/PLAW-107publ243/html/PLAW-107publ243.htm.

24 http://www.hawaii.edu/powerkills/NOTE1.HTM.

25 http://www.washingtonsblog.com/2014/05/90-deaths-war-civilians.html.

26 http://www.washingtonsblog.com/2014/03/2014-gallup-international-poll-us-1-threat-world-peace.html.

27 http://www.washingtonsblog.com/2012/04/us-war-murdered-20-30-million-since-ww2-arrest-todays-war-criminals.html.

28 http://www.washingtonsblog.com/2014/05/90-deaths-war-civilians.html.

29 http://www.washingtonsblog.com/2013/07/obama-celebrates-30-million-us-war-kills-since-ww2-past-hitler-to-3-on-all-time-list.html.

30 https://www.ratical.org/ratville/CAH/warisaracket.html.

31 http://www.bits.de/public/documents/US_Terrorist_Attacks/negroponte.htm.

32 http://www.un.org/Depts/unmovic/documents/687.pdf.

33 https://en.wikipedia.org/wiki/War_of_aggression.

34 http://www.washingtonsblog.com/2014/02/nothing-will-fixed-us-criminals-arrested-top-us-official.html.

35 https://www.theguardian.com/world/2010/jan/12/iraq-invasion-violated-interational-law-dutch-inquiry-finds. For UN Secretary General Kofi Annan's statements, see http://www.theguardian.com/world/2004/sep/16/iraq.iraq.

36 http://www.dailymail.co.uk/news/article-1246312/Chilcot-inquiry-Iraq-war-The-damning-verdict-Whitehall-lawyers-invading-Iraq-ministers-refused-accept.html.

37 http://www.telegraph.co.uk/news/worldnews/middleeast/iraq/7078079/Chilcot-inquiry-Iraq-invasion-had-no-legal-basis-in-international-law.html.

38 http://www.theguardian.com/world/2003/mar/17/iraq2.

39   http://www.un.org/webcast/usa110802.htm.

40   http://www.un.org/webcast/unitedkingdom110802.htm.

41   http://www.wpgaw.org/.

42   http://www.loc.gov/rr/frd/Military_Law/pdf/operational-law
     -handbook_2012.pdf.

43   Also see https://en.wikipedia.org/wiki/War_of_aggression.

44   "The people—the people—are the rightful masters of both Con-
     gresses and courts—not to overthrow the Constitution, but to over-
     throw the men who pervert it," Abraham Lincoln, in "Lincoln in
     Kansas," *Collections of the Kansas State Historical Society,* vol. 7, edited
     by George Martin (Topeka: W.Y. Morgan, 1902), 551.

45   Abraham Lincoln, Speech in U.S. Congress, January 12, 1848. http://
     global.oup.com/us/companion.websites/9780195375701/pdf/ SPD4
     _Opposition_Mex_Am_War.pdf.

46   Abraham Lincoln letter on the Mexican War to William Hern-
     don, February 15, 1848, http://classic-literature.co.uk/abraham
     -lincoln-letter- on-the-mexican-war-1848/.

47   http://www.washingtonsblog.com/2014/05/youd-never-allow
     -favorite-sport-destroyed-psychopathic-officials-allow-us-destroyed.
     html.

48   George Tenet speech to Georgetown University 5 Feb 2004; "CIA
     never said threat was imminent, Tenet says," Deseret News, 6 Feb
     2004, https://www.deseretnews.com/article/590041360/CIA-never-
     said-threat-was-imminent-Tenet-says.html.

49   Neglecting intelligence, ignoring warnings, Center for American Pro-
     gress, 28 Jan 2004, https://www.americanprogress.org/issues/security/
     news/2004/01/28/457/neglecting-intelligence-ignoring-warnings/.

50   Impeach Bush; Bush lied about the aluminum tubes in Iraq; http://
     web.archive.org/web/20070822161544/.

51   WMDgate: fixing intelligence around policy—the aluminum tubes,
     part 2A-3, the left coaster, 19 Nov 2005, http://www.theleftcoaster.
     com/archives/006070.php.

52   https://www.globalpolicy.org/component/content/article/168/37699.
     html.

53 Senate report on whether public statements regarding Iraq by U.S. government officials were substantiated by intelligence information, June 2008; http:// www.intelligence.senate.gov /080605/phase2a.pdf. See also http://www.tomdispatch.com/ post/32550/de_la_vega_bush_s_war_a_case_of_presidential_fraud_.

54 http://www.cnn.com/2003/US/03/14/sprj.irq.documents/.

55 https://www.counterpunch.org/2008/08/16/forging-the-case -for-war/.

56 House of Representatives Committee on oversight and government reform, Memorandum 18 Dec 2008, re: the president's claim that Iraq sought uranium from Niger, http://web.archive. org/web/ 20090814070115/http://oversight.house.gov/documents/ 20081218120632.pdf.

57 J. Wilson, "What I didn't find in Africa," *New York Times,* 6 July 2003, http://www.nytimes.com/2003/07/06/opinion/what-i-didn-t-find-in- africa.html.

58 http://www.washingtonpost.com/wp-dyn/articles/A47812-2004Jun16.html. See also http://www.nbcnews.com/id/14728447/.

59 http://web.archive.org/web/20101214124626/http://crimesofwar.org/ special/Iraq/news-iraq2.html.

60 http://www.un.org/press/en/2001/SC7143.doc.htm.

61 https://www.un.org/en/sc/ctc/specialmeetings/2012/docs/United%20 Nations%20Security%20Council%20Resolution%201373%20 %282001%29.pdf.

62 http://www.globalresearch.ca/guantanamo-military-oaths-confront-the-constitution-in-the-omar-khadr-case/10899.

63 https://www.theguardian.com/world/2001/oct/14/afghanistan. terrorism5.

64 http://query.nytimes.com/mem/archive-free/pdf? _r=1&res=9C04E0D7103EEE3ABC4E53DFB467838A639EDE.

65 http://www.washingtonsblog.com/2012/03/nyc-mayor-john-hylan -house-banking-committee-chairs-on-monetary-reform.html.

66 https://en.wikipedia.org/wiki/The_Guardian.

67 See http://www.bankofengland.co.uk/publications/Documents/

quarterlybulletin/ 2014/qb14q102.pdf.

68 http://www.theguardian.com/commentisfree/2014/mar/18/
truth-money-iou-bank-of-england-austerity.

69 http://www.washingtonsblog.com/2011/11/occupy-facts-federal-re-
serve-causes-unpayable-debt-unemployment-inflation-high-inter-
est-rates.html.

70 http://www.shadowstats.com/alternate_data/inflation-charts.

71 http://www.washingtonsblog.com/2011/07/federal-reserve-at-
torneys-fed-banks-are-not-agencies-but-independent-corpora-
tions-with-private-boards-of-directors.html.

72 http://www.washingtonsblog.com/2015/03/debt-damned-economics-
either-learn-monetary-reform-kiss-assets-goodbye-1-7.html.

73 http://www.treasurydirect.gov/NP/debt/current.

74 https://research.stlouisfed.org/fred2/series/FDHBFRBN.

75 http://www.monetary.org/wp-content/uploads/2014/04/32-page-
brochure.pdf.

76 http://www.themoneymasters.com/monetary-reform-act/.

77 http://www.treasurydirect.gov/govt/reports/ir/ir_expense.htm.

78 https://research.stlouisfed.org/fred2/series/TCMDO.

79 http://www.taxpolicycenter.org/taxfacts/displayafact.cfm?Docid
=203.

80 http://taxfoundation.org/article/rising-cost-complying-federal-
income-tax.

81 http://www.washingtonsblog.com/2012/06/cafr-summary-if-600b-
fund-cant-fund-27b-pension-16b-budget-deficit-why-have-it.html.

82 http://papers.ssrn.com/sol3/papers.cfm?abstract_id=1506452.

83 http://www.federalreserve.gov/pf/pdf/pf_2.pdf.

84 John Williams' shadow government statistics. Alternate inflation
charts. http://www.shadowstats.com/alternate_data/inflation-charts.

85 http://libertyblitzkrieg.com/2013/01/07/chart-of-the-day-
inflation-since-the-american-revolution/.

86 http://www.shadowstats.com/alternate_data/unemployment-charts.

87   Ron Suskind, "Faith, Certainty and the Presidency of George W. Bush", *The New York Times Magazine* (10-17-2004).

88   http://carlbernstein.com/magazine_cia_and_media.php.

89   http://carlbernstein.com/magazine_cia_and_media.php.

90   http://washington.cbslocal.com/2013/0314/obama-says-iran-a-year-away-from-nuclear-weapon/.

91   http://graphics8.nytimes.com/packages/pdf/international/20071203_release.pdf.

92   See http://www.washingtonsblog.com/2012/01/contrary-to-widespread-claims-there-is-no-evidence-that-iran-is-building-a-nuclear-weapon.html.

93   See http://www.washingtonsblog.com/2015/03/iran-wipe-israel-map-read-600-words-confirm-usisrael-criminal-war-lies.html.

94   See http://www.washingtonsblog.com/2012/01/us-overthrew-irans-democracy-1953-1979-armed-iraq-to-invade-1980-1988-now-lies-for-more-war.html.

95   https://dash.harvard.edu/handle/1/4420886.

96   C. Herman, 1917: J.P. Morgan bought US corporate media to be 1%'s lying sacks of spin? 28 Jan 2012, http://washingtonsblog.com/2012/01/1917-j-p-morgan-bought-us-corporate-media-to-be-1s-lying-sacks-of-spin.html.

97   http://www.people-press.org/2007/08/09/internet-news-audience-highly-critical-of-news-organizations/.

98   http://www.people-press.org/2009/09/13/press-accuracy-rating-hits-two-decade-low/.

99   http://cnsnews.com/news/article/michael-w-chapman/gallup-public-confidence-tv-news-all-time-low.

100 M King, "Beyond Vietnam," 4 April 1967, http:// kingencyclopedia .stanford.edu/encyclopedia/documentsentry/ doc_beyond_vietnam.

$$\mathbin{\rlap{\raise0.5ex\hbox{$\sim$}}} 6 \mathbin{\rlap{\raise0.5ex\hbox{$\sim$}}}$$

CHRIS HEDGES ON THE CORRUPTION

OF DCEMOCRACY AND THE COLLAPSE

OF HOPE IN NATIONAL POLITICS

Joseph C. Hough

ABSTRACT: *This essay summarizes Chris Hedges' prophetic writings about climate change, the spread of major military conflicts, the displacement of huge populations, and the globalization of free market capitalism. Corporations now "manage" democracy to benefit their gloval economic interests. Hough agrees with Hedges that the major political parties in the U.S. rely on donations from the richest one percent of Americans but challenges Hedge's call for a third party movement. The history of third party presidential campaigns demonstrates their ineffectiveness. It is better to vote for a major party candidate whose stated positions reflect the primacy of equal justice.*

Chris Hedges is one of the major prophetic voices calling attention to the inevitable catastrophes associated with climate change, the spread of major military conflicts, the displacement of huge populations, and the globalization of free market capitalism. In what follows, I quote sections from a variety of his essays and add comments from other sources relevant to the issues on which I have focused. I conclude with a statement of my major point of disagreement with Chris' position in his essay, "Mania for Hope," and in sections of his book, *Death of the Liberal Class.*

In a 2013 essay, Hedges reports an interview he arranged with political philosopher Sheldon Wollin and philosopher John Ralston Saul, in which he lays out some of the implications of their views for the future of democracy in America. Hedges concludes that the corporate state exploits laws that once protected democracy, in order to extinguish democracy. One example is the decision of the U.S. Supreme Court in the infamous case, *Citizens United v. Federal Election Commission,* in which the Court ruled that money is speech and is protected by the First Amendment to the Constitution. This applies not only to individuals but has also been extended to for-profit corporations, labor unions, and other associations. The result, of course, is the transformation of electoral power from individual voters to those who provide the billions of dollars to fund political campaigns at the state and federal levels.

Furthermore, the state has obliterated privacy through mass surveillance—a fundamental condition for totalitarian rule—and in ways that are patently unconstitutional, has stripped citizens of the right to a living wage, benefits, and job security. The state has destroyed institutions, such as labor unions, that once protected workers from corporate abuse.[1] In other words, the power of money has created in the United States a "managed democracy," a classic case of what Wolin calls "inverted totalitarianism."

Wolin insists that use of the term "inverted totalitarianism" does *not* mean that the United States has morphed into a fascist government like those of Germany under Hitler, Italy under Mussolini, or the Soviet Union under Stalin. In all of these totalitarian states, the aim was to realize "an ideological, idealized conception of a society as a systematically ordered whole, where the 'parts' (family, churches, education, intellectual and cultural life, economy, recreation, politics, state bureaucracy)" are subject to the will of the regime. In short, all of the practice, beliefs, and institutions were subject to the will of the leader and his closest cohorts.[2]

Inverted totalitarianism is quite different. It does not destroy democracy—it "manages democracy." By this is meant that government will be dedicated to the establishment of free markets, the maintenance of world dominance by insuring military supremacy, and the establishment and support of friendly regimes in areas of vital interest to the safety and economy of the nation. Its internal policies are focused on "containing" electoral politics; these policies are essentially hostile to social democracy other than programs furthering literacy, job training, and education necessary for survival in an era of globalization. In Wolin's view, "The United States has become the showcase of how a democracy can be managed without appearing to be suppressed." This has not been the result of the imposition of a leader's will. Rather, it has emerged through certain developments in the economy that have promoted the concentration of wealth and militarization of the nation both internally and externally.

> Voters are made as predictable as consumers, a university is nearly as rationalized in its structure as a corporation; a corporate structure is as hierarchical in its chain of command as the military. The regime ideology is capitalism and all institutions including markets, churches, and entertainment media are eager to enlarge their market share.[3]

In an earlier essay, Hedges turns to what he deems the rise of the security state within American Democracy. Focusing on the plight of Edward Snowden, Hedges writes that government officials who, along with their courtiers in the press, castigate Snowden, insist that congressional and judicial oversight, the right to privacy, the rule of law, freedom of the press, and the right to express dissent remain inviolate. They use the old words and the old phrases, old laws and old constitutional guarantees to give our corporate totalitarianism a democratic veneer. They insist that the system works. They tell us we are still protected by the Fourth Amendment, which states:

> The right of the people to be secure in their persons, houses, papers, and effects, against unreasonable searches and seizures, shall not be violated, and no Warrants shall issue, but upon probable cause, supported by Oath or affirmation,

and particularly describing the place to be searched, and the persons or things to be seized.

Yet the promise of that sentence in the Bill of Rights is pitted against the fact that every telephone call we make, every email or text we send or receive, every website we visit and many of our travels are tracked, recorded and stored in government computers.[4] All of this is, in Hedges' view, a violation of the Fourth Amendment of the Constitution.

According to Hedges, we live in what the German political scientist Ernst Fraenkel called "the dual state." Fraenkel argues that totalitarian states are always so characterized: "In the dual state, civil liberties are abolished in the name of national security. The political sphere becomes a vacuum 'as far as the law is concerned.'"[5] Hedges continues:

> There is no legal check on power. Official bodies operate with impunity outside the law. In the dual state the government can convict citizens on secret evidence in secret courts. It can strip citizens of due process and detain, torture or assassinate them, serving as judge, jury and executioner. It rules according to its own arbitrary whims and prerogatives. The outward forms of democratic participation—voting, competing political parties, judicial oversight and legislation—are hollow, political stagecraft.[6]

In his book, *The Death of the Liberal Class*, Hedges argues that the corruption of democracy has historical roots in times of national peril, especially during the period of World War. He writes that

> [The] hysteria of war destroyed values and self-perceptions that had once characterized American life and replaced them with fear, distrust, and the hedonism of the consumer society. The new mass propaganda designed to appeal to emotions rather than disseminate facts, proved adept at driving competing ideas and values underground.[7] Populists and reformers were vilified. Dissidents and reformers alike were discredited as traitors.

President Wilson pushed through a series of "draconian laws to squelch dissent.... Congress passed the Espionage Act in 1917, which criminalized not only espionage but also speech deemed critical of the government." That plus the passage of the Sedition Act silenced progressives. A few thousand people were arrested. The Socialist politician Eugene Debs was arrested for the "denunciation of the war and calls for draft resistance and strikes." In June 1918 the *Washington Post* denounced Debs as a "public menace," and other reformers who dared speak out against the war were physically attacked or even lynched.[8]

As a result . . . Progressives in World War I shifted from the role of social critics to that of propagandists. They did this seamlessly. The crusades undertaken for the working poor in mill towns and urban slums were transformed into an abstract crusade to remake the world through violence, a war to end all wars . . . The former socialists and activists were, perhaps the most susceptible to Wilson's dreams. . . . Very few found the moral fortitude to resist. And their combined effort to sell the war fatally corrupted the liberal class.[9]

This was a dramatic reversal from an era of social reform that had arisen in the preceding years. This new era led to an age of opulence culminating in the Roaring Twenties when the distribution of wealth exhibited nothing less than obscene economic inequality, and ended in the spectacular collapse of the entire economic order known as the Great Depression.

Hedges clearly believes that the current troubles in the financial sector were rooted in the events surrounding World War I. This view is confirmed and documented in a Pulitzer prizewinning book entitled *Lords of Finance*, written by Liaquat Aamed. Aamed's book is an exhaustive account of the role of the economic elite in the funding of World War I, and the failure of the world's most powerful bankers to avoid the massive and deadly mistakes leading to the Great Depression.[10]

The period of the New Deal under Franklin Roosevelt brought much needed reform focused on those of great need and the restoration of infrastructure, but that was overwhelmed by a new lust for war after the bombing of Pearl Harbor in December of 1941. Once again, a world war and unceasing propaganda overwhelmed civil discourse, and the enormous expenditures required for mobilization cemented the alliance of capitalists and government to a degree greater even than that of World War I. According to Andrew Bacevich, after the end of the Cold War, the United States entered into a state of "permanent war."[11] Following the Korean War, there was Vietnam and then the first Iraq war under President George H. W. Bush. With the election of George W. Bush came the permanent war cabal of Cheney, Wolfowitz, Rice, and Rumsfeld, beginning with the second Iraq war and the war in Afghanistan. We are all aware of the consequence of this ill-fated move that now sees the entire Middle East in chaos from ISIS to Syria to Iraq, Afghanistan, and beyond. For this reason, 80% of our national budget is assigned to the military complex, leaving only 20% of the national budget to address all of the programs of assistance to the unemployed, programs in health care, and assistance to the chronically impoverished in our population that includes as many as 25 million children. That this is immoral is clear, but the control of the political life of the nation by the centers of private and corporate wealth allows little hope for any significant alteration in our current policies.

The control of American politics by the economic elite was not the result of a gradual evolution of political understanding. It was the result of a covert strategy that led to the domination of the political process, a result of careful planning by the economic elite. More than any other single person, it was Lewis Powell, a lawyer for the tobacco industry and, later, a Supreme Court Justice, who was responsible for what Bill Moyers has labeled the rise of an impenetrable plutocracy that has erased any illusion of the "American Democratic Process." Hedges detailed the focused attack on Nader in *The Death of the Liberal Class* that led to the formation of a huge army of conservative "think tanks," and with Bush's presidency, the number of corporate lobbyists increased more than tenfold.[12] Powell's strategy for the control of the American political system began in 1974 when Richard Nixon made a speech to Congress indicating his intent to create a government-based health care system. This enraged conservatives and led to a consistent pattern of organizing to combat any socialist tendencies. These meetings apparently continue from time to time, focusing on the major issues in which corporate leaders have a vested interest.

In Hedges' view:

> the U. S. financial system ... is a mirage. The Federal Reserve purchases $85 billion in U.S. Treasury bonds — most of it worthless subprime mortgages — each month. It has been artificially propping up the government and Wall Street like this for five years. It has loaned trillions of dollars at virtually no interest to banks and firms that make money— because wages are kept low — by lending it to us at staggering interest rates that can climb to as high as 30 percent ... or our corporate oligarchs hoard the money or gamble with it in an overinflated stock market. Estimates put the looting by banks and investment firms of the U.S. Treasury at between $15 trillion and $20 trillion. But none of us know. The figures are not public. And the reason this systematic looting will continue until collapse is that our economy would go into a tailspin without this giddy infusion of free cash.[13]

The consequences are clear. Ellen Brown, in sections **II, III,** and **IV** of her book, *The Web of Debt*, describes in detail the consequences of this alliance.[14] Before 1913, if too many of a bank's depositors came for their money at one time, the bank would have come up short and would have had to close its doors. That was true until the Federal Reserve Act shored up the system by allowing troubled banks to 'borrow' money from the Federal Reserve, which would create it on the spot by selling government securities to a select group of banks that created the money as bookkeeping entries on their books.[15]

Brown concludes that the banks should have been declared bankrupt, and the bankers jailed as embezzlers. However, today the huge banks can be assured that they will be covered, creating a moral hazard that skews the decision-making process when there is a crisis. Meanwhile, the "mega-banks" will continue to engage in highly questionable practices with impunity that will magnify their profits, while at the same time small businesses have no such protection and workers suffer job losses with only minimal provisions to preserve a semblance of a national safety net.

In his essay, "Stand Still for the Apocalypse," Hedges is clear that propaganda supporting those who deny climate change, especially interventions on the part of the major corporations such as the coal and petroleum industries, constitute a major threat to the future of human life and our entire ecosystem: "The political and corporate elites in the industrialized world continue, in spite of overwhelming scientific data, to place short term corporate profit and expediency before the protection of human life and the ecosystem."[16] As a result:

> The ecosystem is at the same time disintegrating. Scientists from the International Programme on the State of the Ocean recently issued a report that warned that the oceans are changing faster than anticipated and increasingly becoming inhospitable to life. The oceans, of course, have absorbed much of the excess CO_2 and heat from the atmosphere. This absorption is rapidly warming and acidifying ocean waters. This is compounded, the report noted, by increased levels of deoxygenation from nutrient runoffs from farming and climate change. The scientists called these effects a "deadly trio" that when combined is creating changes in the seas that are unprecedented in the planet's history. . . . The scientists wrote that each of the earth's five known mass extinctions was preceded by at least one [part] of the "deadly trio"— acidification, warming and deoxygenation. They warned that "the next mass extinction" of sea life is already under way, the first in some 55 million years . . . research from the University of Hawaii says global warming is now inevitable, it cannot be stopped but at best slowed, and that over the next 50 years the earth will heat up to levels that will make whole parts of the planet uninhabitable. Tens of millions of people will

be displaced and millions of species will be threatened with extinction. The report casts doubt that [cities on or near a coast] such as New York or London will endure.[17]

According to William Nordhaus, attempts to organize an international response to this crisis have been very disappointing. A major effort, the Kyoto Protocol, was undertaken in 2008 and ended in 2012. A second commitment period was proposed in 2012, known as the Doha Amendment, in which only 37 countries had binding targets: Australia, the European Union (and its 28 member states), Belarus, Iceland, Kazakhstan, Liechtenstein, Norway, Switzerland, and Ukraine. Others of the original 190 participants have withdrawn from the original agreement or simply have taken no action to reduce carbon dioxide emissions. Negotiations were held in Lima in 2014 to agree on a post-Kyoto legal framework that would obligate all major polluters to pay for CO_2 emissions, but China, India, and the United States have all signaled that they will not ratify any treaty that will commit them legally to reduce CO_2 emissions.

Given this history, Nordhaus indicates that another approach is necessary. He proposes something called "Climate Clubs," in which countries would at least agree to some attempts, such as a carbon tax, to reduce carbon emissions. Countries refusing to participate in the clubs would be penalized through the imposition of a uniform tax on all of their exports to the members of the Climate Clubs. Nordhaus admits that his proposal for Climate Clubs may not be realistic, but he thinks that there is little hope for much success from efforts like the Kyoto Protocol. Thus other means are needed to deal with the threats to life and civilizations.[18]

Later, in the same year that Nordhous expressed his pessimistic view about the Kyoto Protocol, the 2015 United Nations Climate Change Conference was held in Paris from November 30 through December 12. This was actually the 21st session of the Conference of the parties to the 1992 United Nations Framework Convention on Climate Change and the 11th session of the meeting of the parties to the 1997 Kyoto Protocol. This conference produced the Paris Agreement on the reduction of climate change. There were 196 participants. The goal of the conference was to achieve ratification of the agreement by at least 55 nations to limit global warming to less than 2 degrees Celsius. Even though the world's leading sources of greenhouse gas pollution, China and the United States, had already agreed in November of 2014 to limit greenhouse gas emissions, the Paris agreement will not become binding unless the governments of the 55 largest national polluters have ratified the agreement between April 22, 2016, and April 21 2017. Given the current reaction of the United States Congress, the prospects of securing agreement within that time frame are not at all encouraging.

With the Supreme Court decision *Citizens United v. Federal Election Commission* in 2010, the future is more or less permanently shaped. That decision allows virtually unlimited corporate contributions to candidates for political office and for advocacy of particular congressional proposals for enactment of laws. In this situation, it is difficult to generate any substantial hope for significant reversal of state or national legislation except through the intervention of the courts. In this case, both parties are complicit in supporting the agenda of major corporate interests, and there is no indication of a general uprising among negatively affected groups in the society. Hedges writes:

> The yearning for positivism that pervades our corporate culture ignores human nature and human history. But to challenge it, to state the obvious fact that things are getting worse, and may soon get much worse, is to be tossed out of the circle of magical thinking that defines American and much of Western culture. The left is as infected with this mania for hope as is the right. It is a mania that obscures reality even as global capitalism disintegrates and the ecosystem unravels, potentially dooming us all. . . . There is nothing inevitable about human existence except birth and death. There are no forces, whether divine or technical, that will guarantee us a better future. When we give up false hopes, when we see human nature and history for what they are, when we accept that progress is not preordained, then we

can act with an urgency and passion that comprehends the grim possibilities ahead.[19]

A STRATEGY FOR THE FUTURE

So where do we go from here? During a panel discussion in New York in 2014, Hedges said: "We will have to carry out acts of civil disobedience that seek to cripple the mechanisms of corporate power. The corporate elites, blinded by their lust for profit and foolish enough to believe they can protect themselves from climate change, will not veer from our path towards ecocide unless they are forced from power. And this means the beginning of a titanic clash between our corporate masters and ourselves."[20]

And to whom does he refer as "ourselves?" Hedges writes:

> The best opportunities for radical social change exist among the poor, the homeless, the working class, and the destitute. As the numbers of disenfranchised dramatically increase, our only hope is to connect ourselves with the daily injustices visited upon the weak and the outcast. Out of this contact we can resurrect, from the ground up, a new social ethic a new movement.[21]

Yet, he is not optimistic about the possibility for renewal within a foreseeable time frame. The growing danger of the now visible threat of climate change to human life and the whole ecosystem has introduced a powerful strain of pessimism. "Only those who accept the very real possibility of dystopia, of the rise of a ruthless corporate totalitarianism, buttressed by the most terrifying security and surveillance apparatus in human history, are likely to carry out the self-sacrifice necessary for revolt."[22]

Hedges' estimate of the possible bases of renewal in these last two statements rises to the edge of pure fantasy. There is no evidence at all that possibilities for social change will rise from the working class and the destitute. In fact, the evidence, at this time, indicates that vast numbers of working class people have gathered under the banner

of the near neo-fascist Trump movement, and the poor and destitute
have shown no signs at all that they might lead the revolutionary
social change that Hedges advocates.

Furthermore, in response to a question at a public lecture in
Claremont, California, on March 22, 2015, Hedges encouraged a
large audience to consider supporting third party candidates for the
presidency in order to send a message to both of the two major
parties that are both locked in the arms of the richest Americans
and their allies.

I agree with Hedges that both of the major political parties in
the United States are heavily reliant on the largesse of the richest one
percent of Americans for the funding of political campaigns. Though
this is not a new phenomenon, the political power of the so-called
"one percent" has been significantly magnified by the action of the
United States Supreme Court in its January 2010 decision in the
landmark case, *Citizens United v. Federal Election Commission.* In
a 5 to 4 decision, the Court held that nonprofit corporations had a
right to make contributions to political campaigns. This same right
was extended to for-profit corporations, labor unions, and other
associations. The ban on contributions from corporations or unions
to specific candidates' campaigns or political parties remained in place.

This Supreme Court decision, in addition to a decision about three
months later by the Washington, D.C., Circuit Court of Appeals,
SpeechNow.Org v. Federal Election Commission, has opened the gates
for massive infusions of money into every level of political campaigns.
This led to the formation of so-called "super pacs," that could even
engage in the funding of attacks on candidates for public office.[23]

Given the legal context created by these two court decisions, I
seriously doubt that Hedges' call to revolt, or even the call to vote for
third party or independent candidates will yield any national political
challenge to the two major parties at this time, nor has it done so in
the entire history of national elections.

Since 1832, there have been 77 "third party" candidates running
for the presidency, and *none* of them have been elected. However, at

least two of them were widely supported by voters. For example, in 1968, George Wallace carried five states with 48 electoral votes and drew 10 million votes. Though he did not win the presidency, he drew his votes from traditionally Democratic states and his campaign surely was a significant factor in the victory for Republican Richard Nixon over Democrat Hubert Humphrey

Ralph Nader ran as a third-party candidate in six presidential elections beginning in 1972. He was never a major factor in any of the outcomes of the elections until 2008. In that year, he garnered almost 740,000 votes, clearly not enough to challenge the other candidates. Yet according to Eric Zuesse "Nader-voters who spurned Democrat Al Gore to vote for Nader ended up swinging both Florida and New Hampshire to Bush in 2000." Zeusse cites an article in the *New York Times* of March 9, 2004, by Charlie Cook. Zeusse quotes Cook as arguing that

> Mr. Nader, running as the Green Party nominee, cost Al Gore two states, Florida and New Hampshire, either of which would have given the vice president [Gore] a victory in 2000. In Florida, which George W. Bush carried the election by 537 votes, Mr. Nader received nearly 100,000 votes [nearly 200 times the size of Bush's Florida "win"]. In New Hampshire, which Mr. Bush won by 7,211 votes, Mr. Nader pulled in more than 22,000 [three times the size of Bush's "win" in that state.

Zeusse continues:

> If either of those two states had gone instead to Gore, then Bush would have lost the 2000 election; we would never have had a U.S. President George W. Bush, and so Nader managed to turn not just one but two key toss-up states for candidate Bush, and to become the indispensable person making G. W. Bush the President of the United States.[23]

Had Gore won the 2000 presidential election, I seriously doubt that the debacle of war in Iraq would have occurred. In retrospect that alone would be a sufficient reason for Nader voters to have second thoughts.

Given this history, in contrast to voting for any third party candidate, I try to vote for the major party candidates whose stated positions more closely reflect the convictions I have about the primacy of equal justice or "brotherhood" as a norm for political life, as described in the writings of Reinhold Niebuhr. Throughout his writings Niebuhr reminds us that the principles of justice can be seen as servants of the spirit of brotherhood

> in so far as they extend the sense of obligation towards the other, (a) from an immediately felt obligation, prompted by obvious need, to a continued obligation expressed in fixed principles of mutual support; (b) from a simple relation between a self and one "other" to the complex relations of the self and the "others"; and (c) finally from the obligations, discerned by the individual self, to the wider obligations which the community defines from its more impartial perspective.[25]

And yet, judgments about persons and policies remain at best difficult. As Niebuhr puts it in one of his early writings about political organizations,

> Conflict between the national units remains as a permanent rather than a passing characteristic of their relations to each other; and each national unit finds it increasingly difficult to maintain either peace or justice within its common life.[26]

This means that we *never* have the option of voting for candidates whose convictions will coincide perfectly with our own, but we clearly have the option, even the moral obligation, to lend our support to and cast our votes for *viable* candidates whose stated and obvious intentions stand closest to the norms of justice that we see as ideal.

ENDNOTES

1   Chris Hedges, "Let's Get This Class War Started," Truthdig, Oct. 20, 2013, http://www.truthdig.com/report/item/lets_get_this_class

_war_started20131020.

2   Sheldon Wolin, *Democracy Incorporated* (Princeton: Princeton University Press, 2010), 46.

3   Ibid., 46, 47.

4   Chris Hedges, "Our Sinister Dual State" Truthdig, Feb. 114, 2014, http://www.truth-out.org/opinion/item/21925-our-sinister-dual-state.

5   Ernst Fraenkel, *The Dual State: A Contribution to the Theory of Dictatorship* (New York: Oxford University Press, 2006).

6   Hedges, "Our Sinister Dual State."

7   Chris Hedges, *Death of the Liberal Class* (New York: Nation Books, 2010), 64.

8   Ibid., 65.

9   Ibid., 65, 66.

10 Liaquat Aamed, *Lords of Finance: The Bankers Who Broke The World* (London: Penguin Press, 2009).

11 For a comprehensive discussion of the process and consequences of the march to permanent war, see Andrew J. Bacevich, *Washington Rules: American's Path to Permanent War* (New York: Metropolitan Books, 2010).

12 Ibid., 174–83. See also, Thomas E. Mann and Norman J. Ornstein, *It's Even Worse Than it Looks* (New York: Basic Books, 2012).

13 Chris Hedges, "The Myth of Human Progress and the Collapse of Complex Societies," https://www.sott.net/article/272753-The-Myth-of-Human-Progress-and-the-Collapse-of-Complex-Societies.

14 Ellen Hodgson Brown, *The Web of Debt, The Shocking Truth About our Money System and How We Can Break Free* (Baton Rouge, LA: Third Millennium Press, 2007 (December 2008 update), 103–330.

15 Ibid., 328–29.

16 Chris Hedges, "Stand Still for the Apocalypse," Truthdig, Nov. 26, 2012, http://www.truthdig.com/report/item/stand_still_for_the_apocalypse_20121126.

17 Hedges, "The Myth of Human Progress and the Collapse of Complex Societies."

18   William Nordhaus, "Climate Clubs, Overcoming Free-Riding in International Climate Policy," *American Economics Review,* 105:4 (April 2015).

19   Chris Hedges, "Our Mania for Hope Is a Curse," Truthdig, May 24, 2015, http://www.truthdig.com/report/item/lets_get_this_class _war_started20131020.

20   Chris Hedges, panel discussion in New York City titled "The Climate Crisis: Which Way Out" New York, 21 September 2014, http://www. commondreams.org/views/2014/09/22/coming-climate-revolt.

21   Hedges, *The Death of the Liberal Class,* 156.

22   Hedges, "Our Mania for Hope Is a Curse."

23   John Dunbar, "The Citizens United decision and why it matters," The Center for Public Integrity, October 2012, updated; 14 March 2016, https://www.publicintegrity.org/2012/10/18/11527 /citizens-united-decision-and-why-it-matters.

24   Eric Zuesse,"Ralph Nader was indispensable to The Republican Party," Huffington Post, 11 November 2013, updated 23 June 2014.

25   Reinhold Niebuhr, *The Nature and Destiny of Man, Vol. II* (New York: Charles Scribner's Sons, 1941), 247–48.

26   Reinhold Niebuhr, *Moral Man and Immoral Society* (New York: Charles Scribner's Sons, 1934), 3.

≯ 7 ≯

THE "REVOLUTION" WE NEED

Sheila D. Collins

ABSTRACT: *Chris Hedges has called for a new, radical, totalistic move-ment, or "revolution," but he has not spelled out what kind of revolution he is calling for, who would organize it, how it would be organized, or how it would seize power. Drawing lessons from the history of both the successes and failures of past social movements, this article suggests some of the elements that are needed for a successful political revolution in the 21ˢᵗ century that would be both electoral and extra-electoral in character, as well as some of the international law doctrines that organizers could utilize to establish the legitimacy of their revolution.*

BOTH BERNIE SANDERS AND CHRIS HEDGES have called for a political revolution. Beyond using the phrase, Sanders has not spelled out what kind of revolution he is calling for, who would organize it, how it would be organized, or how it would seize power. For Hedges, it means taking to the streets in some unspecified way, despite the fact that he also argues that we have turned into a total-itarian state with all of the police powers that term implies. Hedges sees Bernie's "political revolution," as a cynical form of advertising that will end as an impediment to the mass movements he claims to represent, leading us right back to establishment liberals like Hillary Clinton who, along with her husband, "are responsible as much as anyone on the right for our being sacrificed on the altar of corporate profit."[1] What are we to make of these two calls for revolution? Is Bernie's campaign just a cynical ploy to appease the masses who are clearly fed up with the status quo? Is Hedges' call to take to the streets at all realistic? Is it feasible, given what we know of the character of the American population and the power of the police state? I will argue that we need to outline a position somewhere between the two. But before taking a stab at outlining some of the elements of a feasible revolution, I think we need to take a brief look at both the challenges we face and the opportunities we may have.

THE CHALLENGES

- *The end of liberal democracy.* The almost complete capture of the machinery of government by big money, the Republican capture of state governments, and their gerrymandering of districts have swept away the illusion that we had a democracy that would respond to peoples' needs or even to their votes. Micah White, one of the Occupy movement organizers, argues in his book, *The End of Protest,* that we live in a time when there is no way for ordinary people to influence their governments through protest because there is no democracy left to respond positively to protest as happened in the 1930s and the 1960s. He learned this lesson, he says, from the Occupy movement.[2]

- *A deeply polarized population.* We're polarized by race/ethnicity, gender, age, income, and educational attainment as we have seldom been so polarized before. Our population is too easily manipulated by demagogues like Trump who use racism, xenophobia, homophobia, and sexism to divide and conquer those who should be united around common economic and environmental challenges.

- *A mass media that magnifies the sensational, the food fights, the mean and the violent, while ignoring the positive stories and the information we need to make intelligent decisions.* All of this has created an echo chamber where neither side understands nor can communicate with the other.

- *Unprecedented police state power.* Unlike past periods of social protest, we face a situation of unprecedented (at least in this country) police state power. The militarization of police forces around the country, the extent of the surveillance state, and the ability of those in power to anticipate and prevent mass protest before it even happens means that we are up against a much more powerful set of forces than past protest movements faced.

- *Challenges that go far beyond the ability of one country to meet them.* Galloping climate change (and a Republican majority that is in denial about it), a global refugee crisis, the expansion of Middle East conflicts, and the unsolved nuclear threat that may be greater today than in the last 30 years.

SIGNS OF HOPE

Yet there are signs that the moment we are living in may be riper for significant social change if we can harness and direct the social turbulence that is erupting everywhere. What are some of these signs?

- *The popularity of populist campaigns of both the right and left.* The tremendous level of inequality in our society has made both the Trump and Sanders campaigns possible. It means that millions of people now recognize the unfairness in our economy and are willing to buck political elites to vote for challengers to the status quo.

- *An outbreak of some large and thousands of small social protests.* From Occupy Wall Street, to the largest climate march in history, to the outbreak of Black Lives Matter, to the largest

women's march ever, to the Moral Monday movement, to
the thousands of smaller protest movements against fracking
and pipelines, against plant closures, unjust incarceration,
and for immigrant rights and the minimum wage, etc., we
are seeing an uprising of discontent that has been missing for
some time. For what was called "Democracy Spring," over
3,000 people pledged to risk arrest between April 11-18, 2016.
"Democracy Spring" was planned to be one of the largest civil
disobedience actions in a generation — a sit-in at the nation's
capitol to demand a congress that is not bought by big money
but works for all the people. The action is sponsored by over
100 organizations and many prominent leaders. In addition, a
Poor People's Campaign, modeled after the aborted campaign
organized by Dr. Martin Luther King, Jr., before he died,
and led by the Rev. William Barber of the Moral Monday
movement, is uniting tens of thousands of people across the
country in a series of rallies and civil disobedience campaigns
aimed at calling the country back to policies built on an ethic
of care and compassion both for people and the earth.

- *Demographics are in our favor, but not in the short-run. The
  level of environmental catastrophe is now hitting even the affluent.* The gas leak in the affluent Porter Ranch community in
  Southern California;[3] the discovery by parents of children in
  Malibu, California,[4] that they may be facing the same kind of
  official neglect over an environmental hazard as the parents
  in Flint, Michigan; the wildfires that have engulfed affluent
  communities on the West Coast; and the sea-level rise in
  Miami Beach are the canaries in the coal mine indicating
  that the environmental threat to the planet will eventually
  hit everyone.

- *The realization among many that we are living on borrowed
  time for the planet and that radically new ways of organizing
  our society must be found.* This is evidenced in the proliferation

of networks like the Next System Project, the Transition Towns Movement, the Pando Populus network, the anti-GMO movement, the movement for public banking, and of more localized efforts like farmers' markets and farm-to-food cooperatives.

Although we are in a period of unprecedented challenges, in order to harness this energy we need to start by drawing some lessons from selected social movements of the past. We can learn from history, both from its successes as well as its failures. In what follows, I lay out some of these lessons, then look at some of the resources we have available.

FRAMING THE NARRATIVE

Each movement—whether the Abolitionist movement, the labor movement, the civil rights movement, etc.—had to develop a narrative about its mission in order to persuade people to join its ranks and to appeal to the wider society. In recent years, we have allowed the Right to frame our national narrative. For example, the Right, in its obsession with deficits, manipulated concern for the future by framing running up a deficit (which, in the absence of public banking, is money owed to Wall Street creditors) as "stealing our children's future." The reality of climate change and galloping inequality is what is actually threatening our children's future. The Right has also claimed the phrase, "the right to life," to deny women the right to make choices about their own bodies although that phrase properly belongs to the climate movement that seeks to protect life. In studying past movements we can gain a perspective on what must constitute a successful frame.

- *The cause should be framed as inclusive and universal*—one that affects and resonates with the great majority of the population. Given the fact that we are living in a deeply polarized society, movements that are too narrowly defined will not be able to build the kind of broad-based movement we need. Too often, movements of the Left have been framed either in such sectarian terms that the majority of Americans are turned off by the message, or they have been defined as single-issue movements—the feminist movement (many women did not see themselves as feminists), or the **LGBT** movement (which, with the exception of the parents of gays, leaves out most heterosexuals), or the environmental movement (many workers, especially those in the energy industry, as well as those suffering from economic or racial oppression have not seen themselves as addressed by this movement). Not to negate the critical importance of the issue that it addresses, but the Black Lives Matter movement is another example of such siloing. There is, of course, a tension between the variety of ways in which differing groups of people are impacted by the system and the need to find a universal language that doesn't appear to exclude anyone or to mitigate the more intense suffering that some groups experience. We need to be sensitive to that tension, but we can't go on replicating the competition between forms of oppression if we're going to build a revolution that can be effective. When we do so, it just plays into the divide-and-conquer strategy of those who hold the power. I learned this when I was directing a program funded by a national church agency that brought community organizers from disparately oppressed communities together in the late 1970s. Our early gatherings were food fights over whose oppression was worst: Native Americans, African Americans, women, gays, etc. When participants in the network finally agreed to support each other's campaigns instead of fighting over crumbs it became so effective that it threatened both the source of the funding and the political power structure in an area of the country that the network had decided to challenge.

The Clamshell Alliance provides an example of the kind of inclusivity we need. As one of the most successful of the early environmental movements, the Clamshell Alliance articulated the message that ordinary people had the right, the ability, and the responsibility to challenge and change the direction of energy policy in the U.S. This inclusiveness pulled strength and members from feminist, anti-Vietnam War, Native American rights, labor, environmental and back-to-the-land movements, while quietly sidestepping the approaches of the "hard" Left. Jim Lawson, who led the nonviolent training workshops for the civil rights movement, framed the issue of civil rights in an inclusive manner. Lawson said recently that throughout the entirety of the movement he never heard anyone speak about the struggle as a struggle for "civil rights." It was, rather, a struggle for "dignity, equality, humanity." He explained that by defining the movement as a struggle to reinstate core values shared by Blacks and the wider society, civil rights organizers enabled the struggle to resonate far beyond the African American community.[5]

Jesse Jackson called his insurgent campaign for the 1984 presidential primary campaign the Rainbow Coalition and framed it as a movement that drew together the diversity of populations that were being oppressed in a variety of ways by the dominant political and economic system.[6] People who identified with their oppression as racial minorities, or as women, as gays and lesbians, or as farmers who were losing their land to agribusiness, as peace activists struggling against the war machine, or as environmentalists fighting nuclear power and the poisoning of our air and water could all find a place in the Rainbow Coalition. The Democratic party elite and mass media continually sought to frame the campaign as a black ethnic campaign, and to some extent they were successful. But nonblack people, many even in the South who said they had been racists, resonated to the call, especially when they could hear Jackson in person, not filtered through the distorting lens of the mass media.

The reason the Occupy Wall Street movement took off so quickly and resonated so widely was its use of the term, "the 99 percent." In that way almost everyone but the top 1 percent could feel included in the cause. It may be that the reason the recent fight for the recognition of gay marriage has been successful was because the movement had succeeded in framing the issue, not as one of "gay rights," but of "marriage equality" and "human rights,"—more inclusive terms. Today we need to find a language and strategy that links all of the single-issue movements into a universal, inclusive struggle for life itself.

- *The cause must be framed as moral and ethical.* The most successful movements have framed their cause in moral, ethical terms. Despite the daily diet of violent, competitive messages served up from the media, most people retain a sense of fairness and justice. They know there is something terribly wrong about a society that rewards the wealthy and powerful, punishes the poor, and destroys the environment. Yet too many movement activists seek to explain why they are concerned in terms that are so technical or value-free that the majority has not been moved to see its own stake in the problems that need to be addressed. While 350.org works hard globally to bring about changes in environmental policy, as a slogan or title for a movement it does not resonate as widely as possible because the meaning of 350 is obscure to most people who aren't on the front lines of the climate crisis or are not conversant with climate science. The obscurity of the organization's title lacks moral appeal. Moreover, workers in the energy industry see this movement as their enemy— taking away their jobs and value. The early labor movement, on the other hand, was formed as a movement for human dignity, for bread and roses. Its slogans were: "an injury to one is an injury to all," "the union makes us one," and its theme song was "Solidarity Forever." The early twentieth century social gospel movement, which profoundly shaped a generation of young Christian men and women who went on to become this country's most important social change organizers, was a moral movement that linked racial and economic justice, peace, and democracy. The presidents most beloved by the masses — Abraham Lincoln and Franklin D. Roosevelt — framed the issues in moral terms. Think of the soaring words of the Gettysburg Address, or the words of **FDR** from his first and second inaugurals: "The money changers have fled from their high seats in the temple of our civilization. We may now restore that temple to the ancient truths. The measure of the restoration lies in the extent to which we apply social values more noble than mere monetary profit." Or, "The test of our progress is not whether we add more to the abundance of those who have much — it is whether we provide enough for those who have little." It is also a moral appeal that is the basis of Pope Francis's encyclical on the environment.

- *The cause must be framed as positive and inspirational.* Yes, we are protesting the evils, but what are we *for*? What is the vision of the better life toward which we wish to draw participants? The large and somewhat successful anti-nuclear movement of the 1980s was not just against nukes; it was *for* a nuclear-free world. The slogan of the Social Forum was "a different world is possible." We need to get more specific about what that different world entails and be able to paint a picture of it that will attract and inspire millions of people. Bernie's campaign has resonated so widely among so many because it was more specific than any other candidate in drawing a picture of what a good society looks like.

Music and art, which touch the heart and the soul, provided inspiration for the movements that erupted in the 1930s.

During the Depression, artists, playwrights, musicians, and photographers—thanks largely to the New Deal—sought to give the country a portrait of the diversity of cultures and aesthetic sensibilities that actually existed in the country and the struggles for justice and dignity that the people were waging.[7] And there were public intellectuals who could embody the public mood, articulate its grievances, and provide inspiration—people like the pacifist and labor advocate A. J. Muste, muckraking author Lewis Sinclair, documentarian of the dignity of the poor James Agee, poet Langston Hughes, literary critic Irving Howe, and others. Music and art were also critical to the movements of the 1960s. Folksingers like Pete Seeger, Phil Ochs, Peter, Paul and Mary, Joan Baez, Harry Belafonte, Arlo Guthrie, Bob Dylan, Odetta, and Buffy Sainte-Marie were the movement's troubadours. Martin Luther King, Jr.'s genius was his ability to paint that vision in prophetic terms—his "I Have a Dream" speech being the most emblematic—and the Sixties had its own contingent of public intellectuals in addition to King, like radical lawyer William Kuntsler, political activist and teacher Angela Davis, comedian Dick Gregory, and peoples' historian Howard Zinn, among others. History teaches us that it is a mistake to depend too heavily on charismatic leaders like King or Malcolm to carry a movement. Thus, we have to develop numerous "public intellectuals," or, in Gramsci's terms, "organic intellectuals," who can articulate what we are up against and provide us with inspirational messages and hope. Fortunately, there are many today like Bill McKibben, Naomi Klein, Cornel West, Gar Alperovitz, Richard Wolff, Joanna Macy, Henry A. Giroux, John Cobb, and David Griffin to name just a few, that are providing such inspiration.

FACTORS IN SOCIAL MOVEMENT SUCCESS

In 1929, most Americans were more demoralized than mobilized. Mass unemployment in the 1930s occurred more rapidly and with fewer economic cushions than it did in the aftermath of the 2008 economic meltdown, so in the 1930s, more people were desperate, having nothing left to lose by joining mass movements. And they did. By 1932, mass movements of the unemployed—workers, artists, writers, WWI veterans, and the elderly—were out in the streets or sitting down in factories. Their actions resulted in the greatest shift of power between the masses and the elite in this country's history. Though they didn't overthrow capitalism, they tamed it considerably for about a half century.

Trained and Ideologically Oriented Organizers

Thus, a sudden catastrophe played a role in awakening people to take action. But catastrophe alone does not produce social movement change. An inner change has to happen for people to be willing to contravene the political inertia that is built into the political and cultural system. The presence of ideologically committed organizers during a period of crisis was and is key. Poor people typically lack resources for organized protest. This weakness was overcome with an infusion of external resources. During the 1930s, ideologically oriented and trained members of the Communist Party were the first to organize and were the most active. These organizers were particularly adept at helping jobless workers overcome their tendency to self-blame and to understand their "private" troubles as public grievances. In time, other radical groups provided these resources: the Workers' Committees organized by members of the Socialist Party and other groups of socialists, and the Unemployed Leagues led by the Left-wing minister and activist A. J. Muste. Eventually, elites at various levels of government lent their support.[8]

The 1950s were known as the age of consumerism and conformism. Who would have thought that the conformist fifties would erupt into the rebellious Sixties? But the Sixties rebellions were not spontaneous. When the civil rights movement arose, most of the tactics and strategies had already been developed and honed during the 1940s by organizers who had been shaped and ideologically oriented by the social gospel movement of the 1920s and 1930s, as well as by their study of the nonviolent, direct-action philosophy and practice of Mahatma Gandhi. The first sit-ins were carried out in 1942 by Congress of Racial Equality (**CORE**) activists like Jim Farmer and George Houser, and the first "freedom ride" into the upper South was organized by Bayard Rustin and George Houser in 1947. Thus, the civil rights movement of the Sixties was not starting from scratch.

Perhaps if the student activists of the 1960s had learned from the student movements of the 1930s, they could have avoided some of the mistakes that were made. According to one of its historians, "the student rebels of the Depression era rank among the most effective radical organizers in the history of American student politics."[9] And unlike their counterparts in Germany, they appealed to the better angels of our nature, encouraging students to identify with the working class, to value a more just distribution of income and wealth, and to oppose racism and war. During its peak years, from spring 1936 to spring 1939, the student movement mobilized at least 500,000 collegians (about half of the American student body) in annual one-hour strikes against war. It was the first mass student protest movement in American history. The movement also organized students on behalf of an extensive reform agenda, which included federal aid to education, government job programs for youth, abolition of the compulsory Reserve Officers' Training Corps (**ROTC**), academic freedom, racial equality, and collective bargaining rights.[10]

Safe Spaces

In addition to ideologically committed and trained organizers, safe spaces for meeting, training, and strategizing were critical to the civil rights movement. Black churches were important as safe locations for mass meetings and as sources of inspirational oratory, music, and prayer. Of course, some of these churches were bombed, but it was crucial to have a space that the movement could more or less control. The church bombings also worked to catalyze more sympathetic white support. The Highlander Center in Tennessee played a critical role in the formation of nonviolent activists and cultural workers. One of the problems of the Occupy Wall Street movement was that it eventually had no safe spaces when its encampments were demolished. The drastic curtailing of our public spaces is something we need to strategize carefully about.

New Organizational Structures

New organizational structures like the Southern Christian Leadership Conference (**SCLC**), the Student Nonviolent Coordinating Committee (**SNCC**) and the Southern Conference Educational Fund (**SCEF**) also had to be created to provide the overall coordination and fundraising for the civil rights movement. The anarchists who began the Occupy movement continually eschewed the development of more formal organizational structure and rejected the development of clear policy proposals and demands. The informal structure and lack of a coherent program could not survive the destruction of the encampments. While a great deal of education and informal training went on during Occupy Wall Street encampments, with no long-term organizational support for such education and training, Occupy faltered after the encampments were broken up. To be sure, its remnants remain and many who participated have gone on to organize other movements such as Occupy Sandy, Black Lives Matter, campus fossil fuel divestment campaigns, anti-fracking campaigns, and the like, but as a visible, mass movement it no longer exists. The training and education that went on during Occupy was indeed revolutionary, but it needs to be systematized and institutionalized so that thousands of people can get the training and pass it on to others. We need training centers all over the country to educate and train ideologically committed organizers.

AN INSIDE-OUTSIDE STRATEGY

If mass social protests have lost their efficacy, as Micah White suggests, we must build two kinds of movements, or perhaps one movement with two branches: one that is capable of mounting various kinds of civil disobedience campaigns and remains independent of political parties, and another movement that can mount political campaigns and run people for office on a clear, principled platform. We need to have people massing in the streets, calling a halt to business as usual, but we also need to have people inside government at various levels who are able and willing to respond to the demands coming from the outside. Without that inside power, outside power is impotent. Without that outside power, inside power is easily corrupted. Thus there is the need for an ongoing, independent movement that can continually hold public officials accountable beyond elections. Such a movement must be able to control part of its environment, such as having its own means of communication and education, its own institutions for gathering and strategizing, and its own means of financing the movement. This will not be easy. Most social movements have had a limited trajectory. As Patrick Barrett in a *Truthout* post pointed out, for most people "social movement building is simply too difficult because of the collective action problems it poses, thereby making the simplicity of elections, with their very limited time commitment and narrow objective of electing or unseating individual politicians, that much more seductive".[11]

There have been few times in American history when we have had such a synergy between extra-electoral and electoral politics. The populist movement of the late nineteenth century Gilded Age was one such period. According to Lawrence Goodwyn, its biographer, "it was the last substantial effort at structural alteration of hierarchical economic forms in modern America."[12] Farmers in the Midwest and South who were being driven off their land formed a mass movement that had its own speakers' bureau, its own newspapers, and its own candidates willing to run for office. In a time before mass transit, automobiles, telephones, or the Internet, thousands of people gathered to hear the message of its speakers, to form producer cooperatives, and to engage in civil disobedience. Eventually it formed its own party, the Populist Party, and was successful in winning offices in state houses for several candidates. Key ingredients in this movement were 1) the creation of an autonomous institution where new interpretations that ran counter to those of prevailing authority could be heard; 2) the creation of a tactical means to attract masses of people; 3) the achievement of a heretofore culturally unsanctioned level of social analysis; and 4) the creation of an institutional means whereby the new ideas, shared now by the rank and file, could be expressed in an autonomous political way.[13]

The Populist movement, so promising in its early stages, eventually foundered over racial conflict and differing sectional interests. Although the movement sought to unite poor black and white farmers in a mutual alliance, the racism and nativism of white southern farmers eventually could not be overcome and the movement—largely an agrarian one—was never able to speak the language of urban immigrant industrial workers. And although its electoral victories at the state level were impressive, it made the mistake of throwing all of its eggs into the 1896 Democratic presidential campaign of William Jennings Bryan rather than continuing to build the long-term autonomous Populist movement. Bryan's defeat, by the triumphant business class, spelled the end of the Populist movement. Its dependence on the outcome of the presidential election was a major strategic mistake. Although the Populist movement did not achieve the overturning of capitalist class relations, several of the ideas it had espoused were incorporated into the agenda of Progressives and given legislative voice by both the reforms of the Teddy and Franklin D. Roosevelt administrations.

Another and different take on the extra-electoral/electoral strategy occurred during the Great Depression. The movements in the streets in the 1930s did not spawn an independent party but did help to catalyze a reform-minded Democratic administration that, in turn, provided legislative mechanisms for further activism. One such mechanism was section 7(a) of the National Industrial Recovery Act (**NIRA**) which empowered workers to organize and, when the **NIRA** was declared unconstitutional, to push for the enactment of the National Labor Relations Act (**NLRA**) giving workers for the first time legal power vis-à-vis their employers. Continuously throughout the 1930s, it was radical groups pushing for more radical solutions than they knew government would accept that forced the government to come up with reforms that made a real difference in the lives of the majority. However, the movements of the 30s never cohered into a unified movement, partly because of deep racial and sectarian divisions. And once New Deal reforms were enacted, the movement as an outside force holding government accountable and pushing for more, for the most part dissolved. The Republican Right learned the lesson that the Left failed to learn. After Goldwater's defeat they hunkered down for the long haul, building the institutions and think tanks and political memes and electoral capacity to eventually enact a takeover of the machinery of government. But just as power corrupts, so the successful Republican establishment has spawned its own counterrevolution in the form of the Tea Party.

Since the electoral process today is so corrupted by money, how can an electoral campaign of the Left possibly win against such odds? The answer is that it has to be a different kind of electoral campaign. Those who now own our government may have enormous power as a result of their wealth, but they are a minority of the population. We have the numbers, and if we could use that advantage through old-fashioned grass roots, door-to-door campaigning, as well as the clever use of social media, we might just be able to make headway. The Sanders' campaign did not automatically build a political revolution, just as the Obama election did not build a movement. But several people think that this time might be different. Harold Meyerson thinks things may be different today "chiefly because because Bernie Sanders's campaign didn't create a new American left. It revealed it". Meyerson points to numerous polls that indicate unprecedented numbers of people who identify themselves as socialists. According to Meyerson, a lot of progressives are now talking and strategizing about how to build on Bernie's momentum.[14] Miles Mogulescu in the *Huffington Post* points to several organizations already in place that could be expected to join such an effort including the Working Families Party, National People's Action, Democracy for America,

Progressive Democrats of America, Democratic Socialists of America, MoveOn, and The Progressive Change Campaign Committee.[15]

What would such an electoral strategy look like? Working for the Jackson presidential primary in 1984 provided me with a vision of what an insurgent campaign might look like.[16] The campaign drew its organizers not from traditional electoral political circles but from organizers who had cut their teeth in the various progressive movements that made up the Rainbow Coalition. As a result, their organizing tactics, while using some of the same technical mechanisms as traditional politics—phone calling, town hall meetings, press conferences, etc.—they more often resembled old fashioned social movement building techniques. In every city or town the campaign went into, its organizers gathered up the stories of that city's history of oppression and people's struggles against it. They then fed that information into the candidate's speeches so that when Jackson spoke, he gave back to his audiences a picture of their own lost or suppressed history as well as a picture of their real grievances. Jackson also had a genius for being able to weave into his speeches the issues represented in the rainbow into a coherent picture, showing how they were all interrelated, and often demonstrated those connections concretely; for example, by having struggling family farmers deliver food from their farms to poor inner-city blacks, thus making the connection between the loss of family farms to agribusiness and the overpriced food poor urban people were forced to buy. Whenever working class whites—especially those in the South—heard and experienced such connections, they saw that their racism had been a game the elites had played on them to keep them divided from their natural allies, and they flocked to the campaign. Although Jackson did not become the Democratic presidential candidate, he did win a sizeable vote against great odds. Most of those who participated in that campaign wished to see the Rainbow Coalition continue as an independent political movement, but for reasons known only to himself, Jackson squelched that possibility. The Rainbow Coalition continued, but in a diminished form as a tool of Jackson himself, not as the broad radical movement it could have become. The importance of an ongoing, broad, radical movement not tied to any one political candidate was the lesson that should have been learned from the collapse of both the Populist movement following the 1896 presidential campaign and the Jesse Jackson campaign.

A GOVERNMENT ACCOUNTABLE TO THE PEOPLE

The current emphasis among many social change activists is on localism as a response to corporate domination and unaccountable government. While there is no doubt that we must democratize more of our life at the local and regional levels, the imminent threat of climate change and the need to undo the damage of decades of social and infrastructural neglect cannot be done by local communities alone. We need a large government, but one that is responsive and accountable to the public. It is no accident that the Right in this country has sought to destroy what they call "big government," and to erase the memory of the 1930s when "big government" actually worked to a significant extent for the people. We need a new Reconstruction Finance Corporation, such as the one Roosevelt used in the 1930s, to fund the rebuilding of our crumbling infrastructure, construct mass transit systems, build the grid that will enable us to switch to renewable energy sources, and fund small, locally owned businesses. We need an equivalent of the New Deal's Civilian Conservation Corps (CCC) which employed poor, unemployed youth, WWI veterans, and Native Americans to restore an environment that had been so decimated that we could have faced climate change and species extinction much earlier in our history had the CCC not planted billions of trees, eradicated white pine blister rust and malaria, tamed floods, restored destroyed soils, and saved wildlife. We need the equivalent of the New Deal's Works Progress Administration (WPA) to employ all those who have given up looking for work to educate our children, provide health and elder care, build infrastructure and employ artists to beautify it, as well as providing for all those who can least afford it access to participation in and the enjoyment of the arts as was done in the 1930s. We need a single payer national health care system. The experience of the 1930s[17] teaches us that enlightened leadership, using the power of government, is needed in such a large transboundary undertaking as restoring a depleted environment. When large government is put into such service, the earth proves resilient. Moreover, Roosevelt's programs created the leaders for the environmental movement that erupted in the 1960s, and that movement gave us whatever protections for our environment that now exist—protections that the corporate elite are working hard to eliminate. We also need a strong national government to work at the international level to limit greenhouse gas emissions and provide developing countries with the tools they need to adapt to climate change.

At the same time that we need to work toward a strong national government, the electoral movement needs to learn a lesson from the Tea Party: that if you can't move the mountain, start with the foothills. City, state and country governments can often initiate changes that are later adopted at the national level or can undermine intransigence at the national level. What if we were to start running candidates for office that come out of the leadership of the movements themselves? Progressives have for too long neglected the lower levels of government where it is often easier for candidates to run and get elected. Thus, an electoral strategy has to focus on building local and state-level electoral institutions and running candidates at these levels.

PROSPECTS FOR A NEW MOVEMENT TODAY

Bernie Sanders' campaign has demonstrated that large numbers of people are ready for a political revolution and that they are willing to pay for it. His grassroots fundraising via the internet shows us how such a political movement can now be funded.

But how is the polarization that currently paralyzes such a revolution to be overcome? There is, first, the polarization within the Left over tactics. To some extent this is a generational problem. Those mostly older folks who come out of strong organizational backgrounds like trade unions and political party formations want strong organizational structures while the younger generation, raised on social media, have a tendency toward anarchism. That dichotomy has to be acknowledged and worked out. It was a constant frustration in Occupy Wall Street. There is also the racial polarization. An effective movement will have to overcome this perennial barrier to progressive achievement.

But a real revolution must also mobilize the majority of the population, not just those who identify as leftists or progressives. What could be the source of the interconnections we need? People on both the Right and the Left are registering their anger with a government that has capitulated to Wall Street and that it has become unresponsive to their needs. As the environmental crisis deepens, affecting more segments of the society, even segments of the affluent may be persuaded to join the revolution. But it must be a revolution that is based on some kind of legitimacy. We're not talking about armed insurrection.

We might think in terms of what Jeremy Brecher has termed a "constitutional insurgency," in which participants declare that the perpetrators of economic, racial, and environmental injustice — whether by private corporations or by governments doing their bidding — are acting illegally.[18] Participants in such a movement would declare themselves as acting to uphold the true spirit of the law even if they have to resort to civil disobedience, strikes, and boycotts.

Just as the civil rights movement insisted that it was simply calling for the enforcement of rights already provided by our Constitution, so a new movement could draw on several instruments of international law to support its actions.[19] Progressives have too often failed to use mechanisms like these that have already achieved legitimacy but are rarely enforced. One, of course, is the Universal Declaration of Human Rights. The movement we would hope to build might draw up a new Bill of Rights for the 21st century, modeled after the Universal Declaration and F. D. Roosevelt's Second or Economic Bill of Rights but extended to include populations that are still denied basic rights, as well as the right of all to a healthful and sustainable environment. This could be used as an educational tool as well as a way to test the legitimacy of candidates for office.

Another possible instrument is the obligation of governments embedded in the U.N. Charter for the protection of individuals and peoples within their territories. Clearly individuals and peoples (as in Flint, Michigan) are being harmed by the actions of private corporations and governments when they destroy the environment and human health. "We the people" thus have an obligation to protect if governments controlled by the corporate elite are unwilling to do so.

Another instrument is the principle of the "common heritage of mankind." This ethical and general concept of international law establishes that some localities such as the deep international seabed, the Arctic, Antarctica, and outer space, belong to all humanity and that their resources are available for everyone's benefit, taking into account future generations and the needs of developing countries. This concept could be applied beyond the localities already specified to include the atmosphere, the seas in general, and all living resources.

Still a third instrument is the public trust doctrine whose roots date back as much as fifteen centuries. Under this doctrine, certain resources are to be preserved for public use, and the state is supposed to serve as a trustee on behalf of the present and future generations. This principle is widely accepted today but rarely enforced. The people, acting on behalf of a state that has abandoned this duty, must then serve as trustees.

The preamble to our own Constitution provides for yet another avenue of defense. It states that the country was founded "to provide for the common defense and promote the general welfare." There is no common defense when the people who attempt to exercise their right of assembly are labeled and arrested as trespassers or, worse, labeled as terrorists and fired upon; nor do we have promotion of the general welfare when corporations are allowed to drill for oil in common waters or take minerals from under protesting property owners.

This is the revolution that we need, but is it possible? Evan Handler, in a *Huffington Post* article, argued that the American people aren't ready for revolution.

If mass numbers of people wanted a revolution, then one would be happening. They would have taken to the streets along with Occupy Wall Street, and they would never have left. Not tens of thousands. Millions. They would have replaced each other more quickly than any jail could have held them. It didn't happen. That doesn't mean people don't want change. It means they're not authentically enthusiastic about toppling the very structures of politics and the economy, or of the fallout such a toppling would provoke.[20]

If Handler is right, it may take a major catastrophe on the order of a new Great Depression or a major environmental disaster to awaken us.

ENDNOTES

1   Chris Hedges, "Voting with our Feet," TruthDig, 20 March 2016 (accessed March 31, 2016), http://www.truthdig.com/report/item/voting_with_our_feet_20160320.

2   Interview with Micah White, https://www.micahmwhite.com/crisis-in-activism-interview.

3   Nathaniel Rich, "Invisible Catastrophe," *New York Times Magazine,* 31 March 2016 (accessed March 31, 2016), http://www.nytimes.com/2016/04/03/magazine/the-invisible-catastrophe.html.

4   Ian Lovett, "Health Scare at Malibu Sets Off Media War," *New York Times,* 4 April 2016 (accessed April 4, 2016), http://www.nytimes.com/2016/04/05/us/an-exclusivity-malibu-could-do-without-pcbs.html?_r=0.

5   Matt Mulberry, "Civil Resistance in North America: Themes from the James Lawson Institute," Open Democracy, 9 September 2014, https://www.opendemocracy.net/civilresistance/matt-mulberry/civil-resistance-in-north-america-themes-from-james-lawson-institute.

6   For more on this campaign, see Sheila D. Collins, *The Rainbow Challenge: The Jackson Campaign and the Future of U.S. Politics* (New York: Monthly Review Press, 1987), http://www.amazon.com/Rainbow-Challenge-Sheila-D-Collins/dp/0853456917/ref=sr_1_5?s=books&ie=UTF8&qid=1459980879&sr=1-5&keywords=

Sheila+D.+Collins.

7   For more on this see Sheila D. Collins and Naomi Rosenblum, "The Democratization of Culture," in *When Government Helped: Learning from the Successes and Failures of the New Deal,* ed. by Sheila D. Collins and Gertrude Schaffner Goldberg (Oxford University Press, 2014), 207–32.

8   For more on the radical organizing of the 1930s, see Gertrude Schaffner Goldberg, "Where are Today's Mass Movements?" *Dollars & Sense* (January-February, 2015):10–17. See also, Gertrude Schaffner Goldberg, "A Decade of Dissent: The New Deal and Popular Movements," 86–119, and Richard McIntyre, "Labor Militance and the New Deal: Lessons for Today," 120–45, in Sheila D. Collins and Gertrude Schaffner Goldberg, eds., *When Government Helped: Learning from the Successes and Failures of the New Deal* (New York: Oxford University Press, 2014).

9   Robert Cohen, *When the Old Left Was Young: Student Radicals and America's First Mass Student Movement, 1929-1941* (New York: Oxford University Press, 1993), xiii.

10 Cohen, "Student Movements, 1930s."

11 Patrick Barrett, "Can We Change the Political System? Strategic Lessons of the Bernie Sanders Campaign," Truthout, 25 March 2016 (accessed April 6, 2016), http://www.truth-out.org/opinion/item/35375-could-we-change-the-political-system-strategic-lessons-of-the-bernie-sanders-campaign.

12 Lawrence Goodwyn, *The Populist Moment: A Short History of the Agrarian Revolt in America* (New York: Oxford University Press, Oxford/New York, 1978), 264.

13 Ibid., xviii.

14 Harold Meyerson, "The Long March of Bernie's Army," *The American Prospect,* 23 March 2016 (accessed April 4, 2016), http://prospect.org/article/long-march-bernie%E2%80%99s-army.

15 Miles Mogulescu, "Time to Turn Bernie's Campaign into a Permanent Organization," Huffington Post, 25 March 2016 (accessed April 4, 2016), http://www.huffingtonpost.com/miles-mogulescu/time-to-transform-bernies_b_9547060.html.

16 For more on that campaign see: Sheila D. Collins, *The Rainbow*

Challenge: The Jackson Campaign and the Future of U.S. Politics (Monthly Review Press, 1986), http://www.amazon.com/s/ref=nb _sb_noss?url=search-alias%3Daps&field-keywords=The +Rainbow+Challenge%3A+The+Jackson+Campaign+and+the+ Future+of+U.S.+Politics.

17   For the role of government in environmental governance during the Great Depression see Sheila D. Collins, "The Rightful Heritage of All: The Environmental Lessons of the Great Depression and the New Deal Response," in *When Government Helped: Learning from the Successes and Failures of the New Deal* (Oxford University Press, 2014), 233–65.

18   Jeremy Brecher, "A Nonviolent Insurgency for Climate Protection?" *Foreign Policy in Focus,* December 2013, (accessed May 25, 2015) http:// fpif.org/wp-content/uploads/2013/12/A-Nonviolent-Insurgency -for-Climate-Protection-Foreign-Policy-In-Focus.pdf.

19   For an elaboration of these instrumentalities, see Laura Westra, *Revolt against Authority* (Leiden/Boston: 2014).

20   Evan Handler, "We All Want to Change the World," Huffing- ton Post, 4 April 2016 (accessed April 4, 2016), http://www. huffingtonpost.com/evan-handler/we-all-want-to-change -the_b_9610568.html?utm_hp_ref=politics.

HOW AMERICA BECAME AN OLIGARCHY

Ellen Brown

ABSTRACT: *The voters' collective will no longer prevails because democracy has been captured by big money. The culmination of this process has taken place through globalization and transnational corporations. One way for governments to recall their sovereign powers is by creating money rather than allowing money to be created by banks making loans.*

> The politicians are put there to give you the idea that you have freedom of choice. You don't. . . . You have owners. ~ George Carlin, *The American Dream*[1]

According to a study from Princeton University,[2] American democracy no longer exists. Using data from over 1,800 policy initiatives from 1981 to 2002, researchers Martin Gilens and Benjamin Page[3] concluded that rich, well-connected individuals on the political scene now steer the direction of the country, regardless of — or even against — the will of the majority of voters. America's political system has transformed from a democracy into an oligarchy, where power is wielded by wealthy elites.

"Making the world safe for democracy" was President Woodrow Wilson's rationale for World War I, and it has been used to justify

American military intervention ever since. Can we justify sending troops into other countries to spread a political system we cannot maintain at home?

The Magna Carta, considered the first Bill of Rights in the Western world, established the rights of nobles as against the king. But the doctrine that *"all"* men are created equal"—that all people have "certain inalienable rights," including "life, liberty and the pursuit of happiness"—is an American original. And those rights, supposedly insured by the Bill of Rights, have the right to vote at their core. We have the right to vote but the voters' collective will no longer prevails.

In Greece, the left-wing populist Syriza Party came out of nowhere[4] to take the presidential election by storm; and in Spain, the populist Podemos Party appears poised to do the same. But for over a century, no third-party candidate has had any chance of winning a U.S. presidential election. We have a two-party winner-take-all system, in which our choice is between two candidates, both of whom necessarily cater to big money. It takes big money just to put on the mass media campaigns required to win an election involving 240 million people of voting age.

In state and local elections, third-party candidates have sometimes won. In a modest-sized city, candidates can actually influence the vote by going door to door, passing out flyers and bumper stickers, giving local presentations, and getting on local radio and TV. But in a national election, those efforts are easily trumped by the mass media. And local governments, too, are beholden to big money.

When governments of any size need to borrow money, the megabanks in a position to supply it can generally dictate the terms. Even in Greece, where the populist Syriza Party managed to prevail in January, the anti-austerity platform of the new government is being throttled by the moneylenders who have the government in a chokehold.

How did we lose our democracy? Were the Founding Fathers remiss in leaving something out of the Constitution? Or have we simply gotten too big to be governed by majority vote?

DEMOCRACY'S RISE AND FALL

The stages of the capture of democracy by big money are traced in a paper called "The Collapse of Democratic Nation States" by theologian and environmentalist John B. Cobb, Jr. [Chapter One of this book.] Going back several centuries, he points to the rise of private banking, which usurped the power to create money from governments:

> The influence of money was greatly enhanced by the emergence of private banking. The banks are able to create money and so to lend amounts far in excess of their actual wealth. This control of money-creation . . . has given banks overwhelming control over human affairs. In the United States, Wall Street makes most of the truly important decisions that are directly attributed to Washington.

Today the vast majority of the money supply in Western countries is created by private bankers. That tradition goes back to the 17th century, when the privately owned Bank of England, the mother of all central banks, negotiated the right to print England's money after Parliament stripped that power from the Crown. When King William needed money to fight a war, he had to borrow. The government as borrower then became servant of the lender.

In America, however, the colonists defied the Bank of England and issued their own paper scrip; and they thrived. When King George forbade that practice, the colonists rebelled.

They won the Revolution, but lost the power to create their own money supply when they opted for gold rather than paper money as their official means of exchange. Gold was in limited supply and was controlled by the bankers, who surreptitiously expanded the money supply by issuing multiple banknotes against a limited supply of gold.

This was the system euphemistically called "fractional reserve" banking, meaning only a fraction of the gold necessary to back the banks' privately issued notes was actually held in their vaults. These notes were lent at interest, putting citizens and the government in debt to bankers who created the notes with a printing press. It was something the government could have done itself debt-free, and the American colonies had done with great success until England went to war to stop them.

President Abraham Lincoln revived the colonists' paper money system when he issued the Treasury notes called "Greenbacks" that helped the Union win the Civil War. But Lincoln was assassinated, and the Greenback issues were discontinued.

In every presidential election between 1872 and 1896, there was a third national party running on a platform of financial reform. Typically organized under the auspices of labor or farmer organizations, these were parties of the people rather than the banks. They included the Populist Party, the Greenback and Greenback Labor Parties, the Labor Reform Party, the Antimonopolist Party, and the Union Labor Party. They advocated expanding the national currency to meet the needs of trade, reform of the banking system, and democratic control of the financial system.

The Populist movement of the 1890s represented the last serious challenge to the bankers' monopoly over the right to create the nation's money. According to monetary historian Murray Rothbard,[5] politics after the turn of the century became a struggle between two competing banking giants, the Morgans and the Rockefellers. The parties sometimes changed hands, but the puppeteers pulling the strings were always one of these two big-money players.

In *All the Presidents' Bankers*,[6] Nomi Prins names six banking giants and associated banking families that have dominated politics for over a century. No popular third party candidates have a real chance of prevailing, because they have to compete with two entrenched parties funded by these massively powerful Wall Street banks.

DEMOCRACY SUCCUMBS TO GLOBALIZATION

In an earlier era, notes Dr. Cobb, wealthy landowners were able to control democracies by restricting government participation to the propertied class. When those restrictions were removed, big money controlled elections by other means:

First, running for office became expensive, so that those who seek office require wealthy sponsors to whom they are then beholden. Second, the great majority of voters have little independent knowledge of those for whom they vote or of the issues to be dealt with. Their judgments are, accordingly, dependent on what they learn from the mass media. These media, in turn, are controlled by moneyed interests.[7]

Control of the media and financial leverage over elected officials then enabled those other curbs on democracy we know today, including high barriers to ballot placement for third parties and their elimination from presidential debates, vote suppression, registration restrictions, identification laws, voter roll purges, gerrymandering, computer voting, and secrecy in government.

The final blow to democracy, says Dr. Cobb, was "globalization"—an expanding global market that overrides national interests:

> [T]oday's global economy is fully transnational. The money power is not much interested in boundaries between states and generally works to reduce their influence on markets and investments. . . . Thus transnational corporations inherently work to undermine nation states, whether they are democratic or not.[8]

The most glaring example today is the secret twelve-country trade agreement called the Trans-Pacific Partnership.[9] If it goes through, the TPP will dramatically expand the power of multinational corporations to use closed-door tribunals to challenge and supersede domestic laws, including environmental, labor, health, and other protections.

LOOKING AT ALTERNATIVES

Some critics ask whether our system of making decisions by a mass popular vote easily manipulated by the paid-for media is the most effective way of governing on behalf of the people. In an interesting Ted Talk, political scientist Eric Li makes a compelling case[10] for the system of "meritocracy" that has been quite successful in China.

In *America Beyond Capitalism,*[11] Gar Alperovitz argues that the U.S. is simply too big to operate as a democracy at the national level. Excluding Canada and Australia, which have large empty landmasses, the United States is larger geographically than all the other advanced industrial countries of the OECD (Organization for Economic Cooperation and Development) combined. He proposes what he calls "The Pluralist Commonwealth," a system anchored in the reconstruction of communities and the democratization of wealth. It involves plural forms of cooperative and common ownership, beginning with decentralization and moving to higher levels of regional and national coordination when necessary. Alperovitz is co-chair, along with James Gustav Speth, of an initiative called The Next System Project,[12] which seeks to help open a far-ranging discussion of how to move beyond the failing traditional political-economic systems of both left and Right.

Alperovitz quotes Prof. Donald Livingston, who asked in 2002:

> What value is there in continuing to prop up a union of this monstrous size? . . . [T]here are ample resources in the American federal tradition to justify states' and local communities' recalling, out of their own sovereignty, powers they have allowed the central government to usurp.[13]

TAKING BACK OUR POWER

If governments are recalling their sovereign powers, they might start with the power to create money, which was usurped by private interests while the people were asleep at the wheel. State and local governments are not allowed to print their own currencies; but they can own banks, and all depository banks create money when they make loans, as the Bank of England has acknowledged.[14]

The federal government could take back the power to create the national money supply by issuing its own Treasury notes as Abraham Lincoln did. Alternatively, it could issue some very large denomination coins[15] as authorized in the Constitution; or it could nationalize the central bank and use quantitative easing to fund infrastructure, education, job creation, and social services, responding to the needs of the people rather than the banks.

The freedom to vote carries little weight without economic freedom — the freedom to work and to have food, shelter, education, medical care and a decent retirement. President Franklin Roosevelt maintained that we need an Economic Bill of Rights. If our elected representatives were not beholden to the moneylenders, they might be able both to pass such a bill and to come up with the money to fund it.

ENDNOTES

1   Geroge Carlin, The America Dream, https://www.youtube.com /watch?v=acLWivFO-2Q.

2   Brendan James, "Princeton Study: U.S. No Longer An Actual Democracy," TPM, April 18, 2014; http://talkingpointsmemo.com/ livewire/princeton-experts-say-us-no-longer-democracy.

3   Martin Gilens and Benjamin I. Page, "Testing Theories of American Politics: Elites, Interest Groups, and Average Citizens," *Perspectives on Politics* 12, no. 3 (2014): 564–81, online: doi:10.1017/S1537592714001595.

4   Sylvia Poggioli, "In Greece, the Election May Have Been the Easy Part," June 18, 2012; http://www.npr.org/2012/06/18/155263974/greek-parties -to-hold-coalition-talks.

5   Murray N. Rothbard, *Wall Street, Banks, and American Foreign Policy*, Second Edition, Auburn, Ala.: Ludwig von Mises Institute, 2011; online: https://mises.org/system/tdf/Wall%20Street%2C%20 Banks%2C%20and%20American%20Foreign%20Policy_2. pdf?file=1&type=document.

6   Nomi Prins, *All the President's Bankers*, New York: Nation Institute/ NationBooks, http://www.nationinstitute.org/blog/nationbooks /3977/all_the_presidents%27_bankers/.

7   See Dr. Cobb's article on page 18 of this volume.

8   See Dr. Cobb's article page 19 of this volume.

9   Sarah Lazare, "TPP vs. Democracy: Leaked Draft of Secretive Trade Deal Spells Out Plan for Corporate Power Grab," Common Dreams,

March 25, 2015, http://www.commondreams.org/news/2015/03/26/ tpp-vs-democracy-leaked-draft-secretive-trade-deal-spells-out-plan- corporate-power.

10   Eric X. Li, "A Tale of Two Political Systems," Global TedTalk, recorded June 2013 at TEDGlobal 2013; http://www.ted.com/talks/ eric_x_li_a_tale_of_two_political_systems?language =en.

11   Gar Alperovitz, "Is a Continent too Big? excerpt from *America beyond Capitalism,* Truthout, September 7, 2012, http://www.truth-out .org/opinion/item/11391-democracy-is-a-continent-too-big.

12   See: http://www.thenextsystem.org/.

13   Donald Livingston, "Dismantling Leviathan," from *Chronicles* (January 2002), reprinted in Harper's, vol. 304, no. 1824 (May 2002), 13-17, especially 17.

14   Michael McLeay, Amar Radia and Ryland Thomas, "Money Creation in the Modern Economy," Bank of England Quarterly Bulletin 2014, https://www.bankofengland.co.uk/-/media/boe/files /quarterly-bulletin/2014/money-creation-in-the-modern-economy.

15   See: https://en.wikipedia.org/wiki/Trillion_dollar_coin.

❧ 9 ❧

HOW PRIVATE CURRENCIES AND
CREDIT CLEARING EXCHANGES
CAN HELP SAVE CIVILIZATION

Thomas H. Greco, Jr.

ABSTRACT: *The fundamental role of money is to provide a convenient and efficient means of facilitating the exchange of value in the marketplace. Modern money is essentially a credit instrument which the issuer is required to accept back in payment for real value. But money has been politicized to serve the interests of a corporate, banking, and political elite. The resulting concentration of power and wealth has undermined democratic government, despoiled the environment, and put our very civilization at risk. But people, businesses, and communities have the power to allocate credit directly amongst themselves, using private and community currencies and credit clearing circles to bypass the dysfunctional, interest-based, debt-money system and reclaim the credit commons.*

EDMUND BURKE HAS OFTEN BEEN QUOTED as saying, "Those who don't know history are destined to repeat it."

I would add that those who don't know the history of *money* cannot possibly understand today's geopolitical situation or the peril that is imminent. But very few today know anything at all about money, its evolutionary history, its essential nature, or how it has

165

become the fundamental tool for centralizing power and concentrating wealth.

One need not subscribe to any particular conspiracy theory or believe in nefarious plots, but simply to observe the trajectories of politics, economics, banking, and finance as they have unfolded over the past many decades. The most striking of these have been:

- The increasing centralization of power and the erosion of democratic government;

- Continual ceding of sovereignty from governments to transnational banks and corporations by means of trade agreements and preferential legislation;

- Ever growing disparities in incomes and the concentration of wealth in the hands of a small "super-class";

- Exponential growth in both private and sovereign debts;

- Recurrent financial and economic crises;

- The growth and consolidation of banking institutions that have made them "too big to fail"; with subsequent

- Bank bailouts by governments; and

- Ever more regressive tax policies that shift the costs of government from the wealthy to the middle class.

All of that is indicative of a money and banking system that is seriously flawed.

In modern societies, we all live by exchange. Most of the goods and services we need are produced by others. For the most part we acquire them by paying money. That means we first need to get money before we can get the goods and services we need. Money is first and foremost a medium of exchange, a kind of placeholder that enables a seller to deliver real value to a buyer, then use the money received to claim from the market something that s/he needs from someone else. As Nobel prizewinning chemist Frederick Soddy wrote long ago, *"Money now is the nothing you get for something before you can get anything.*"[1] Soddy's statement correctly conveys the point of our utter dependency upon conventional money that is provided for us by some remote agency by means which people by and large know nothing about.

Here in a few pages I will try to explain the transformational stages through which money has passed, and how money, or more accurately, the exchange process, is now once again being transformed. I will describe the most efficient and equitable alternatives that are now emerging and show how it is possible to create economic exchange mechanisms that better serve the causes of equity, justice, personal freedom, peace, and sustainability.

POWER SHIFT

It is clear to me that civilization is at a critical juncture. The world is trending toward social, political, economic, and ecological disaster. It is not widely recognized, but the main driver of this trend is the global interest-based, debt-money system. The exponential growth of debt, worldwide, derives from a structural flaw in the dominant system of money, banking, and finance. The creation of money by banks as they lend it into circulation *at interest* creates a debt/growth imperative that is driving not only debt-slavery, but also social decay, environmental degradation, and international conflict. The breakdown of that system is inevitable. The question is, when will there be widespread recognition of the flaws inherent in the global interest-based, debt-money system, and what will be done about it? There seems little chance of systemic reform since the banking and political elite have structured it to put control in their own hands, so it's up to people, businesses, and communities to build new innovative exchange mechanisms from the ground up.

KINDS OF ECONOMIC INTERACTION

As we try to grapple with these problems, it is first necessary to realize the precise role which money is intended to play, and to do that we must distinguish among the various modes by which real economic value changes hands. These are (1) as gifts, (2) by involuntary transfers, or (3) by reciprocal exchange.

In the case of a gift, if it is truly a gift, something of value is transferred without any particular expectation of the giver receiving anything in return. In the case of involuntary transfers, such as theft, robbery, extortion, or taxes, some form of threat or force is applied to coerce the transfer of value from one person or entity to another. In reciprocal exchange, two parties voluntarily agree to exchange one thing for another. Each ostensibly values the thing received more than the thing surrendered, so both parties are enriched by the bargain.

It is within the realm of reciprocal exchange that money plays its fundamental role. Any feature of a monetary system that subverts reciprocity is dishonest and destructive to the intended outcome of mutual benefit among those who use money.

THE EVOLUTION OF MONEY[2]

We can summarize the mechanism for reciprocal exchange in order from primitive to advanced as follows:

- Barter trade
- Commodity money
- Symbolic money
- Credit money
- Credit clearing

Barter is the most obvious but primitive form of reciprocal exchange. Barter involves only two parties, each of which has something the other wants. However, if Jones wants something from Smith, but has nothing that Smith wants, there can be no barter trade between them. So barter depends upon the "double coincidence" of wants and needs. Money, in its most fundamental role, enables traders to transcend this barter limitation. Money bridges the gap in both space and time, acting as a "placeholder" that enables the need of a buyer to be met wherever and whenever the needed good or service may be found, by agreement of the seller to defer satisfaction and to find his needed goods or services elsewhere. Thus, the first evolutionary step in reciprocal exchange came when traders began to use as an exchange medium some useful commodity that was in general demand and could be easily passed along in payment to other sellers.

Commodity money carries value in itself and can fulfill all of the classical functions attributed to money. It is at once a payment medium, a measure of value, and a store of value. Throughout history, a wide variety of commodities has served as money, including cattle, tobacco, grains, nails, shells, hides, and, of course, metals, especially the so-called precious metals, gold and silver. Because they are durable, easily portable, and easy to divide into smaller amounts (fungible), certain metals, notably silver and gold, became commodities of choice for mediating the exchange of all other goods and services.

As banking developed, customers would deposit their gold or silver at a bank and receive redeemable notes which themselves could be used by traders to pay one another. Being redeemable for gold or silver, these notes were "symbolic" money, in essence "warehouse" receipts for the metal that had been deposited.

What I call "the great monetary transformation" was the shift from metallic money (commodity money) and "claim check" money (symbolic money) to *credit money*. This transformational development provided a major leap forward in the potential efficacy of exchange media but, unfortunately, it also opened the door for greater abuse. The failure to distinguish between the different kinds of paper money that came into circulation caused much confusion and enabled subtle forms of cheating to proliferate. The important question to be answered with regard to any piece of paper currency is, what does the paper represent; what is behind it?

Bankers eventually came to realize that redeemable bank notes were seldom presented for redemption so they could lend their banknotes instead of gold. This was the birth of "credit money."

Nowadays of course, when banks make loans they typically do not hand over bank notes but simply credit the borrower's deposit account. So long as the loan was based on the pledge of real marketable value, that was legitimate, and so long as depositors maintained their faith in the bank, it was a workable way of expanding the supply of money in accordance with the needs of commerce. But quite often banks would (and still do) make such loans on the basis of something that had little or no marketable value. That not only puts the bank at risk of insolvency, but also in today's centralized banking system, causes inflationary rises in prices.

It is important to realize that those who would have us revert to commodity money, like gold and silver, do so because they see no other way of imposing discipline upon the powers that have gained control over the process of money creation and allocation, namely bankers and politicians. But by understanding the fundamental nature of modern money as credit, it becomes possible to liberate and perfect it and to avoid throwing out the more evolved credit money "baby" with the "bath water" of perverse centralization of power.

To summarize the present situation, we can say that money today is a credit instrument whose main purpose is to facilitate the exchange of goods and services by providing a means of payment. But our present money system has become an instrument of power that allows a small banking and political elite to control not only money and finance, but economics, politics, and virtually everything else. Because of the way money is created and allocated, and because of its scarcity and interest burden, we have become slaves to money and those who control money.

RECLAIMING THE CREDIT COMMONS[3]

The Commons is an age-old concept that refers to those resources and forms of wealth that are the common heritage of all. It is comprised of those gifts of nature — the land, the air, the seas, the sunlight, the genetic material of plants and animals, and all those things that humankind did not create. It also includes the social, cultural, and intellectual treasures that we have inherited from past generations, including our accumulated knowledge and creative works. All of these must be protected and managed for the good of all, including future generations. In modern times, the Commons has increasingly been privatized and exploited for short-term, private gain that benefits a few at the expense of the common good and the health of the planet.

One crucial but overlooked aspect of the commons is the "credit commons." Few people understand that money today is simply a credit instrument, i.e., a claim against the resources of the money issuer, be that a government, a bank, or a private issuer of currency. Thus, the users of a currency provide credit to the currency issuer when they accept it as payment for real goods and services. By using national currencies, we have allowed the banks to decide for us how our credit is to be allocated and on what terms. That is, we give our collective credit to the banks and then beg them to lend it back to us, and we pay them interest for the privilege.

The good news is that we need not be victims of a system that is so obviously failing us. We have in our hands the power to reclaim the credit commons. We can do it peacefully and without attacking the entrenched regime. It only requires that we each take control of our own credit and give it to those individuals and businesses that merit it and withhold it from those that do not, and for us to apply our talents and energies to those enterprises that enhance community resilience, sustainability, self-reliance, and the common good.

In brief, any group of people can organize to allocate their own collective credit amongst themselves, interest-free. This is merely an extension of the common business practice of selling on open account—"I'll ship you the goods now and you can pay me later"—except it is organized, not on a bilateral basis, but within a community of many buyers and sellers. Done on a large enough scale that includes a sufficiently broad range of goods and services, such systems can avoid the dysfunctions inherent in conventional money and banking. They can open the way to more harmonious and mutually beneficial relationships that enable the emergence of true economic democracy.

Think about how you personally manage your material affairs. Most of us work at some job or profession. You provide goods or services to someone, you receive money in return, then you use that money to get the goods and services you need and want. So in a very real sense the goods or services you provide pay for the goods or services you want. Money is merely an intermediary device. The fact that it is universally accepted as a payment medium gives money enormous power. But why do we trust the money that has been provided for us by the banking system? There are several reasons. Foremost among them is the fact that central governments have been partners in creating this system, supporting and underwriting it. Declaring it to be "legal tender" makes the central bank currency and bank deposits denominated in central bank currency units generally acceptable as payment. Further, such currencies are easy to exchange for one another through well developed currency exchange (forex) markets, the public is habituated to their use, their true costs and "side-effects" are obscured and unrecognized, and heretofore there has been a lack of any viable exchange alternatives.

That is not to say that exchange alternatives have been entirely lacking. History is replete with examples of private and regional currencies circulating within limited bounds. Some of these were issued by private entities, like individual companies, associations of businesses, grassroots organizations, nonprofits, and NGOs, and some by municipal and/or provincial governments. Now, if we are to transcend the destructive effects of the dominant monetary paradigm and promote local resilience and self-reliance, communities and producer groups need to assert even more strongly their control over the exchange process.

As I wrote previously, "The most graceful and promising approach to empowering ourselves and our communities is through voluntary entrepreneurial activities that can liberate the exchange process and reclaim the credit commons. While we may not be able to do much in the short-run to change the legal privileges of political currencies or bank-created credit money, we can reduce our dependence upon them. The way to do that is by taking control of our own credit, and organizing independent means for allocating it directly to those individuals and businesses that we trust and wish to support."[4]

There are two basic approaches to doing that — private currencies and credit clearing circles.

PRIVATE AND COMMUNITY CURRENCIES

Imagine what would happen if a major airline were to make its frequent flyer miles available in a form that was easily transferable from person to person, allowing you to routinely transfer miles from your account to someone else's account. You might then be able to make a purchase at some online marketplace and pay for it using miles instead of dollars. This is an example of a private currency spent into circulation by a trusted issuer.

Has anything like this ever been done before? Indeed, it has. During the nineteenth and twentieth centuries, some railway companies in Europe did something like that, but instead of giving railway money as a rebate to customers, as the airlines do, the companies spent their currencies into circulation by using it to pay their contractors and employees.[5]

In Argentina during the 1990s, the governments of several provinces paid their workers in part with "provincial bonds" that were printed in convenient denominations that could pass from hand to hand. They did this because there was an insufficient supply of Argentine pesos circulating in their regions, and they realized that providing a supplemental means of payment would stimulate local economic activity and increase their tax revenues.

These cases illustrate that it is possible to circumvent the monetary scarcity and other dysfunctions that are inherent in the dominant centralized bank money system. Whether issued by private companies, or by municipal or regional governments, private and local currencies empower people by shifting some degree of economic control from remote external agencies, like banks, to private businesses and people within the community. When properly designed and managed, they can enhance the vitality of a local economy and provide a greater measure of community self-determination.

Unlike public legal tender currencies, however, the acceptance of private currencies in the market is voluntary. This makes private currencies self-regulating in that the issuers themselves will manage their issuance in such a way as to avoid having it discounted or refused in the marketplace.

CREDIT CLEARING—PURE AND SIMPLE[6]

A credit clearing system is an arrangement in which the members of an association of traders, each of whom is both a buyer and a seller, agree to allocate to one another sufficient credit to facilitate their transactions amongst themselves. That means they simply keep a record of their purchases, sales, and account balances. By allowing some trusted members to buy before they sell, an internal currency is created that can circulate among the members. In the long run, each member is expected to earn (from their sales) as much as they spend (on their purchases).

When a member buys something from another member, the price is subtracted (debited) from the account of the buyer and added (credited) to the account of the seller. Thus, members' balances will fluctuate over time, being sometimes negative (in debit) and sometimes positive (in credit).

In such a system, the total amount of credit outstanding at any point in time can be thought of as the money supply within the system. That will be the sum of either the positive balances or the sum of the negative balances. These two sums of course must always be equal to one another, the total of all account credits must always be equal to the total of all account debits.

Following is a table that illustrates the credit clearing process. In this example we have just four members and 10 transactions. Note how the money supply (total credits outstanding) fluctuates up and down as credit balances are spent and debit (negative) balances are reduced when sales are made by those who previously had a debit balance.

Credit clearing is the highest stage in the evolution of reciprocal exchange, which, in effect, makes money as we've known it obsolete. The fact is that goods and services pay for other goods and services, whether we use money as an intermediate payment medium or not. Direct credit clearing makes the use any third party credit instrument, like conventional money, unnecessary.

We can see then that the quantity of money (total credits) at any point in time is unimportant. What *is* important is the prearranged right of some members ("issuing members") to buy before they sell up to some limit that we refer to as a "line of credit." We then have a system in which trade credit is created automatically as needed in the process of making transactions.

On this basis, we can see that money can be thought of as simply a system of accounting for credit in which the quantity can fluctuate according to the needs of traders to exchange value with one another, and the quantity of credit allowed is determined only by the amount of valuable goods and services that members make available for sale.

The fact is that present day banking is mainly a credit clearing process in which additions and subtractions are made to bank customers' account balances. However, banks perpetuate the myth that money is a "thing" to be lent. If a client's balance is allowed to be negative, the bank considers that to be a "loan" and will charge "interest" on it. Has the bank loaned anything? Not really. What they have done is to allocate some of our collective credit to the "borrower." For this they claim the right to charge interest.

It is clear from the example below that any group of traders can organize to allocate their own collective credit among themselves interest-free. Done on a large enough scale that includes a sufficiently broad range of goods and services spanning all levels of the supply chain from retail, to wholesale, to manufacturing, to basic commodities, as well as employees, such systems can avoid the dysfunctions inherent in conventional money and banking and open the way to more harmonious and mutually beneficial trading relationships. *(Figures 1 and 2).*

Transaction Number	Buyer	Seller	Item	Amount	Amy			Brad			Carl			Doris			Total Amount Cleared System	Money Supply
					Sales	Purchases	Balance	Sales	Purchases	Balance	Sales	Purchases	Balance	Sales	Purchases	Balance		
1	Amy	Brad	200	200		-200	-200	200		200			0			0	200	200
2	Doris	Amy	200	200	200		0			200			0		-200	-200	400	200
3	Brad	Carl	300	300			0		-300	-100	300		300			-200	700	300
4	Carl	Doris	200	200			0			-100		-200	100	200		0	900	100
5	Carl	Brad	100	100			0	100		0		-100	0			0	1000	0
6	Doris	Amy	300	300	300		300		-200	0			0		-300	-300	1300	300
7	Brad	Doris	200	200			300	100		-200			0	200		-100	1500	300
8	Amy	Brad	100	100		-100	200	100		-100			0			-100	1600	200
9	Amy	Doris	100	100		-100	100			-100			0	100		0	1700	100
10	Amy	Brad	100	100		-100	0	100		0			0			0	1800	0
Totals				500	500	-500		500	-500		300	-300		500	-500			

Figure 1: Credit Clearing Simple Illustration —Transaction Spreadsheet, Thomas H. Greco, Jr.

TOTAL AMOUNT OF TRANSACTIONS CLEARED

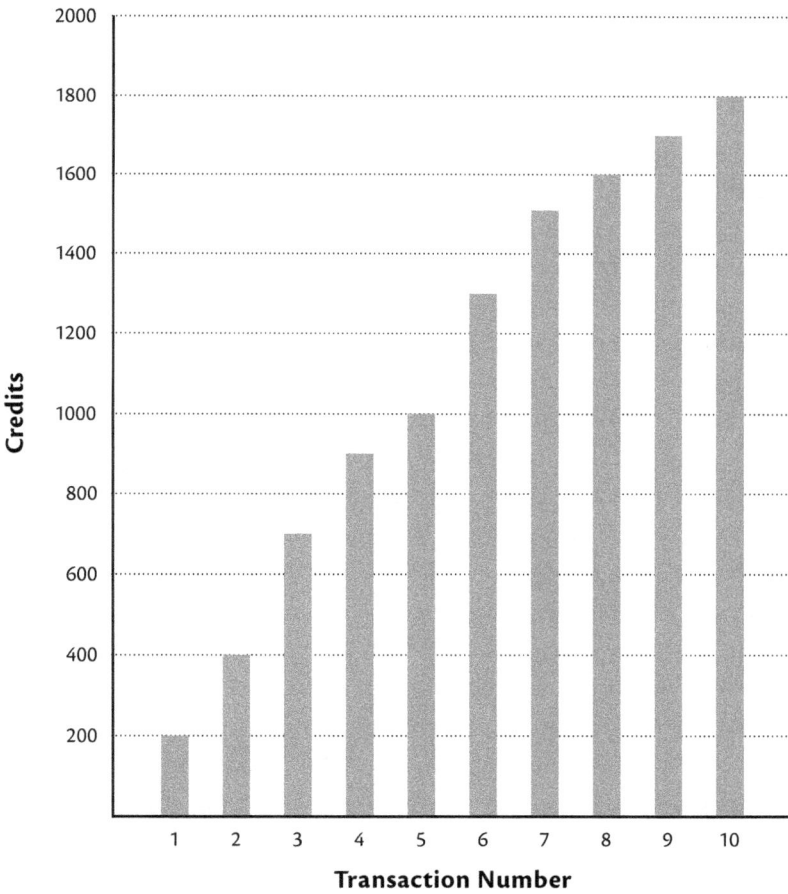

Figure 2: Total Amount of Transactions Cleared, Thomas H. Greco, Jr.

The credit clearing process can be applied at any economic level from trading amongst individuals, to business-to-business exchanges within a regional or national economy, to international trade amongst member nations of a trading union.

By providing the associated members with a "home-grown" source of interest-free liquidity (means of payment), credit clearing exchanges reduce their members' need for bank borrowing and provide a large measure of independence from national currencies and international financial institutions while at the same time encouraging domestic sourcing and production instead of reliance upon imports.

There are numerous examples of the credit clearing process being successfully applied amongst traders. Presently there are scores of commercial trade exchanges (also known as "barter" exchanges) operating all over the world that enable their member businesses to buy and sell amongst themselves without the use of money. Together these exchanges manage transactions amounting to tens of billions of dollars a year. These trade exchanges are typically for-profit businesses that have between a few hundred to a few thousand members that pay some combination of membership and/or transaction fees.

Perhaps the best example of a credit clearing exchange that has operated successfully over a long period of time is the **WIR**[7] Economic Circle Cooperative. Founded in Switzerland in the midst of the Great Depression as a self-help organization, **WIR** provides a means for its member businesses to continue to buy and sell with one another despite a shortage of Swiss francs in circulation. Over the past 80 year, in good times and bad, **WIR** (now known as the **WIR** Bank) has continued to thrive. Its more than 60,000 members throughout Switzerland trade about $2 billion worth of goods and services each year, paying each other, not in official money, but in their own internal currency called **WIR** credits.

At the grassroots level, over the past thirty years, hundreds of community trade exchanges called **LETS** have been organized around the world to enable people to exchange goods and services without the use of scarce official money. Most of these have enabled casual trades between individuals and have not involved very many business members. Therefore, very few have grown to any significant size. But, while the economic benefits may not have been great, people's experience with LETS circles has provided them with a better understanding of reciprocal exchange and the liberating potential of credit clearing.

CONCLUSIONS

So who, precisely, is qualified to issue a currency or receive a line of credit within a credit clearing circle? In brief, we can answer as follows:

1. Any entity that produces goods or services that are in general demand and offers them for sale at competitive prices in the market is qualified to issue either as an individual or collectively within an association of traders.

2. Any entity that has the power to appropriate revenues, i.e., local or regional governments and their authorities,

3. Non-profit organizations that receive pledges of financial contributions.

Every unit of currency (or ledger credit) is a credit instrument, it's value rests upon this ultimate foundation—that the issuer be ready, willing, and able to receive it back again as payment for something of value that he offers in the market. It is instructive to enumerate what kinds of value that might be. Here is my augmented list of those that have historically been identified:

- Inventories of goods (goods foundation)
- Ability to provide needed services of some sort (Service foundation)
- Anticipated tax revenues (tax foundation)
- Donor pledge foundation

By now, it should be clear that sound and credible exchange media can emerge from a variety of sources. There is no valid economic argument for the exchange process to be limited by centralized power, i.e., governments or banks. Competition among currencies and exchange options is both possible and desirable and will result in a stronger, less costly business environment, more resilient economies, and healthier communities.

Opportunities for Business: Companies of all kinds, either individually or in association with one another, can economize on their need for conventional working capital by using their own merchandise credits/coupons or service credits/coupons to pay suppliers and employees. To the extent that they can persuade others to accept their currency as payment, they will be able to reduce borrowing from banks and other sources. One immediate benefit would be a reduction in the companies' interest expense.

Opportunities for Governments: Municipalities and provincial governments can fund a large proportion of their current operations by using their own currencies to pay part of what is owed to local suppliers and employees. Infrastructure development can also, to some degree, be financed by making payment in municipal currency. Again, the possibilities for significant interest savings exist. Even more importantly, it enables the funding of important activities and projects that are presently starved for capital because of the artificial scarcity of national currency and reduced support from state and national governments.

Opportunities for Nonprofit Organizations: In considering the possibilities inherent in complementary currencies, we should not overlook the nonprofit sector. Nonprofits depend primarily upon donations to accomplish their mission. Supporters are able to donate only so much in cash, but since most companies have unused capacity, they are more able to donate goods and services. These so-called, *in-kind donations* constitute a large proportion of total support for many nonprofits, but they could be even greater.

Some of the donated items, like computers and office supplies can be put to use directly in the organization. Others, which the organization cannot use, must somehow be marketed. This can be a major headache. One way around this difficulty is for donations to be received in the form of pledges of goods and services or discounts on goods and services. Vouchers representing these donated values can be issued by the nonprofit and used to pay employees and suppliers. This approach can eliminate the need to market, or handle in any way, in-kind donations.

SUMMARY OF BENEFITS

To sum up, the direct benefits of interest-free private and community currencies and credit clearing exchanges include:

- Allow credit to be allocated locally and democratically.

- Supplement the supply of scarce bank credit.

- Provide saving on interest costs.

- Reduce risk of default compared to loans of cash.

- Promote community self-reliance and the health of the local economy because it recirculates locally.

GUIDELINES TO ASSURE FAIRNESS AND SUCCESS

In any human interaction, especially those involving economic values, there is always the possibility of error, mismanagement, or fraud. In the case of complementary currencies and exchange systems, there are some basic features that can be built in to minimize, if not eliminate these problems. Here are the minimal requirements for circulating a sound currency and maintaining public confidence in it.

- Currency must be issued on a sound foundation or basis.

- The amount issued must be in proper proportion to the foundation upon which it is issued.

- Administration must be fully accountable to the users of the currency.

- Full and timely disclosure of all information needed
  to assess the credibility and value of the currency.

Private currencies that are *spent* into circulation by trusted producers and mutual credit clearing exchanges have a much greater potential for promoting local community prosperity, resilience, and self-determination because they allow a community to *monetize the local value created by local businesses and professionals*. That enables a community to greatly reduce its dependence upon official money and bank borrowing. Anyone can be a member of a credit clearing exchange but lines of credit should be allocated only to those accounts that have demonstrated their willingness and ability to reciprocate by accepting it back as payment for the goods and services they sell at their customary prices.

As properly designed and managed private currencies and trade exchanges begin to be deployed, they will become models for others to follow, then the rapid growth phase will begin, leading eventually to an Internet-like global trading network that will make conventional money obsolete and enable a freer, more equitable and harmonious society to emerge.

ENDNOTES

1   Frederick Soddy, *The Role of Money* (Routledge, 1935), https://archive. org/details/roleofmoney032861mbp.

2   For a much more complete description of this evolutionary process, see Chapters 9 and 10 in my book, *The End of Money and the Future of Civilization* (White River Junction, VT: Chelsea Green, 2009), https://beyondmoney.net/the-end-of-money-and-the-future-of-civilization/ https://beyondmoney.net/monographs/ reclaiming-the-credit-commons/.

3   Based on my article, "Reclaiming the Credit Commons: Toward a Butterfly Society," in *The Wealth of the Commons: A World Beyond Market and State,* M.R. Bollier and Silke Helfrich, eds. (Amherst: Levellers Press, 2012), https://beyondmoney.net/monographs/reclaiming -the-credit-commons/.

4   Ibid., Chapter 11.

5   For details on historical precedents and an elaborated proposal
    see "Railway Money And Unemployment," by Dr. Walter Zander
    at https://reinventingmoney.files.wordpress.com/2018/06/railway
    -money.pdf.

6   For further discussion of credit clearing and its current and historical
    applications, see my *The End of Money and the Future of Civilization,*
    especially Chapters 11 and 12.

7   WIR, an abbreviation for "Wirtschaftsring-Genossenschaft," is the
    German word for "we."

Part Three

Actualizing Possibilities
through Elections,
Volunteers, and Technology

꩜ 10 ꩜

RICHMOND, CALIFORNIA:

A Local Community Defines Its Destiny[1]

Gayle McLaughlin

ABSTRACT: *Richmond's story since the turn of this century is one of the genesis and rise of progressive politics in a mid-size Bay Area city, of how a metropolis was transformed, and how an organized movement of activists and an elected leadership of progressives prevailed against a multinational, billion-dollar industry that for a century had kept a stranglehold on the community and city government. The Richmond Progressive Alliance developed in order to address economic, social, and environmental issues facing the city. Some of these problems stemmed from Chevron's contamination—land, sea, and air—and its political reach. By working to elect Gayle McLaughlin to the city council and as mayor, a new direction was set that led to numerous projects benefiting the environment and the city's diverse population. Through continuing reform of the alliance and the city, Richmond offers both a model of progressive politics and a challenge to others to take action to realize democratic ideals.*

RICHMOND IS SITUATED at the east side of the Bay Area with a landmass of just under 53 miles, thirty-two miles of shoreline, and a vast expanse of hills, plus an inner city. The population includes 107,000 residents, nearly a fifth of whom live in poverty. Our people

187

come from diverse communities and are 40% Latino, 27% African American, 17% White, 13% Asian American, and smaller portions are Native American and Pacific Islander.[2] A majority of our population is people of color; one-third of our residents are foreign-born; and we have a working class identity that cuts across all demographics. Richmond, in other words, is a window to the present day United States.

Since the 1980s, significant numbers of immigrants have fled to Richmond, bringing about a large demographic shift. In the post-Vietnam War era, Laotians, Cambodians, Hmong, Vietnamese, and other Asian populations settled here; they were followed by large numbers of Latino arrivals having fled war and poverty from Mexico, Central, and South America.

Richmond is home to an exquisite natural landscape on one side, buttressed on the other by a gargantuan oil refinery with smokestacks spewing toxins. Predictably, the more privileged citizens live closer to the shoreline, and huge swaths of people live downwind of the refinery's emissions. The refinery belongs to Chevron Corporation, an industry with a legacy of 100-plus years of fossil fuel development in this geographical locale.

Richmond is a city of contrasts—great natural beauty of land and homesteads on one side, and remnants of heavy industry and squalor in the inner city. We have parks aplenty amid performing arts centers, and violence and destitution in other parts. And, of course, there are a plethora of activist groups working on issues of progressive politics, environmental justice, immigration, and criminal justice reform, to name a few.

CHEVRON

The fossil fuel industry has a home here in Richmond with the Chevron Richmond refinery, a corporation that has been in place for over a hundred years both in its physical structure as well as its political reach. The refinery takes up just over 13% of city land, sitting on 2,900 acres. But the refinery's emissions have not only discharged pollutants into Richmond's air, land, and water, their toxic presence in city government has left equal parts of contamination as they have bought and owned countless city government officials for scores of years, setting the agenda for what problems have or have not been addressed. Extreme poverty and violence were left untended for years. Chevron also managed to escape paying its fair share of taxes, so the city coffers had little means to uplift its people.

I arrived on the political scene in 2003 and soon became aware of some stark facts about the corporation:

- Few Richmond residents work at the refinery. For some reason Chevron refuses to release the data, but we estimate that a mere 5–10% of the refinery's 1,200 employees are Richmond residents, and Chevron has not refuted that assertion.[3]

- Chevron's worldwide sales and profits include $25 billion in sales, and $2.5 billion in profits. The corporation has $40 billion for capital budget, 94% of that for oil and gas exploration and only 3% for making their refinery and chemical plants safe and lowering emissions.

- Despite Chevron's extraordinary profit margins, the refinery did not compensate the city its share of taxes for many years. City council members, most of whom had their campaigns paid for by the industrial giant, neither questioned nor addressed this issue.

- Chevron ran its refinery with years of neglect and lax oversight. This carelessness would affect worker health and safety as well as pollute the air and land for residents living near the refinery. Like any industry of this size and reach, Chevron would experience intermittent catastrophes including spills, leaks, heavy flaring, toxic gas releases, and fires. Most of these were cited as business as usual with no consequences for the company.

The oil giant's dominion over the land and air surrounding Richmond, plus its deep pockets for funding in the city's political arena, left many serious issues unaddressed, and the people needed advocacy and change. While a number of activist groups had risen up to tackle certain problems, no one group had formed to take on the political environment that was allowing Chevron to continue its reign.

Origins

In 2003, a group of activists gathered around a kitchen table in the home of Juan Reardon and Kay Wallis and began forming a group specifically focusing on progressive politics and democracy. The Richmond Progressive Alliance (RPA) is a group of progressive activists who have come together over local issues without emphasizing party affiliations. The RPA unites itself on shared values and vision, with keen focus on our neighborhoods—housing, schools, the environment, criminal justice, immigration, and income inequality. RPA members have been registered with a variety of political parties: the Green Party, Peace and Freedom Party, Democrats, Independents, and some are non-aligned. We describe ourselves as progressive. Most of us have rich experiences of activism from antiwar movements, to advocacy for the environment, for public health and education, etc. But for this alliance, our focus has been changing local government in order to bring justice to members in our own community who have been disenfranchised and left behind.

Agenda

While addressing Chevron's reach and control of the city was the biggest target, RPA also called for ending excessive use of force by the police, stemming gun violence, standing up for immigrants, and focusing on homelessness among the poor in our city—all issues screaming out for attention. We wanted to chart a new course in Richmond based on our values of peace, grassroots democracy, social justice, equity, and ecological sanity. Our organizing started with the following vision:

Our mission is to create a space for public discussion of issues affecting Richmond; to propose solutions and ideas to address Richmond problems (or create an alternative platform); to expand grassroots organizing in Richmond to demand change; and to endorse progressive candidates running for City Council.

Elections and Government Leadership

From the early beginnings of the RPA, we realized that we would need seats at the table of city government if we were to implement the changes we were proposing. I entered that arena and was elected to the City Council in 2004. That was followed by being elected to two terms as mayor, beginning in November 2006, and 2010. The city's charter only allows two mayoral terms, so in November 2014, I ran and won another city council race along with other progressives, triumphing over Chevron's $3 million political war chest in opposition. All of the Chevron candidates lost their electoral bids, and all the progressive candidates won.

As mayor I led the city in a progressive direction that kept city workers in jobs and city services in place, even in tough economic times. Under my leadership, the city council passed a Minimum Wage Increase Ordinance, raising the minimum hourly wage for Richmond workers to be phased in and reach $13.00 by 2018. Later, we amended the ordinance to reach $15.00 by 2019. This huge victory helps local residents to work and live with dignity, and it serves as an inspiration for other jurisdictions throughout the country to follow suit.

Also during my time as mayor, violent crime and property crimes showed significant declining trends. Homicides decreased nearly 75% over my tenure. By 2014 the homicide rate had dipped to its lowest since 1971. This reduction was brought about by new innovative programs such as the Office of Neighborhood Safety, with outreach teams hired by the city, made up of formerly incarcerated individuals who had turned their lives around, and who helped quell violence before it began in neighborhoods hard-hit by crime. We put the focus on the roots of the violence, offering healthy youth activities, mentorship, and job training. We also hired a police chief with a commitment to community-involved policing who changed the culture of our police force.

My attention to environmental justice helped the city move forward as a leader on many environmental initiatives. Our focus on a healthy environment moved the city to create community gardens, bike paths, bay trail construction, and park renovations in neighborhoods throughout the city. In 2010, I successfully led the opposition to a proposed casino at Point Molate. The opening and dedication of the beautiful Point Molate Beach Park in 2014 was a key step in establishing our community's vision to keep this land available to the community and sustainably developed.

In the area of environmental responsibility, I also helped advance the implementation of solar power throughout our city. Richmond became a leader in the Bay Area for solar installed per capita in 2010. Subsequent to that, Richmond received numerous awards for its model green job-training program that certified hundreds of Richmond residents who are now working in the green economy.

In 2007, I joined other East Bay mayors and leaders in a partnership for a "green corridor" for research and jobs for the new green economy. In 2012 Lawrence Berkeley National Lab agreed to build its second campus in Richmond. That project experienced a financial setback, and eventually UC Berkeley took over and has made plans to develop that same land for a global campus. The Berkeley Global Campus at Richmond Bay is expected to bring many changes to Richmond. With the help of RPA and many alliances, I am working to make sure the new campus offers substantial benefits for our city, does not displace current residents, and accurately reflects the city's healthy, sustainable, and equitable direction for its residents.

As the mayor of Richmond and as a council member, I advocated, through the introduction of policies to hold Wall Street accountable, for residents evicted by banks and speculators. I stood up in opposition to the big banks with foreclosure prevention programs. We are working to help homeowners stay in their homes, avoid foreclosure, help neighborhoods stabilize, and help the local Richmond economy recover.

On schools, I voted to assist Kennedy High School and other Richmond schools with $3 million. I have been in the forefront defending immigrants' civil rights. This advocacy included a municipal ID for all Richmond residents, so everyone, including immigrant residents, can access services such as bank accounts.

My more recent council work included protection for renters; sponsorship of environmental and public health and safety initiatives, such as banning glyphosate; advocating for refinery emission reduction, as well as regulations on the transport of toxic substances; and the initial start-up of a homeless task force.

WORKING WITH ALLIES

Richmond is home to hundreds of people in organizations that address a plethora of causes, including housing, poverty, police brutality, the environment, and multi-faith peace and justice groups. The following is a list of some groups that have worked closely with the RPA: ACCE, Alliance of Californians for Community Empowerment; APEN, Asian Pacific Environmental Network; CBE, Communities for a Better Environment; CEASEFIRE; Lifelines to Healing; 350. org; CCISCO, Contra Costa Interfaith Supporting Organizations; CUIDO, Communities United in Defense of Olmstead (a Bay Area grassroots disability rights activist organization); Disability Brigade; East Bay Center for the Performing Arts; Groundwork Richmond; Idle No More; NIAD Art Center; Reach Fellowship International; Reentry Solutions Group; Richmond Art Center; Richmond CARES, Richmond Community Action to Restore Equity; Richmond Native Health Center; *Richmond Pulse*, a community newspaper; Richmond Regla Friendship Committee; RYSE Youth Center; Safe Return Project; Saffron Strand (homeless membership organization); Solar Richmond; Sunflower Alliance (environmental issues); Sierra Club; TANC, Tibetan Association of Northern California; TRAC, Trails for Richmond Action Committee (completing the San Francisco Bay Trail along the Richmond water's edge); Urban Tilth (developing urban gardens); and YES, Nature to Neighborhoods. At one point or another each of these groups energizes and organizes their members to step forward as occasions call for their support and presence.

SOME NOTABLE ACCOMPLISHMENTS

In just under a decade and half, the progressive community has made great strides in Richmond. We began organizing in 2003, were instrumental in getting me elected to city council and mayor, and subsequently helped in the election of three other activists to the city council with a team slate to press progressive ideals. Our accomplishments are profound and have gained us certain notoriety on the national stage. Below is a list of some of some significant accomplishments:

- Chevron agreed to pay $114 million in additional taxes over a 15-year period.

- We stopped a major casino development in our city that threatened to bring about more poverty, addiction, and crime.

- In 2013, we experienced a 75% reduction in the homicide rate — the lowest since the 1970s.

- Richmond became a leader in the Bay Area for per capita solar installations.

- We raised the minimum wage to $13 per hour, to be phased-in over time, leading the way before the "Fight for 15" campaign spurred other cities in the region and across the nation.

- Richmond joined with a Community Choice Aggregator — Marin Clean Energy—and transferred 85% of our homes and businesses to a healthier energy supplier.

- We supported immigration rights by affirming ourselves as a city with a non-cooperation policy with Immigration Custom

Enforcement, ended police driver license checkpoints, and created an official Richmond Municipal ID for all our residents, regardless of immigration status.

- We defended homeowners and put forward innovative programs to prevent foreclosures by reducing mortgage principal through acquiring loans.

- We attracted UC Berkeley to bring its new second campus to Richmond (in competition with other, more prosperous neighboring Bay Area cities).

- Richmond has received national attention for its efforts. The *New York Times*, PBS News Hour, *LA Times*, *The Nation*, Bill Moyers, Chris Hayes of MSNBC, and Amy Goodman of Democracy Now have all covered the news that progressive politics in America is alive and well.

RPA TODAY AND BUILDING PROGRESSIVE ALLIANCES FOR THE FUTURE

Like many progressive groups around the state, the RPA leadership, although diverse in its composition from its inception, realized the need to more fully diversify both its leadership and its membership. After a decade of solid engagement with many progressive issues, RPA set out to enlist the efforts of more young people and people of color. In a year of earnest recruitment, a new steering committee was formed with twenty-three people—six each of African American, Latino, and Asian American heritage. Some of the previous steering committee members remained on the committee to serve as a bridge from the former days to the new. The ages of the new steering committee on average are at least a decade or two younger than the prior committee, and gender parity is nearly equal. The purpose is to diversify leadership and mentor the next generation of progressive politics in Richmond.

Over the past couple of years, we have worked to encourage the development of progressive alliances in other cities throughout the State of California based on the Richmond model. To date, at least a dozen new alliances have emerged in the state. With the success we've had in Richmond, activists have taken the cue that the time is now ripe for progressive politics to take root far and wide. The challenge now is to continue to encourage local organizing and unite all progressive groups around democratic ideals working together for real change.

ENDNOTES

1   I thank Diana Wear for her editorial work on this article.

2   See http://www.bayareacensus.ca.gov/cities/Richmond.htm (accessed 9 May 2016).

3   See http://www.contracostatimes.com/ci_23394901/chevron-announces -change-leadership-at-richmond-refinery (accessed on 24 May 2016).

$\rightarrow$ 11 $\rightarrow$

LOCAL RESPONSE TO CRISIS AND COLLAPSE

Tina Clarke

ABSTRACT: *In times of crisis, voluntary groups and local community efforts are essential to increasing social stability, functioning, and well-being. This essay explores the role of community-based relationships, local groups, citizen-led structures, and voluntary action in facing, handling, and recovering from crisis, system deterioration, and ecological collapse. The Transition Towns movement, launched in the U.K. in 2005, is a model for how voluntary networks can support the development of collaborative responses catalyzing positive, effective action in the face of extreme stress and system collapse.*

VOLUNTARY ACTION IS ESSENTIAL. The actions of individuals, families, neighborhoods, and local community groups and networks can make a crucial difference in times of crisis and collapse. Existing structures will prove to be insufficient. Locally organized structures of individuals and groups can often respond more effectively.

EXISTING STRUCTURES AND SYSTEMS WILL BE INSUFFICIENT

System crisis and "collapse" mean that existing structures are overwhelmed. In ecological collapse, systems upon which we rely

197

for daily life will be intensely impacted. Water, food production and transport, waste management, health care, education, and most economic activity will cost more, be delayed, be inadequate, or, in situations of complete disruption, not be available. Complex societies, dependent upon massive movements of goods, people, and services, and on complex technologies, will become unable to cope with the severity of impacts and change. This "import-dependency" will become acutely apparent as extreme weather events increasingly disrupt daily life. Institutions that sustain daily life, including businesses, government, nonprofit, and civic associations all rely heavily on imported food, energy, manufactured products, expertise, and many complex technologies and services. These institutions need time to shift and adapt to conditions of scarcity and crisis, assuming they even can.

Existing levels of local cooperation and coordination — levels of mutual support that may be sufficient today — will prove totally insufficient to cope with extreme events, let alone ecological collapse. For example, a suburban neighborhood might have a small level of social cooperation with 90% of neighbors maintaining tidy, mowed lawns. Residents might expect that the worst they will have to handle is a stray pet, noisy car alarm, or unweeded flowerbed. But what happens when storms, fire, flooding, job loss, crime, depression, obesity, illness, and rising costs of food and other essentials take down one family after another, or many at once? Whether change comes as a rapid crisis or a slowly unfolding deterioration, ecological and social traumas affect neighborhood stability. Socially isolated individuals and families — those who lack connections, mutually supportive communities, resources, or alternative ways to meet their needs — will be forced to move. Another home deteriorates. The tax base weakens, putting more pressure on remaining neighbors. Meanwhile, those forced to move become part of a growing number of people living on the edge or in chaos.

While large institutions can be essential structures of cooperation, they are no substitute for neighbors acting voluntarily to create supportive neighborhoods. The difference between modern import dependency and old-fashioned neighborhood mutual support became clear in Detroit's meltdown: some neighborhoods were plundered for copper pipes and other valuables, while others had systems of neighborhood watch, community caring, and voluntary helping.

In short, our current technology-focused, complex, consumption-oriented system has enticed many to believe in the reliability of individualistic, import-dependent, environmentally disconnected ways of living. Those ways of living put us at risk in times of crisis and collapse. Many Americans lack the skills, human-powered equipment, attitudes, and community connections to survive even modest drops in system functioning. The more our population expects experts, engineers, banks, governments, corporate businesses, and other institutions to "take care of everything," the greater our risk of falling deeper in a crisis.

Depletion of certain non-renewable industrial inputs (e.g., phosphorous for industrial farming), and deterioration of biological diversity below the point of reliable regeneration (especially in a changing climate), are already at disconcerting levels. In the U.S. and most of the world, we are not yet seriously transitioning from an extractive economy to a regenerative economy. Every year of delay makes devastating climate change—runaway climate instability, biological deterioration, economic meltdown, and social instability—more likely. In short, we're not on the road to resilience, and the longer we wait to take strong action, the more inadequate our current institutions will be to handle the significant crisis and collapsing ecosystems. Now is the time to act to stop runaway climate change—the rapid cascading of earth system changes that will shorten, even more severely, the time and resources for transitioning to a better future.

While many of us live as if we are separate and autonomous, our fates are intertwined. For any of us to be resilient through a crisis in food, water, shelter, health care, sanitation, disease prevention, security, or other system breakdown, our community must have groups of people with resources, simpler technologies, technical skills, social skills, and attitudes that support everyone in meeting basic needs. In addition to material preparations, communities will need to cultivate sufficient cooperation, respect, trust, participation, specialization of labor, and systems of coordination to fill the gaps where large institutions do not, or cannot, go. Below are a few of the challenges that will be faced by existing institutions.

1. Government lacks sufficient public trust and resources

Federal government funding for emergency responses and reconstruction from weather disasters will not be able to keep pace.

In addition, some government policing agencies are mistrusted, which compromises their ability to facilitate community volunteerism, emergency preparedness, and trust building. Police shootings of unarmed people, evidence of racial discrimination, fear of the loss of firearms, police armed with military equipment used in warfare, and other challenges for local law enforcement have created greater controversy and weakened overall public confidence in the ability of police to facilitate community well-being. In addition, unlike Europe, where citizens expect and fund government to provide extensive social and emergency services, resources for longer-term crisis response are low to non-existent in many areas of the U.S. For example, the state of South Carolina has no system of emergency response and follow-up social services for people with low incomes who lose their home in a fire.

2. Large nonprofits lack sufficient resources

Extreme weather events and climate change impacts can quickly outpace existing social service capacities. As the number and scale of climate catastrophes rise, the inability of large-scale non-profit organizations to keep up with local human needs will become increasingly clear. Voluntary responses will be increasingly important.

While regional, state, and national nonprofit groups will hopefully be able to provide some support and coordination of crisis response, the most reliable infrastructure will be what local people have built in their own local communities. The resilience of a community will significantly depend upon an alternative or parallel localization of communications, coordination, and decision-making. The strength of the community will depend upon local collaborations of civic associations, faith communities, schools, businesses, social service organizations, health facilities, local government, and other local groups.

3. Large-scale, corporate businesses are not purposed to ensure public well-being

Investor-owned corporations, and larger companies with little geographical loyalty, are not in the business of rescuing communities and society from crisis, unless there is payment. In our current economic policy framework, the wealthy will hire the help they need, some governments will be able to raise taxes to cover the needs, and the majority will be left to cope however they can.

4. Monetary structures will be insufficient

Monetary systems designed to maximize profit for shareholders are ill suited for supporting public needs and security. Large, corporate banks and investment firms will instead try to exploit a crisis as a moneymaking opportunity.

In times of economic instability, banks may close or change policies, restricting access to currency. Hyperinflation can make paper money worthless. In crisis, locally accountable methods and structures for exchanging goods and services will be an essential complement to national currency.

5. Current technological systems are complex and fallible

We depend upon complex technologies to provide for our essential needs. We depend upon functioning transportation and power systems to deliver additional technologies and services that sustain the complex technologies that provide for our essential needs. This chain of inputs is a chain of dependency upon imported technology, services, personnel, and expertise that adds to the vulnerability of the system.

Complex technologies, and even relatively simple ones, are susceptible to failure because of the many components, conditions, and types of skills they require. Our nation has become so dependent on human and mechanical, energy and materials systems that are manufactured elsewhere—or mostly elsewhere—that most people can no longer endure extended energy and supply disruptions. Take the example of vehicles (let alone computers). We rely on multi-country supply chains for refining fuels, manufacturing tires and repair parts, operating electronic diagnostic systems, accessing fluids and lubricants, etc., etc. Another example is water and sewer pumping, trash removal and other sanitary services—all requiring specialized skills, tools, and personnel. Grocery store shelves will be largely bare within a couple of weeks. In a crisis, that will be only one of our big problems.

Complex energy, water, food, telecommunications, and transportation systems carry security vulnerabilities. Al Qaeda apparently contemplated dropping a bomb on a nuclear power plant instead of flying planes into the World Trade Center. Chlorine used to disinfect public water supplies is an explosive gas that increases the vulnerability of communities. Oil trains can explode. Pipelines can explode and leak. Transitioning to less dangerous, more local, more reliable technologies and alternatives can reduce community vulnerability.

INDIVIDUALS AND LOCAL GROUPS CAN
SOMETIMES RESPOND MORE EFFECTIVELY

In situations of ecological and social collapse, local, voluntary, grassroots initiatives will be essential to surviving, healing, and restoring stability. Individual and group action will make the difference between deepening deterioration and restoration. When large institutions and existing structures cannot respond quickly, effectively, or sufficiently, what are the alternatives? A police state can restore a superficial form of "stability," but rights and freedoms may be at risk. Government rationing can delay shortages, but dependency on government programs may develop. Businesses might find new economic opportunities, but the profit motive can push aside, neglect or damage individual needs, local priorities, and the public good. Achieving economic resilience and ecosystem regeneration will require labor, skills, resources, and work far greater than most of our existing structures are yet contemplating.

Voluntary action makes three important contributions in situations of crisis and collapse:

1. Individuals and local groups can often respond more rapidly

In times of crisis, individuals and groups often respond more quickly because individuals and small groups have fewer decision-making procedures and restrictions. An example is severe weather events. Help rushed in from individuals and groups after Katrina: donations, medical supplies, workers, transportation vehicles, emotional support, and more. Government and other institutions (in this case, the Red Cross) can play essential coordinating and management roles. Individuals and group support can be unhelpful and chaotic. Yet in times of crisis, large-scale support is needed. The challenge is to educate and inform the public, train volunteers, and support the development of small groups in networks of mutual accountability that can flexibly respond to diverse types of disasters and needs. Policy changes, as noted at the end of this chapter, are essential to maximize the benefits of voluntary action.

2. Individuals and local groups can often respond more flexibly, creatively tailoring their responses to unique needs

Volunteers can give personalized attention. They may be more familiar with individuals and needs in the community. Their volunteering may be more accountable to the community as a whole—both because they may have connections to the community and because they may be more easily refused or ignored if their volunteering does not serve local needs. They may be able to comprehend local needs more fully. They may face fewer constraints, consult with other members of the community, and come up with more creative solutions. For all these reasons and more, sometimes a community that knows a person or family is far more able to provide care and support than a large, distant organization or business. In addition, organizations and businesses typically have needs and goals that interfere with their willingness or capacity to respond to individual needs.

3. Individuals and voluntary groups can respond less expensively

Individuals give money as well as time, and ask others to give. Neighbors and local businesses often respond more readily to local, community-based projects. More intensive engagement of local organizations can mobilize resources beyond what people would otherwise be willing to pay in taxes or willing to give to more distant organizations.

In addition, local communities can generate a wider range of support: materials, labor, land, new collaborations, social capital, and information. Personal connections and local accountability also make it possible for alternative types of exchange such as uncompensated "favors," barter, credit, local currencies, time banks, volunteer exchanges, business swaps, technical assistance support, and other types of non-formal, relationship, or community-based exchanges and contributions.

Local social networks and groups can play crucial roles in responding to stressful, traumatic or crisis situations. A strong network of relationships, trust, communications, and collaboration can make an enormous difference when a community lacks resources, technology, security, and essential services.

SUPPORTING VOLUNTEERISM: FACING THE POTENTIAL FOR COLLAPSE

Downsides of volunteer support can be the lack of familiarity or commitment to health, public safety, equity, infrastructure, and other needs or regulations that are important to protecting the well-being of a community. Volunteerism is a great benefit, but also carries risks of harm or disregard that can damage a community.

The more that nonprofit, for-profit, and government organizations can face the potential for collapse, the better able they will be to support citizen, volunteer, and small group involvement in regional responses to crisis and collapse. The more existing institutions can transition to collapse-aware structures, the more they can support the energy, talent, and community spirit of volunteers while also ensuring greater understanding of public health and safety rules and practices that protect a community.

CHALLENGES FOR VOLUNTEERISM AND CIVIC ACTION

Can necessary levels of local, voluntary action and cooperation be achieved? When individualism, competition, and consumption are promoted as the "rational" and desirable ways to live, the values of cooperation, caring relationships, voluntary support, and non-economic exchanges are arguably lowered. In many parts of the U.S., volunteerism has declined. So has voting. Challenges for promoting volunteerism and civic action include:

1. The decline of job compensation and security

Economic stress and insecurity distract citizens, making them more vulnerable to addictions and "escape-isms," reducing their capacity to participate in social system maintenance. Fewer people have the capacity, financial security, or energy to volunteer, even when doing so would feel rewarding to them.

2. The decline of respect for political activities

Frustration with government, political parties, and politicians is high. The complexity of the system, neglect of the needs of the majority, and concentration of economic power make it difficult for citizens to access understandable, accurate information. Citizens are intentionally misled and unknowingly vote against their own interests and the common good. Many citizens don't know that "democracy" depends upon a set of citizenship practices and values, including respect, fairness, participation, and dialogue.

3. The cultivation of selfishness

Production of consumer goods by global industrial giants has made high levels of spending and consumption essential to the growth and "health" of "the economy." As depicted in Annie Leonard's entertaining videos, "The Story of Stuff," citizens are told that "our economy" depends upon high levels of consumer buying. Communications scholars suggest that as the marketing industry becomes ever more effective in convincing us that consumer purchases will fulfill our desires, we are becoming more selfish. By promoting selfish pursuits and consumerism, these scholars argue that our society is becoming more selfish. Meanwhile, civic concerns, public issues, community well-being, and volunteerism suffer.

4. The rise of imaginary realities in an electronic society

Imaginary worlds and stimulating story telling in ubiquitous electronic media further distract people from substantive human connections, place-based experiences and conversations, and civic participation.

Engaging citizens in their democracy and their community, along with creating collaboration among diverse people and groups, are challenges that can appear daunting. Yet every generation in human history has experienced both intransigent problems and surprising accomplishments by groups of people drawn together for common purpose. In fact, researchers increasingly speak of "meaning" and "purpose," social connections, and caring relationships, as more important for happiness, health, and quality of life than classic economic theory purports.

A growing body of science is finding that affiliation with others—community and caring connections—is biologically hardwired into our species. Painful experiences in life can trigger fear, anger, and competitiveness, which may become powerful visceral memories held in areas of the brain associated with emotional regions of our reptilian brain. As neuroscientists learn more about brain chemistry and the social impacts of trauma, loneliness, social rejection, and inequality, we will have the potential to build institutions and social structures to encourage peaceful, secure, high-functioning, responsible citizens. A beginning is to observe the state of volunteerism and civic participation and notice what obstacles and challenges prevent Americans for creating more of the kind of happy, secure, healthy, and socially connected life most of us seem to deeply want.

Historically, the United States has been seen as a nation of citizen associations. Sociologists and historians have noted the extensive networks of voluntary organizations, neighborhood groups, and civic associations that structured connections, work, and identity in American communities. More recently, observers have noted the rise of electronic networks and the growing impact of media on society, with television, social media, and electronic communications structuring patterns of thought, behavior, and social relationships in new ways. Yet, just as it seemed that urban areas were dying and neighborhood life was declining, millennials and many others have been rediscovering urban neighborhoods, backyard and container gardening, bicycling, storefront businesses, and local beer. Neighborhood affiliations are emerging in new ways, with social media assisting in networking and connecting.

BUILDING COMMUNITY RESILIENCE: THE
GLOBAL TRANSITION MOVEMENT

A terrific example of how grassroots initiatives can encourage coop-eration for mutual benefit is the global Transition Town movement. Towns, neighborhoods, islands, counties, cities, universities, and other geographical entities are part of a global network of grassroots groups sharing ideas, models, skills, resources, and support. People all over the world share resources for building (and expanding) resilient local structures of mutual aid.

The global Transition Town network has become an inspiring movement of voluntary action that supports people taking initiative locally to prepare for a world of lower economic means and greater environmental and social stress. The movement is global in perspective and local in action. The global organization, Transition Network, offers inspiring and useful, largely free resources to support people and groups in taking visionary, globally conscious but locally focused action. The fantastic success and viral spread of the movement's ideas is an example of how global, national, and local transformation can happen quite quickly when certain conditions are met. Below is a brief history of the Transition movement, along with a description of core concepts, philosophy, practices, and practical expressions.

THE EMERGENCE OF "TRANSITION" TO "COMMUNITY RESILIENCE"

The idea of "Transition" began in 2004 in the U.K., when a permaculture teacher, Rob Hopkins, realized that the challenges posed by climate change and depletion of non-renewable resources meant that conventional ways of living could not last. Rob coined the word "transition" to describe the process needed to change, and focused on the community as a scale of human organization essential to well being. Through his teaching, Rob worked collaboratively with a group of students to design a local food, energy, materials, social, and economic initiative, with a flexible, adaptable structure, and a positive vision of the future outlined in an "Energy Descent Plan" for the town of Kinsale, Ireland. In 2005 Rob moved to Totnes, a small market town in southwest England. There he and Naresh Giangrande, with several similarly concerned neighbors, formed "Transition Town Totnes" to support their community in transitioning "from oil dependency to community resilience."

The success and enthusiasm generated in Totnes by this handful of "Transition Initiators" quickly attracted interest from dozens of other towns in the U.K. Within a few years the Transition model had spread virally to a thousand communities in the U.K., and to tens of thousands of people in thousands of communities and organizations around the world. By April 2014, more than 1,120 registered Transition Initiatives had formed in 43 countries, with many thousands of people inspired to organize a wide range of local, resilience-building projects. As the Transition Towns model spread virally and rapidly, Rob and colleagues formed the Transition Network (www.TransitionNetwork. org) to support local initiatives and regional and national "hubs" around the world.

Transition Initiatives also organize at the neighborhood level, many of them inspired by Transition Town Totnes' hugely successful Transition Streets program. Approximately 70% of the 8,000-plus residents of Totnes have participated in one or more Transition Town activities or programs, with Transition Streets attracting large-scale funding to install solar panels and pay staff to expand the project. Neighbor-to-neighbor outreach, public events, practical projects, and sustained, town-wide outreach and collaboration with existing groups, have successfully engaged the community to extraordinary levels. Meanwhile the movement has transformed environmental politics and organizing in dozens of countries across the world.

With a central focus on local economies and supporting locally based "livelihoods," the Transition movement has inspired and supported a wide variety of imaginative local enterprises and economic projects. Transition brings together people and organizations from across communities to agree on joint actions, to influence decision makers, and to improve community quality of life. Beyond the "official" Transition initiatives, the movement has sparked an enormous shift in thinking—a global transformation among environmental groups, community organizations, governments, educational institutions, businesses, and nonprofit groups. Local, national, and regional levels are increasingly incorporating the language, goals, principles and action ideas of the Transition—community resilience—movement. After interviewing leaders and studying the Transition movement, editors of the most recent U.N. climate report extensively incorporated the concepts of the Transition approach.

Concepts in the Transition Movement

In a recent strategic plan, leaders in the Transition movement summarized the shared analysis, always evolving, that led to the popularity of the idea of "transition":

- The era of cheap and easy fossil fuels is over, leading industry to resort to extreme methods of extraction with enormous environmental and economic costs.

- For the first time in human history, the concentration of climate-warming carbon dioxide in the atmosphere has passed the milestone level of 400 parts per million.

- Extreme weather events are increasing in frequency, and the connection with man-made climate change is becoming ever harder to ignore.

- There is a mainstream expectation that we can maintain and even increase our current levels of consumption, although we live on a finite planet and have come to rely on resources that are becoming scarcer.

- Despite the connections between resource use, carbon emissions, and economic growth, most governments and commentators continue to focus their policies and pronouncements on achieving growth at all costs.

- Inequality is increasing globally and within individual countries, as wealth and power is concentrated withhin a minority; some countries struggle to raise living standards and others implement cuts in public services, which hit the most vulnerable.

- Growing numbers of people and organizations *are* asking questions, getting in touch with their fears for the planet and their yearning for a healthier, more connected way of living.

From this analysis, Rob Hopkins and colleagues in the first Transition Town Totnes identified several core concepts.

1. Acknowledge the Severity of Our Situation

The Transition movement acknowledges the severity of our situation. The risk of severe and multi-faceted crises is recognized as a core concept in the movement.

When the movement began, the risk of runaway climate change and catastrophic ecosystem collapse was just beginning to be discussed beyond climate science and environmental circles. At the time, conversations about political, social, environmental, and economic collapse were almost nonexistent. Leaders in the Transition movement publicly raised awareness of the risk of severe climate disruption and other catastrophic events. Unlike many leaders in environmental and economic circles, they did not sugarcoat bad news but instead acknowledged major risks and threats.

Instead of denying the possibility of collapse, the Transition approach is to encourage ongoing inquiry, sharing of information, and discussion. The Transition movement's willingness to honestly name the great risks humanity faces, yet to launch a movement focused on respect for different opinions and positive responses to locally-defined threats, is a positive model for environmentalists who are upset that other people are not recognizing the threats of climate change.

2. Choose Optimism and Positive Action

Instead of dwelling on horrific scenarios, the Transition movement proposes that the best response is positive action and building local community resilience. Instead of debating the risk of collapse, Transition focuses on strengthening local community resilience — transitioning from dependency on importing essential food and other products.

The rapid spread of the Transition movement was due, in part, to an emphasis on fun, hope, and positive, collective action. Information about climate instability and crisis, when presented with an attitude of "doom and gloom," led to widespread despair. The Transition movement references the crisis, grounded in the alarming science and sobering indicators of our time. Yet Transition consciously chooses a positive, community-focused response.

In 2006 the Transition Movement summarized the paradoxical messages of crisis and positive action with a list of "Recognitions":

- Climate change and the peaking of (conventional) oil require urgent action.

- Life with less energy is inevitable. It is better to plan for it than to be taken by surprise.

- Industrial society has lost the resilience to be able to cope with energy shocks.

- We have to act together, now.

- Infinite growth within a finite system (such as planet Earth) is impossible.

- We demonstrated great ingenuity and intelligence as we raced up the energy (consumption) curve over the last 150 years. There's no reason why we can't use those qualities, and more, as we negotiate our way back down.

- If we plan and act early enough, and use our creativity and cooperation to unleash the genius within our local communities, we can build a future far more fulfilling and enriching, more connected to and gentler on the Earth, than the life we have today.

Courage in truth-telling is a type of leadership that is essential in crisis. History is often the stories of coping with crisis, change, and disaster. When individuals and groups accurately assess danger and crisis, and calmly lead or support others to better outcomes, we see that hope, determination, caring, and positive action can sometimes achieve far greater results than we imagined were possible.

3. Focus on Local Communities Taking Initiative

The Transition movement popularized the words "resilience" and "transition," thus shifting from problem-focused thinking to solution-focused action. The first "Transition Concept" states: "A town using much less energy and resources than we presently consume, could, if properly planned for and designed, be more resilient, more abundant, and more fulfilling than the present." Building community resilience—the principles and practices of the Transition model—are ways to encourage the personal connections and attitudes that help communities thrive and make democracy work. Collaborative, practical projects, and connections with neighbors lead to information sharing and awareness of real world cause-and-effect. Instead of imaginary realities created by media and electronic storytelling, neighbors invite neighbors to experience the realities of growing food, protecting water, generating locally owned renewable energy, constructing and insulating shelters, delivering local services, and exchanging mutual support when monetary systems prove inadequate, etc. Local, voluntary, grassroots initiatives can help transform attitudes, communications, actions, and behaviors to support cooperation. Individuals and small groups can initiate positive projects and community activities that generate local culture and create greater social cohesion and resilience.

The Transition Town Totnes model emphasizes individual and small group action: "average people" and small working groups taking initiative, in their local communities. This approach appeals to people of all political perspectives. Rather than a "top-down" model, Transition emphasizes local people creating together, helping their community move "from where we are now to an abundant, fulfilling, and resilient future." Instead of looking to a handful of leaders, Transition emphasizes community relationships and teamwork. "Initiators" support the emergence of many projects and activities by scores of neighbours. The Transition model emphasizes that ordinary people taking initiative and working together in small groups can create a "buzz" of local community action—cooperative, creative, voluntary, neighborhood, and local institutional action—to build resilience from the bottom up.

One of the central ideas of the movement is that each local community is unique—and so will have its own way of transitioning.

As we say, "There is no right way to do Transition...and that's part of the fun of the whole thing." The movement emphasizes that each local community has its own history, local talent, knowledge, abilities, and culture. Each place has its own unique environment and local resources. Therefore, each local community will create its own path—its own ways of transitioning.

In another impressive example of handling the paradox of "think global, act local," Transition initiators also share globally. While each community is unique, and will create its own unique pathway to resilience, we all face similar global problems. While we each face a unique local situation, we all face some similar stages and challenges in "transitioning" from various types of dependency (e.g., dependency on imported energy and food) to community resilience.

4. View Change as a Process, a "Transition"

Rob Hopkins' idea of "transition" shifted thinking across the world. Instead of environmental solutions needing to be fully identified and planned, the concept of transition helped leaders and citizens take steps without knowing exactly how bad a crisis might be or what structures would be ideal for their community. People with different perspectives or differing degrees of understanding about the "threats" and the "solutions" could move forward toward resilience without knowing or agreeing upon ultimate answers.

In support of the idea of transition as a process, Transition Network leaders identified five distinct stages in community transitioning: beginning with meeting equally enthused people and deciding to give Transition a go ("Starting out"), to finding that you are now becoming a viable, vibrant project ("Deepening"), then trying to broaden your engagement with the local community ("Connecting") and scaling up what you are doing in order to make localization a reality on the ground ("Building"). Lastly, there is a visionary, speculative stage of looking forward to how things might be if this happened everywhere ("Daring to Dream"). That's where things get really interesting.

5. Find Gentle Ways to Encourage "Inner Transition"

Inner transition, as well as outer transition, is a crucial resource for building resilience. Transition Town Totnes members Hilary Prentice and Sophy Banks started an "Inner Transition" group in Totnes, England, and drew attention to the emotional and psychological impacts of all the "doom and gloom" information. They responded to information about the ecological-energy-economy-equity crisis from the perspective of neighbor/citizen/volunteer, instead of academically or politically. Focusing on local community engagement, they and others in Transition Town Totnes realized the importance of addressing the feelings, beliefs, and social isolation that might hamper people from responding to warnings of impending crisis. Here is some of their language:

> This [information] may make you feel:
> - Disconnected from ourselves and others around us
> - Anger
> - Frustration
> - Despair
> - Numbness
> - Powerlessness
>
> You might be feeling overwhelmed by the gloomy forecasts for our future. Often we just switch off from it, and can look as though we don't care. But actually most of us care deeply. Not just about our families, but also about our community, the places we live, and the future our children will inherit.
>
> We just need to feel we can do something about it, and that we have the support of others. We need to see the possibility that our actions can actually make a difference.
>
> And the more of us that do this, the bigger those changes will be.
>
> Transition Network is here to help you and your community build healthy, resilient, local responses to these challenges.

We don't claim to have all the answers — we give no guarantee as this is an ongoing experiment and we're all learning as we go — but we've learnt a lot already that we can share with you.

An empathetic, compassionate approach to people not interested in sustainability turned out to be pivotal in the growth of the Transition Towns/community resilience movement. Instead of judging people negatively, Transition encourages local leaders to initiate positive, friendly, supportive, inclusive, and fun local events and practical projects. Instead of complaining about people who deny the climate crisis, or distaining people are not aware or active, the Transition approach is to listen, to be supportive and positive, and to find what practical projects can bring at least part of the community together.

Transition Principles for Building Local Resilience

Eight Transition Principles formed the foundation of the movement that spread virally to over 50 countries and tens of thousands of people in just a few years. Together these principles can build community across a diversity of beliefs, priorities, ethnicities, and political perspectives. The principles point local citizens toward ways of building community that increase neighborhood collaboration and community well-being.

1. Positive Visioning

- We dedicate ourselves to creating tangible, practical visions of a positive future.
- Our primary focus is not campaigning *against* things, but rather on positive, empowering possibilities and opportunities.

2. Respectful and Engaging Awareness-Raisings

- Raising awareness in respectful, nondirective ways
- Sharing the truth as we understand it in engaging, fun, playful, accessible, and empowering ways.

- Helping people access good information and trust them to make good decisions.

3. Inclusion and Openness

- Seek an unprecedented coming together of the broad diversity of society.
- Dedicate ourselves to open and inclusive decision-making.
- Seek to engage our local business community, the diversity of community groups, and local authorities.
- In the challenge of energy descent, we can have no room for "them and us" thinking.
- Every skill is valuable. Everyone is needed.
- Encourage people to bring their passion and create a project!

4. Enable Sharing and Networking

- Transition Initiatives dedicate themselves to sharing their successes, failures, insights, and connections at the various scales across the Transition network, so as to build up a collective body of experience. We are learning together.

5. Build Resilience

- To deal with shocks—impacts, drastic change.
- Build strong local communities (local food, energy, sustainable livelihoods, etc.)

6. Re-skill: Increase Basic Skills

- Inner *and* outer transition
- Need to change both our technologies and our worldview.
- Information about the state of our planet can generate fear and grief.
- Unconscious processes, behaviors, and patterns sabotage change.
- Transition thrives by enabling and supporting people to do what they are passionate about, what they feel called to do.

7. Scale and Complexity

- Work with the whole system in your local environment and mimic nature.

8. Subsidiarity: Self-organization

- Decision-making at the appropriate level, but as decentralized and easy to replicate as possible.
- Self-organizing: Encourage people to organize themselves rather than pushing for "top-down" solutions.
- Solutions at the most appropriate, practical, and empowering level.
- Models are easy to copy

Advice from the Transition movement: Start where you are—the place where you live, the people, the strengths and assets of your community. Work with what exists. Instead of trying to impose ideas on others or persuade them to do what you think they should do, listen and work with others in a more collaborative, personal, local, human scale.

Follow great leaders and successful social change movements throughout history. Instead of focusing only on problems and obstacles, focus on possibilities and practical projects that achieve real improvements in people's lives, and developing positive collaborative relationships.

Practical Expressions of the Transition Movement

Transition Woodstock, New York, created a local, alternative health clinic. Community volunteers worked with caring medical professionals and alternative health practitioners to build the resilience of the community by offering free and low-cost health services to low-income residents. The health center became a network, a community asset, a circle of friendship, and a vital support for people without the means to access health services or the full range of healing modalities.

Transition Port Townsend, Washington

Transition Town Media, Pennsylvania, created a "FreeStore" in their suburban town near Philadelphia. Open to everyone, the store, located in a local c hurch, is stocked with donated, "gently-used" items. A website displays pictures of "What's New" and explains: "We accept small household items no larger than what one person can carry. Food and clothing can be given to the food/clothing pantry," which is also located in the church. The store has been a great success, bringing people together for sharing and friendship. The message to the community is: "All items in the store are free. You are welcome to come and take whatever you like or need. In this way we keep things out of landfills, support a reuse ethic, and help one another without the use of currency" (http://www. mediafreestore.com/).

Transition Guelph, Ontario, has catalyzed and encouraged many local initiatives and celebratory networking in a city of 110,000. Their hugely successful Resilience Festival has become an annual event. Partnerships with inspired individuals and community-minded projects have grown into a network of caring, creative collaboration. Among many food-oriented projects is the Transition Guelph TreeMobile, a volunteer-run project that "can provide fruit-bearing trees and shrubs at low cost, deliver them to your door, and even do the planting!" The goals of the annual TreeMobile are:

- To increase our community's resilience by planting more food-bearing trees and shrubs in the urban environment;

- To increase the urban tree canopy, thus improving air quality, soil stability, temperature moderation, and carbon sequestration;

- To accomplish the above by making hardy, disease-resistant, climate-appropriate, and flavorful food-bearing trees and shrubs available at reasonable cost; and . . . to increase FUN!

Since 2011, TreeMobile has planted 2170 fruit trees and plants. In 2014 they partnered with Transition Toronto for the first annual

Toronto TreeMobile (http://www.transitionguelph.org/project-list/treemobile/).

Transition Putney, Vermont, created over 18 working groups, with projects touching many aspects of resilience: aging in place, alternative higher education options, food shelf, renewable energy, community garden, Inner Transition, creating jobs and livelihoods, health and wellness, and more. Many of the working groups and projects were launched at public forums. Over several years, many hundreds of people attended events and forums where local leaders and organizations shared information about their work and explored how to strengthen the community. Key to their success was a strong core group of positive, visionary community members who saw their mission as both accomplishing practical projects and nurturing a caring community.

POLICIES TO SUPPORT COMMUNITY VOLUNTEERISM AND INITIATIVE

As local communities work to become more resilient, less dependent, more technologically flexible, and more socially cohesive, a number of federal, state, and municipal policies support the development of local, voluntary, resilient structures.

First, federal, state, and municipal policies need to prioritize building local resilience for times of crisis. This includes policies to lower dependence on imported "essentials": basic levels of food, water, energy, waste management and recycling/reuse, shelter, health care, transportation, and mutual support. It also includes policies to strengthen the local economy—to support resilient jobs (unlikely to move away, such as home repair and weatherization) and jobs that support community well-being in times of crisis

Second, we need federal, state, and municipal policy strategies to prioritize simplifying essential technologies—or at least create parallel infrastructure—that support local communities in shifting from highly complex, resource intensive, import-dependent technologies to systems and technologies that support communication and coordination for delivering local essentials like food, water, health care, shelter, etc..

Third, we need federal, state and municipal policy strategies to prioritize relocalization of:

- agriculture, food processing, and storage,
- economic activity and sustainable job development,
- health care and community care services,
- emergency services and community-based security/ neighborhood protection, and
- flexible and alternative exchange systems (i.e., materials swaps, "Time Bank" volunteering, local currency, barter, internships and experiential learning for young people and career-changing, and labor for housing, labor for food opportunities, etc.).

Fourth, we need federal, state, and municipal policies that support local, individual, and group initiative. Government and other institutions need to support and encourage individuals, small groups, and local organizations taking initiative and achieving successes in crisis response.

Finally, federal, state, and municipal policies must walk their own paradox of both supporting local initiatives and implementing the larger principles that protect the global biological support system. Where scientists have identified dangers and vulnerabilities in the biological/ecological systems that sustain life and health for everyone, communities have a responsibility to prevent biological system change and collapse in their own local region as much as possible. In short, it is not enough to prepare for local resilience. The global dangers of ecological collapse must be addressed locally as well as prepared for locally.

CONCLUSION

We do not know how severe change will be, how deep our global crisis will go, and what types of crisis or resource constraints will hit first or most painfully. We don't know what inventions might be possible, what creative solutions may emerge, or what positive action and collaboration might accomplish. There will be no perfect preparation, no ideal institutions, and no fully resilient structures. We face a multitude of unknowns.

Lack of knowing is a characteristic of crisis and collapse. Not being able to predict the troubles of the future is an ongoing human challenge. The best we can do to prevent disintegration and prepare for possible collapse is to assume that some of the harrowing predictions could happen, but that succumbing to despair will only make things worse. We can experience a richer, more satisfying life by engaging in meaningful activities with other people who care.

Where people do not understand or seem to care about global dangers that will affect them, neighbors inviting neighbors to join in practical, positive, community-building projects is an excellent first step towards relationship-building and preparation for change and crisis. Instead of expecting people to study, comprehend, and act on abstract, complex, overwhelming, depressing, and frightening future potential crises, a focus on local, community resilience and neighborhood mutual support can be a more effective response. There are enormous economic, social, energy, food, security, and aesthetic benefits in building networks and structures for more resilient, less globally dependent, less environmentally destructive, local ways of living.

In the process of strengthening our communities in practical ways and improving our local quality of local life, we achieve something potentially even more valuable for crisis prevention: psychological resilience. History shows that what helps people through the most devastating crises is qualities of character and community cohesion such as: the strength of community collaboration, caring, common purpose, flexibility, patience and compassion towards other members of the community, sharing information, "collective genius," analysis, calm consideration of options, and resilient spirits. The Transition movement gathers these attitudes and practices and delivers this ancient wisdom in a secular, accessible way that crosses divisions and boundaries. Storm clouds are forming. We cannot afford to be divided and unfamiliar with our place and community.

When crisis hits, voluntary action and local structures of mutual support can make an enormous difference. With time, new structures of community organizations, municipalities, state and federal government, businesses, and nonprofit systems can create new structures for society and economic activity and specialize in handling more complex aspects of collapse. The more that local institutions face potential collapse and publicly prepare for a major crisis, the more they can support the growth of volunteerism and civic action in protecting and sustaining local communities.

Regardless of how much we prepare, however, the return of the growth economy and industrial society as we know it today will prove impossible. Those who have the courage to face the severity of our biological and climate vulnerability, the mental flexibility to question the appearance of normalcy, and the vision to act locally, regionally, nationally, and globally to transition to community resilience, will create a better life for themselves and help strengthen the well-being of all.

People and communities are finding many ways to use less energy while enjoying a high quality of life. Engineers have found technologies to help us to reduce our use of polluting, nonrenewable energy. In particular, The Solutions Project (www.TheSolutionsProject. org) and the 2000 Watt Society (http://www.2000-watt-society.org/) offer excellent responses to make the best of our situation. These two initiatives offer a more comprehensive set of approaches and technologies to increase global equity and well-being. Combined with lifestyle, educational, political, and economic action, these two approaches show essential ways to prevent much worse outcomes and to transition to the best possible future for our precious earth.

TRANSITION RESOURCES

News, information, and support:

- Transition Network: www.TransitionNetwork.org
- Transition US: www.TransitionUS.org

- Transition Training: www.TransitionNetwork.org/training

Videos, books, articles, websites, and other media:

- U.S. TeleSeminars: http://transitionus.org/training/past-events.
- Transition Culture blog: https://transitionnetwork.org/blogs /rob-hopkins.

Projects:

- Transition Streets neighborhood project: http://transitionstreets. org/.
- REconomy: www.REconomy.org.

⧉ 12 ⧉

SANDIEGO350 ACTIVISM

James Long, Ashley Mazanec, and Michael Brackney

ABSTRACT: *A brief history of the founding of SanDiego350, a volunteer climate action organization affiliated with 350.org international, plus descriptions of its mission, organizing structure, day-to-day operations, membership building, action teams, and activities.*

SANDIEGO350 IS A VOLUNTEER-LED Southern California non-profit organization promoting action on climate change. In a few short years, effective grassroots organizing and collaboration with many community groups resulted in San Diego becoming one of the first cities to adopt a climate action plan to target 100% renewable energy by 2035. We demonstrate that local activism can bring positive change in government policies to mitigate climate change. We explain how SanDiego350 organizes itself to advocate change at the local level. In this chapter, we offer a brief event history of SanDiego350, describe our grassroots organizing, day-to-day operations, membership building, and action teams, and then conclude with a vision of what we're trying to achieve here in San Diego and beyond.

SanDiego350 had its beginnings in September 2011 when local climate activists who were to become our founding members staged a "Moving Planet" event in San Diego along with many other such events worldwide inspired by the international organization 350.org. After some folks met at St. Paul's Episcopal Cathedral for an interfaith panel discussion on earth-keeping, about 350 of us (really!) gathered in Balboa Park and marched across Cabrillo Bridge to the Plaza de Panama, right past the Organ Pavilion, and left on Presidents Way for a rally on the grass featuring speeches by several local politicians including Mayor Bob Filner. This event was well covered by local news media. Co-founder Simon Mayeski, a native San Diegan, "saw the smarts, the dedication, and the excitement" of those who organized that rally and felt inspired to join in. Two months later the SanDiego350 group formed and soon became familiar faces advocating for climate action at public meetings with local officials, and by staging more public events.

Since our beginning in 2011, SanDiego350 is affiliated, but independent of, the international organization 350.org.[2] Our local SanDiego350 group has a self-governing board and steering committee, so all decisions are completely at the local level. Of course, SanDiego350 works closely with the international 350.org movement, and draws inspiration from its founder Bill McKibben. SanDiego350 co-founder Masada Disenhouse explains that SanDiego350 coordinates large rallies and protests in conjunction with 350.org events. SanDiego350 shares common principles of climate justice, strength in collaboration, and mass mobilization to create change. We share our SanDiego350 name with the 350.org movement. The number 350 means the safe number of greenhouse gas concentration. Humanity must reduce carbon dioxide in the atmosphere from greater than 400 parts per million down to 350 parts per million in order to avoid bad consequences of changing climate.

In May 2012, we organized our "Connect the Dots" rally at Mission Beach where we staged a human wave holding up and rippling long pieces of blue cloth to show the sea level rise projected for 2050 if we don't stop global warming.[3] During press coverage of the event, SanDiego350 member Janina Moretti told San Diegans "If we don't address [climate change], there will be bad consequences in our community. We are out here today to try to raise awareness to do something before it is too late."[4]

Later that year (2012) and well on into the next, we worked with other local environmental organizations to stop the construction of a natural gas-fired power plant. The proposed plant was to be built on the state's largest municipal park in Mission Trails Regional Park. The San Diego City Council voted unanimously against the project. The press credited SanDiego350 along with seven other community groups opposed to the plant.[5] But battles are not always successful. Later, the California Public Utilities Commission approved a natural gas power plant in Carlsbad California, despite heavy opposition from the community.[6]

In February 2013, SanDiego350 staged one of many nationwide rallies against the Keystone XL Pipeline, again featuring our mayor calling for much more renewable energy in San Diego. Afterward we walked our 55-foot long *"Stop the Keystone Pipeline. Fight Climate Change"* banner out onto the nearby bridge over Interstate-5 for all the motorists passing underneath to see. This event, too, was well covered by local news media.[7]

Come spring (2013), we established our own SanDiego350 booth at EarthFair in Balboa Park, the world's biggest Earth Day celebration, mobilizing many volunteers to talk with many fairgoers about the reality of our climate emergency, and signing up more newsletter subscribers and potential active members than at any other event of the year.

Our biggest climate change-related event so far was our own People's Climate March in September 2014, in concert with over 2600 People's Climate March events worldwide. While nearly 400,000 people from all over the country marched in New York City, 1500 turned out in San Diego, nearly twice as many as expected, to march in support of the city's proposed climate action plan after hearing its authors, past interim mayor Todd Gloria and his environmental policy director Nicole Capretz, give fiery speeches for it.[8]

GRASSROOTS ORGANIZING

SanDiego350 members build grassroots support by engaging the public through petitioning, flyering for events, staging marches and rallies, presenting talks, slideshows, and movies, and doing creative outreach at fairs and festivals. We then leverage this support to help further the formation and implementation of local public policies that combat climate change as discussed below in the Public Policy Team section.

We make a lot of use of petitions and pledges to gain support for issues. A good example of this is our gathering of hundreds of signatures before and during our People's Climate March on a pledge to drive less, eat less meat, use less water, support sustainable business, get involved in local climate actions, and call on our elected representatives to implement a strong climate action plan for the City of San Diego.

Another good example of our grassroots organizing is the advance work done by the members of our Creative Engagement Team before staging their *High Water Line* art project as discussed below in the section on this team.

Having found that project evaluation is critical for our success, we review completed projects in terms of what worked and what did not. We use evaluation forms to gather feedback from volunteers and event attendees, team leaders report feedback to the Steering Committee, and the Steering Committee evaluates each project and suggests improvements for the next event.

In addition to evaluating projects, we recognize the efforts of volunteers by thanking them publicly at monthly meetings, and by sending them hand-written thank-you cards for accomplishing extraordinary tasks.

DAY-TO-DAY OPERATIONS

There are many keys to the successful operation of SanDiego350 including our leadership, democratic approach, communication channels, and record keeping.

Our Steering Committee, anchored by co-founder Masada Disenhouse, oversees our activities. Any member may attend and speak at Steering Committee meetings, as well as at our monthly general meetings, and we strive to make our decisions by consensus. Moreover, since SanDiego350, like all other local 350 groups, is established, governed, and funded independently of the national organization, we make our own decisions and seek local solutions for local problems.

We communicate with each other through several key channels including our webpage (for our events, projects, resources, photos and videos, blogs, and press releases), Email (for our monthly newsletter and one-on-one communication), Google Groups, Google Docs, and social media.[9] Our SD350 Google Group is an effective way for all our members, except those without email, to connect, ask questions, get feedback, and keep up on the latest news. Each team has its own Google Group for team-specific communications. Google Docs provides us with the capability of sharing documents on the cloud without having to send them back and forth to each other. In addition, we have Facebook, Twitter, and Instagram accounts, as well as a YouTube channel onto which we upload composite newscasts of SD350 events.

Last but by no means least, we keep and track records — member contact records, event records, member event attendance records, and media contact records — using CiviCRM, the web-based, open source, Constituent Relationship Management database geared toward meeting the needs of nonprofits and other civic-sector organizations.

MEMBERSHIP BUILDING

We inspire and sign up new members at all of our events using paper forms or, for the first time at Earth Day, using electronic tablets which greatly facilitate the process at large events. Shortly after each event we call the people we've signed up to welcome them to SanDiego350, ask them about what interests them in what we're doing, answer any questions they may have, offer to meet in person with any who show strong interest—an excellent technique for building relationships—and invite them to attend our next Intro Chat to learn more about what we do and how they can get involved. Then we invite them to attend their first general meeting to meet more of us, see how we work together, hear reports from all our action teams, and discover how they'd like to work with us. Currently SanDiego350 has a mailing list of over 6000 people and over 100 active volunteers.

A key tool for organizing and member building is the SanDiego350 monthly volunteer meeting. The meeting location rotates around the county to be accessible to a wide area. The steering committee creates the agenda each month. A different member volunteer is chairs each meeting, reading each topic on the agenda. Volunteers also keep time during the meeting, keeping track of the time allotted for each topic. Volunteers also serve as meeting greeters, looking for new faces, greeting them, and making sure they are oriented and can ask questions when they arrive. The meetings are fast paced. Meetings open with a motivational minute where members usually talk about what inspires them in climate change. Then a 5–10 minute ice breaker usually breaks into smaller groups for people to talk about a question, or do an activity together to meet people in the group. Each team in the organization gives a report during the monthly meeting. A portion of the meeting is for an invited group to come and speak about a project or about their group. SanDiego350 seeks active collaboration with other groups. We also discuss upcoming events and announcements at the end of the meeting. The monthly meeting is a good way for new people to find out what our organization is doing.

Relationship building is a key principle to building membership. SanDiego350 uses social media like Facebook to outreach to the community. However, old-fashioned grassroots organizing through person-to-person contact creates the most impact at our events. SanDiego350 actively executes phone banking, tabling, canvassing, and speaking at presentations to build membership. We make it a priority at each event to capture all attendee names, email addresses, and phone numbers to enter into our CiviCRM contact management system.

ACTION TEAMS

SanDiego350 currently has seven action teams: the Bridge, Public Policy, Fracking, Planet-Based Diet, Community Presentation, Creative Engagement, and Media teams.

As mentioned above, our *Bridge Team* follows up on the initial phone calls we make to new members by introducing them to the workings of SanDiego350 in order to help them find their own place in the organization. Team members organize introductory meetings for new members called "Intro Chats," which consist of introductions to the reality of global warming and climate change, to 350.org national and international, and to the teams and activities that SD350 has to offer. After Intro Chats, the hosts make follow-up support calls to all the participants.

Our *Public Policy Team* is our original SD350 action team, dedicated to furthering the formation and implementation of local public policies that combat climate change. Accordingly team members 1) investigate current legislation and regulation bearing on climate change, and present concerns and recommendations thereon to elected officials in letters, comments at public hearings, and conversations in private meetings; 2) focus on the regional transportation planning work of **SANDAG**, the San Diego Association of Governments, in order to encourage them to reduce vehicle miles traveled (**VMT**) and associated greenhouse gas emissions by implementing a viable mass transit system instead of expanding our freeways; and 3) encourage and support the development of strong, measureable, and enforceable climate action plans in the city of San Diego and surrounding municipalities.

Our *Fracking Team* is focused on ending fracking in California. Team members have taken a busload of SD350 members with fine homemade signs and banners up to Sacramento to join many others in calling for a moratorium on fracking. They have also taken two busloads—including one full of the high school students of one team member—up to Oakland to join many others in calling on Governor Brown to show real climate leadership and declare a moratorium on fracking. Since both of these ventures failed to achieve their immediate goal, the team joined Californians Against Fracking (CAF) in calling for an outright ban on fracking in California and in working for legislation to bring this about. Meanwhile, team members continue their ground work of educating the public about the hazards of fracking by giving presentations, operating their own booth at EarthFair, and putting on special events like taking a busload of the same high school students mentioned above on an earlier field trip to Kern County to see the fracking operations there.[10] Indeed, our Fracking Team members have done so well that they've received two $5000 grants from Patagonia to keep up their great work!

Our *Planet-Based Diet Team* is dedicated to showing everyone that shifting from an animal-based diet to a plant-based diet, along with cutting back on food waste, is the single most effective thing every one of us can do to mitigate climate change and the depletion of global forest, soil, and water resources. Team members give presentations, screen videos, hold monthly book discussions, and operate booths at local fairs and festivals. At EarthFair in 2015, they engaged many people at the "Garden of Eating" booth, with a display of colorful fruits and vegetables fished out of local dumpsters that was so striking it made the front page[11] of the San Diego Union Tribune, and helped the volunteers at the SD350 booth next door to sign up more mailing list supporters than ever before. The photo showed Rob Greenfield eating an apple he got from out of a dumpster behind a San Diego grocery store.[12]

Our *Community Presentation Team* creates and gives presentations on climate change at a variety of venues—community, educational, political, religious, senior, youth—to increase climate change literacy and develop relationships for future collaboration. The presentation includes an introduction to climate change, its causes, impacts, and urgency, climate change denial, personal and collective solutions, and time for questions and answers. This team formed soon after the founding of SanDiego350. Team leader Janina Morretti explains that they quickly learned how to create more effective presentations by making them interactive. The presentations include lots of time for questions, and for small group discussions. Another strategy they employ is to create an "ask" for an attendee to perform. They invite attendees to an upcoming rally or event. They ask attendees to talk to their family and friends about climate issues.

Our *Creative Engagement Team* is focused on engaging and educating people about our climate emergency through the use of audio, visual, and performing arts. Team members have paraded our *"Stop the Keystone Pipeline. Fight Climate Change."* banner at several venues, chanting along the way. They have sung songs and performed skits at rallies, approached folks at EarthFair by clowning in costume or presenting them with bottles of yucky-looking "fracking water" in order to engage them in conversation. In 2015, team members staged a High Water Line art project in Mission Beach, chalking a line along Mission Boulevard to show where the high tide flood line is projected to be in 2050 if we don't stop global warming.[13] This event generated extensive TV news coverage, community discussion, and many signatures by local business owners and voters on a petition calling for a strong climate action plan for the city of San Diego. Team members ascribe much of this success to their advance work of canvassing all the businesses along the planned route for their support in signing the petition and posting flyers for the event in their windows, and of presenting the project to the town council. A video describes the project and what people can do.[14]

Our *Media Team* works to increase public awareness of our climate emergency, of what people can do about it, and of what we of SanDiego350 actually are doing about it. Team members work closely with our other teams to get news media coverage for their events, help news media staff get the interviews and footage they need, keep track of their coverage, and sometimes serve as team spokespersons. They also track letters to the editor by SD350 members and edit writings by SD350 members for publication in local media including our own blog. The Media Team plans to train more members on how to get and support media coverage for our events, share and store photos of our events, make effective use of social media, and build closer relationships with local journalists.

CONCLUSION

In achieving our initial goal of establishing SanDiego350 as a leading, well-organized and operated climate action organization, we had the great good fortune of being recognized, appreciated, and celebrated as an inspiration to other local 350 groups by 350.org founder Bill McKibben at our big fundraiser in 2014. In addition to conducting our ongoing work and growing our membership, we look forward to hiring our first intern this summer, transitioning into our next phase of promoting community choice energy in San Diego, encouraging more municipalities in San Diego County to develop strong, measurable, and enforceable climate action plans, pushing local governments and organizations to divest from fossil fuels, and building the organizing skills of our members through regular trainings. If life as we know it on Earth is going to survive global warming and climate change, the people of San Diego must help lead the way. We of SanDiego350 are doing all we can to encourage all of them — all of us — to do so.

ENDNOTES

1   See https://www.facebook.com/SanDiego350 (accessed 4/5/2015).

2   See www.350.org (accessed 5/8/2016).

3   See https://www.youtube.com/watch?v=3SCG5EqigbA for news report of event.

4   Ibid.

5 For a news report of this event, see http://www.kpbs.org/news/2012/sep/24/san-diego-city-council-consider-quail-brush-power-/ .

6 For a news report of this event, see http://www.sandiegouniontribune.com/news/2015/may/21/cpuc-carlsbad-power-plant/.

7 For a news report of this event, see https://www.youtube.com/watch?v=-rD7H4Aocjc.

8 For a news report of this event, see http://sandiegofreepress.org/2014/09/a-photo-essay-of-sundays-san-diego-peoples-climate-march-the-time-for-change-is-now/. For another news report, see https: //www.youtube.com/watch?v=2rHiO6LYysM.

9 https://trainings.350.org/for/organisers/and https://350.org/resources/.

10 For a photo essay of this event, see http://sandiego350.org/blog/2015/01/05/student-fieldtrip-environmental-justice-vs-oil/.

11 For a news report of this event, see http://www.sandiegouniontribune.com/photos/galleries/2015/apr/19/earth-day-2015/.

12 See http://www.sandiegouniontribune.com/news/2015/apr/19/earth-fair-environment-dumpster-food-recycling/.

13 For a photo essay of this event, see http://sandiego350.org/blog/2015/02/06/photo-essay-high-water-line-2/.

14 For the video made by SanDiego350 of the High Water Line event, 19 January 2015, see https://www.youtube.com/watch?v=I-yk_Zh_vG4.

REBUILDING THE FOUNDATION:

The Critical Role of Materials for a Sustainable World

David Stone

ABSTRACT: *It is well known that our global civilization needs to decrease its dependence on fossil fuels to avert an ecological collapse. It is less well known that most of the materials we use for construction and manufacturing are themselves unsustainable. The processes of producing steel, cement, glass, and other common building materials consume huge amounts of fossil fuels and generate equivalent amounts of CO_2 and other pollutants. Changing how we build and what we build with is fundamental to transforming our thermo-industrial culture into one based on green processes that imitate the low temperature and highly sophisticated chemistry of biology. Here we discuss the efforts of the Tohono O'odham Native Americans to adapt their construction materials to the predicted mega-drought in their homeland due to climate change. By starting with an innovative material called Ferrock, we hope to revive not only their ancient desert-adapted architecture, but also their lost way of life that was both environmentally and socially stable. This specific project will also promote a wider vision that might serve as a guide to other places and peoples suffering the first effects of global warming.*

ANCIENT CONSTRUCTION

With hand tools our group of Native-, Mexican-, and Euro-Americans carves an ever-deepening circle into the hard, dry desert ground. We are digging down to make a living space protected from the heat. The domed roof will be buried under a thick layer of the soil we are piling up. The opening will be on the east side, facing the rising sun. I step into the shade and look again at the design on the computer screen. It is one thousand years old. But the materials piled around us among the saguaros speak of the decay of industrial culture: iron dust, broken glass, coal ash. We will mix them with saltwater, pour our walls, and then feed them exhaust gas. The carbon dioxide will seep into the pores, make acid in the water, and dissolve the metal iron. In turn the free iron will trap the gas in a solid crystalline matrix that grows by forming microscopic shells around the dust particles. The shells will grow together, interlock like clenched teeth, and harden our walls. It is a mix of ancient and modern technologies.

We are building down into the ground and making a traditional pit house with an innovative green material that is being used here and nowhere else on earth. The work is interesting and satisfying, but there is an underlying tension because we are preparing for the arrival of an enemy. The day is very hot, going over 110, and in the coming decades the summer days will get hotter still. The earth is heating up. This desert will become extreme and may change beyond what can be tolerated. We are hoping that the new material will help our children survive here.

ENVIRONMENTAL IMPACT OF MODERN CONSTRUCTION MATERIALS

Our project is one small effort to address a fundamental yet often overlooked global challenge. Among the wide variety of topics considered from an environmental perspective there is one major category that has not received as much attention as it deserves. Unlike our energy sources, the materials we use for construction and manufacturing are receiving less scrutiny despite their major contribution to pollution, resource depletion, and global warming. How do materials themselves cause such problems? Are they not inert? Though materials might seem innocuous when not in use, the processes that brought them into being are often surprisingly energy greedy and environmentally dirty.[1]

When we consider the automobile's environmental impact, for example, we are concerned with miles per gallon and exhaust gases, not what it is made of. We think that a car must be running to impact the environment, and we assume that when our Prius sits quietly in the garage all is fine. But that is a serious delusion. Production of the steel that makes up most of the automobile, and much of our industrial civilization, as well, is an energy-intensive process that burns vast amounts of fossil fuels and therefore generates huge volumes of CO_2—approximately 6% of the entire world's annual total output of this greenhouse gas.[2] Steel itself is not sustainable, at least not as it is commonly produced now.

The concrete slab under the car is also not innocent. Though it appears as cold, gray, and dead as rock, its active ingredient and binder, Portland cement, was once red hot at the center of an inferno. The raw materials for making cement, mostly limestone, are chemically transformed in a rotating kiln, which is a giant tube with a roaring burner at one end that typically consumes tens of tons of coal or other fuel per hour. Approximately half of the CO_2 comes from this combustion and the other half from the transformation of limestone to lime, the main ingredient. About one ton of CO_2 is created for every ton of cement and the global cement industry is responsible for almost as much of this greenhouse gas as the steel industry.[3] So we are already at over 10% of the global output just with these two materials, and that is before even making anything functional. Steel and concrete, the materials with which we build the foundations of our world, are themselves unsustainable. We must find new materials and rebuild in a new way.

For other building materials the story is similar. Plaster for the massive dry wall industry is made from ground gypsum (calcium sulfate) that is run through a hot kiln process very similar to that used to make cement. Bricks, tiles, and other ceramic products are vitrified (hardened) in a glowing-hot kiln burning fossil fuels. Glass products are formed from the molten state using high heat, again from burning fossil fuels. Many plastics are made from petroleum derivatives and during their multi-step manufacture burn still more fossil fuels for the heat to drive the reactions. Processes using heat from electricity like electric arc furnaces for melting steel are still indirectly using fossil fuels that are burned at the coal and gas-burning power plants. We live in a thermo-industrial civilization based on processes driven by heat from fire.

The evolution of our relationship with fire has been traced from the warming campfire through the steam boiler and open-hearth furnace to the rocket engine propelling humans into space. The transformative power of heat became enculturated along the way and sometimes reached a cult-like obsession, as it did among the alchemists in the Middle Ages. They explored the mysterious change of matter from one form to another using various glassy contraptions like steaming retorts, fuming crucibles, and bubbling beakers. Though their metaphysical approach ultimately proved misguided, many of their physical methods were adopted by science. Today technology continues to push the frontiers of thermal transformation and, notably, in the quest for nuclear fusion of hydrogen isotopes like deuterium. The plasma must be held by magnetic fields without contact with any material, because it reaches temperatures hotter than the surface of the sun.

But there are other ways besides heat to transform matter. We need look no further than any green plant as a model. The near-miracle of photosynthesis converts the most unlikely raw materials, carbon dioxide gas and water, into a phantasmagoria of living matter ranging from rot-resistant hardwoods to the most ephemeral flowers. CO_2 and H_2O are unpromising because they are both oxides. The carbon and hydrogen have already become bound to oxygen, the most electron-hungry element in the universe besides fluorine. It is difficult to break the bonds with oxygen to enable other reactions that produce familiar hydrocarbons such as sugars, proteins, carbohydrates, and fats. Photosynthesis deftly uses the high energy of sunlight to cleave oxidized molecules by adding electrons and assembling them into much bigger bio-molecules. It is a game of chemistry masterfully played against entropy though no matter how well played it is always lost. Entropy is always winning, always increasing in the universe. But plants use high quality light energy with such exquisite efficiency in their cellular factories that they can convert even lowly CO_2 to energy-packed matter that is rich in nutrients such as nuts, fruit, and grains. High quality energy (sunlight) is "degraded" to lower but still useful and delicious forms (like oranges), and entropy is served. But there is almost no waste heat, a very low-grade form of energy.[4]

Our factories are not nearly so efficient, and almost everything is based on processes that lose vast amounts of waste heat. We quickly burn the finely wrought carbon materials created by plants in a fiery sacrifice to entropy. Some of this energy-rich carbon that we use as fuel is fresh like wood and some is ancient like coal. "Fossil" fuels are doubly worrisome. First, their incineration is raising the CO_2 levels in our atmosphere with the resulting climate change. Second, they are finite and our massive dependence on them therefore sets us up for an inevitable crash. We, the self-described most intelligent species on the planet, are undoing millions of years of work in storing carbon performed by the mindless plants. The staggering biodiversity and proven stability of this entire global system is being affronted in an unplanned Promethean experiment reversing the ageless trend by life to capture and conserve carbon.

We can do much better at making our industrial plants more like green plants. The basic technological approach to this challenge has been developing for 150 years and is now having a renaissance. Electrochemistry uses electricity rather than heat to drive chemical reactions. So far it has given us batteries, solar cells, fuel cells, and other less well-known technologies. One of the first major industrial uses was for plating metals, especially copper, and a form of this process called "electrowinning," continues to be the standard industrial-scale method of extracting the pure metal from copper ore dissolved in acid. The pioneers in metal plating were Italian artists who made permanent coppery sculptures this way without the high heat of melting and pouring bronze into molds. Iron, too, can be plated out from an aqueous solution of a salt, like ferrous sulfate. Though electrodeposition of iron is not as straightforward as copper, it can be done, and more efficient methods are under development. There are novel hybrid thermo-electrochemical approaches that pull iron out of a molten salt. The important point is that iron, still the most essential metal of our modern world, can be produced without heat. The electricity used to plate metals is direct current, which could come directly from solar panels. One form of electrochemistry serves another.[5]

GREEN MATERIALS WITH LIMITED IMPACT ON ENVIRONMENT

All this may seem like an arcane **R&D** project carried out only in the cutting-edge labs of big corporations that run the industrial world. Certainly much important work is being done at such facilities. But sunlight shines everywhere and offers the potential to de-centralize our energy systems as well as our innovative spirit. The vision is growing ever more practical that clean rooftop solar power can replace the big dirty coal and gas-burning power plants. With the change to a distributed energy system, the other electrochemical technologies will also be more widely implemented. Excess solar energy can be stored in batteries or in the form of hydrogen gas to be used in fuel cells. The plating of metals, now a minor but essential supportive technology, could gradually become the primary way the industrial world does metallurgy. The giant, carbon-spewing, energy-draining steel mills will go the way of the power plants. This transformation is possible now, but the necessary motivation to fully commit will come only with a real international agreement to mitigate climate change.

One of the best places in the U.S. for daily cloud-free sunshine is southern Arizona. Scientific research on solar-based energy systems is happening at Arizona State University near Phoenix and at the University of Arizona in Tucson. A less likely location for the development of sustainable technology is the Tohono O'odham Nation, a vast Indian reservation of 2.8 million acres at the center of the state's boundary with Mexico. Like many Native Nations, the Tohono O'odham (meaning "desert people" in their language), suffer from several centuries of intergenerational trauma due to colonization, which in turn manifests itself in a variety of social problems including poverty, high unemployment, and alcoholism. Yet, there are positive efforts to rebuild their shattered culture and even recover some of their ancient traditional life ways (himdag). There have been notable successes in recovering and maintaining their language, stories, ceremonies, and agriculture. But one core part of their traditional culture that has been more conspicuously lost is architecture.

One thousand years ago the ancestors of the Tohono O'odham, the Hohokam ("those who are gone"), lived very differently. At the villages that have been excavated, such as Casa Grande, Pueblo Grande, and Snaketown, the most distinguishing feature was immediately apparent. The village center was one large building, a sprawling multi-room compound that gained many benefits from this style of construction. The defensive advantages of being within this fort-like structure are obvious, though it is uncertain that this was the primary motivation. Structurally, one wall could conveniently serve two rooms, and the interconnected geometry helped stabilize the whole. The well-fitted but loosely consolidated walls of rock and mud all needed to help each other keep standing against the elements over centuries. They also helped shade each other and, in an era without electricity and insulation, the ingenious design of creating rooms within rooms was quite effective at moderating both extreme summer heat and cold winter winds. The walls were also very thick, up to almost five feet at Casa Grande, and this also moderated the interior temperature. Socially, everyone lived, worked, ate, slept, played, prayed, and died in close proximity with everyone else. There is nothing like this architecturally mediated tight-knit culture today.

People live and suffer the effects of intergenerational trauma mostly in their own homes, in neighborhoods modeled after the suburbs of the dominant culture. They live in the dysfunctional limbo between village and city.

Some of us are attempting to pull synergistically from both sources, both the traditional village and the modern city. We are reviving the proven architectural principles of the ancient desert masters but using advanced materials and construction methods to build stronger, more durable structures. This integrated approach will combine the best of both cultures in what might be called an ecological civilization. For the Tohono O'odham Nation, as for other Native American Nations, the ongoing struggle to at least maintain or hopefully revive their traditional culture is another guide for how we all can find our collective way forward in the 21st century. We can follow them in their struggle to keep connected to the past while selectively utilizing some aspects of the dominant culture's technological progress.

While others work on language and agriculture, our group focuses on another basic aspect of life, creating shelter. For the Desert People who learned to respectfully and sustainably harvest from the spare landscape, the ground provided another essential resource that we have all but forgotten—a stable temperature. That is, just going down a few feet the temperature swings from day to night and summer to winter flatten out. This "thermal moderation" is well known in caves. Tapping this old resource does not mean returning to the Stone Age. In the coming Ecological Age, this can be done in a sophisticated way that provides well-lit and energy-efficient buildings. With the Tohono O'odham we can return to the earth with space age technology.

One specific material technology can serve as an example of this transformation to a revived past. We take a new approach to building with iron. Instead of fighting the natural propensity of iron to rust, we cultivate this process to create something useful. In imitation of the earlier human achievement of taming fire for our purposes, we aspire to use corrosion for creation. Corrosion is another natural electrochemical process that reverses the electrically driven purification of metal from its ore discussed earlier. On a warm, wet, oxygenated planet like ours, the natural state of iron is not metal but oxidized minerals like hematite ("blood stone"). Iron wants to rust and this entropy-driven reaction can cause other reactions that are beneficial to us, just as the heat from fire can be used for cooking. Other bonds besides those with oxygen alone are possible. We use carbon dioxide and water to create iron carbonate or siderite ("star rock," from the early association of iron with meteorites), which is a mineral that effectively cements itself together along with aggregate-like crushed glass. As a result, carbon dioxide is trapped in the solidifying mineral matrix, making the process carbon negative. We call our new old cement Ferrock (a fusion of the words "ferro," or iron, and "rock").

In 2003, the author made the initial discovery of this method of making synthetic siderite in a lab by accident (still a common form of invention). In the early stage the motivation to develop it further was to simply find a way to utilize the millions of tons of nonhazardous waste steel dust that is not recycled but dumped into landfills every year. But then further research at Arizona State University unexpectedly revealed that Ferrock is actually structurally superior to Portland cement in several important ways. It has almost five times the flexural strength, which is the ability to resist bending and to bend more without breaking. Ferrock is also tougher and more resistant to cracking.[6] The practical consequence is that this is the ideal material to use to make dome-shaped structures designed to bear heavy loads of soil and especially where they might be subjected to the dynamic stress of earthquakes. With a new, innovative material we will return to the architectural designs of the Hohokam, who hand built water canals tens of miles long as well as the great village compounds like Pueblo Grande, which is now a mound of soil and rubble in the middle of the vast Phoenix metropolis.

A more modest architectural style that we are starting with is the so-called "pit house" (in the O'odham language, olas ki, or round house). It was common in the southwest as a basic family dwelling.

The round or oval structure is nestled into the thermally moderating ground and also covered with a layer of protecting soil. The internal structure was built with branches and supported by tree trunks used as posts. This design goes back thousands years, but our approach is modern, or rather postmodern. For wood we substitute scrap steel like machine shop shavings and old barbed wire. For caleche (a form of clay with high calcium carbonate) we substitute Ferrock, a carbon-negative alternative to Portland cement. Instead of rock we use crushed glass from liquor bottles that have been collected by hand at drinking sites along roads through the desert lands of the reservation. In this way we transform a residue of alcoholism into something positive and useful. Those tribal members who have done this work express a sense of personal renewal. This act of recycling has become a kind of environmental ritual among the communities. Our project is being encultured. But the goal is to do more than just clean up. We are going back into the ground and starting to rebuild an ecological civilization from the foundation up.

The skyscraper, that architectural icon of the modern city, is not appropriate for the Tohono O'odham culture, for cities of the Southwest, or for a world going into climate change. A tower of steel anchored in concrete and sheathed in glass is, environmentally speaking, the worst possible design. In cold weather it radiates heat through the uninsulated glass on all sides and couldn't be more inefficient. On hot days exposed to the sun, the buildup of heat must be countered with constant artificial cooling. The energy used to heat and cool skyscrapers is exorbitant and archaic in this era of climate change. We must rethink how we build and what we build with. We must build in response to climate change and in ways that mitigate its effects.[7]

The Hohokam are gone, according to archeologists, because they faced a mega-drought that even those masters of desert living could not overcome. Based on the evidence, starting roughly about 800 years ago, the climate changed due to natural causes. The U.S. Southwest became much more arid. Despite their prayers, the rains did not come and even many of the rivers eventually dried up. The

Hohokam and other ancestral agricultural peoples of the region like the Anasazi apparently dispersed in smaller bands to survive by reverting to an earlier hunting and gathering way of life. As the centuries passed and conditions moderated, they gradually began to gather back together in farming communities. But then came another disaster, the European invasion, which initiated a deeper and more prolonged cultural attack. After many generations of transmitted grief, the Tohono O'odham, who once lived throughout much of southern Arizona and northern Sonora, were left with a much-diminished reservation allocated to them by the new American government, one that revolted against its original foreign masters while dominating harshly over its own first citizens. As a result, there is now no place else for them to go as they face another mega-drought, this time a byproduct of the dominant industrial culture.[8] Unlike their ancestors, the Hohokam, "those who are gone," the modern Tohono O'odham must become the Wi'ikam ab Jewed (WE ee kahm ahb JEH ehd) "those who remain on the land."

We all need to learn how to stay on the land. We must be with the Desert People and other Native Peoples as we all adapt to climate change. This critical effort will require a synthesis of the best practices from both cultures. We will start at the foundation, literally, and rebuild a more sustainable ecological civilization with new and better materials. This effort requires a renewed, more respectful perspective inspired by Native sensibilities that see all of nature, including the primal elements, as animate, beneficial gifts. Even iron has an existence beyond our utilitarian intentions for it. How can we work differently and more naturally with iron? Good science can still be done from this organismic philosophical foundation, and this will help guide it toward the development of technologies that are integrated better with our living planet. This multifaceted reconstruction of our world must begin with all of us in our individual moment-to-moment engagement with it. On principle, this work cannot be relegated to the corporate elite and their plans contrived only for profits. As we rebuild our physical world, so we rebuild our culture and our selves.

Despite the current dominance of the industrial culture, the world is still as interrelated as my Native coworkers tell me. Together we are rediscovering and rebuilding the connections.

ENDNOTES

1 For example, see the EPA's document "Materials Management: the Road Ahead," https://www.epa.gov/sites/production/ files/2015-09/ documents/vision2.pdf

2 For annual updates on energy consumption and CO_2 productions for the steel and other industries see the International Energy Agency: https://www.iea.org/media/workshops/2017/ieaglobalironsteeltechnologyroadmap/ISTRM_Session1_A._PURVIS_241117.pdf.

3 https://www.iea.org/newsroom/news/2018/april/cement-technologyroadmap-plots-path-to-cutting-co2-emissions-24-by-2050.html.

4 Schneider, Eric D., and Dorian Sagan, *Into the Cool: Energy Flow, Thermodynamics, and Life* (Chicago: University of Chicago Press, 2005).

5 Bockris, J. O'M., and Z. Nagy, *Electrochemistry for Ecologists* (New York: Plenum Press, 1974)

6 For a brief visual summary of this research see this PBS news report: https://www.pbs.org/newshour/show/cement-alternative -absorbs-carbon- dioxide-like-sponge.

7 For a thorough review of social, economic, and environmental criticisms of skyscrapers see Al-Kodmany, Kheir, "The sustainability of tall building development," *Buildings* 2018, 8, 7, www.mdpi. com/2075-5309/8/1/7/pdf.

8 For one example of the ongoing discussion of "mega-droughts," past and pending, see http://origins.osu.edu/article/west-without -water-what-can-past- droughts-tell-us-about-tomorrow.

CONTRIBUTORS

MICHAEL BRACKNEY is an activist in San Diego working with Climate Mobilization Coalition, Fair Elections Coalition, Peace Resource Center, and Jewish Voice for Peace San Diego Chapter..

ELLEN BROWN is an attorney, founder and chair of the Public Banking Institute, and author of twelve books including the best-selling *Web of Debt.* Her latest book, *The Public Bank Solution,* explores successful public banking models historically and globally.

TINA CLARKE has a B.A. from Macalester College and an M.A. from the University of Chicago. Tina has been a professional community organizer, trainer, and facilitator since 1985, directing national citizen participation programs in D.C., coalitions and programs on environmental issues, and several nonprofit education and resource organizations in New England. Since 2008, Tina has been a Transition Towns Trainer, served over 240 communities worldwide, delivered 65 Transition Training courses, and provided hundreds of presentations. She is currently consulting for Ecolise, a coalition of 38 organizations in Europe that includes the Transition Network.

SHEILA D. COLLINS is Professor Emeritus of Political Science at William Paterson University, where she taught courses on public policy and social movements and directed the Graduate Program in Public Policy and International Affairs. She has lectured widely in the U.S. and abroad and is the author and editor of six books on American politics and public policy. As a member of the Global Ecological Integrity Group, she has contributed many book chapters on environmental politics.

JOHN B. COBB, JR. is a retired theologian, philosopher, and environmentalist. Most of his career was spent teaching at the Claremont School of Theology and Claremont Graduate University. His many publications include reflections on the assumptions of economic and political theory as well as the traditional teaching of the church. He was chief organizer of the conference that produced these papers.

JOHN CULP is Emeritus Professor of Philosophy at Azusa Pacific University, with special interest in philosophy of religion. Among his publications is the "Panentheism" entry in the Stanford Encyclopedia of Philosophy.

THOMAS H. GRECO, JR. is a preeminent scholar, author, educator, and community economist who is widely regarded as a leading authority on moneyless exchange, community currencies, and financial innovation. Greco is a sought-after speaker internationally and has conducted workshops and lectured in 15 countries on five continents, and has been advisor to currency projects in many countries. He has authored numerous articles and books, including *The End of Money and the Future of Civilization*. Many of his presentations, interviews, and writings are available via his website, Beyond Money, at http://beyondmoney.net.

CARL HERMAN worked with both U.S. political parties over 18 years and with two U.N. summits for heads of state with the citizen's lobby **RESULTS** for U.S. domestic and foreign policy to end poverty. He is a National Board Certified Teacher of U.S. government, economics, and history (also credentialed in mathematics), with all economic factual claims receiving zero refutation since 2008 among ~2,000 Advanced Placement Macroeconomics teachers on the group's discussion board. He can be reached at Carl_Herman@post.harvard.edu

JOSEPH C. HOUGH is the retired president of Union Theological Seminary, dean of Vanderbilt University Divinity School and professor of social ethics at Claremont School of Theology and Claremont Graduate University. He is author of *Black Power and White Protestants*.

KATSUNORI IHA is a research economist, responsible for tracking Ecological Footprints in global supply chains through the use of the multi-regional input-output model, which also applies to sub-national and personal calculator projects. His next project will be building a platform to connect interdisciplinary scholars and leaders in Asian regions that are facing sustainability challenges. He holds an M.S. in economics, specializing in environmental economics, from Okinawa International University, Japan.

JAMES LONG is a Certified Public Accountant, working for the City of San Diego. James has B.S. in electrical engineering from Cal Poly, San Luis Obispo. James joined Climate activist group SanDiego350 to do something for a future that is threatened by climate change.

GAYLE MCLAUGHLIN is the former two-term elected mayor and councilmember of Richmond, CA (2005-2017), and a co-founder of the Richmond Progressive Alliance. As mayor, she led Richmond's remarkable transformation, reducing homicides 75%, passing rent control, increasing the minimum wage, acquiring over $100 million in additional city taxes from Chevron, and promoting Richmond's inclusion in a Community Choice Energy program. Gayle ran as an independent, corporate-free candidate for California Lt. Governor and was endorsed by Bernie Sanders' Our Revolution (www.gayleforcalifornia.org).

LÍLIA DIAS MARIANNO is a researcher in the PhD program in history of sciences and technology and epistemology, Federal University of Rio de Janeiro UFRJ. She is a member of the International Process Network, board and fellow researcher of the Center for Process Studies, coordinating the Latin American Network for Process Research.

ASHLEY MAZANEC has her Masters of International Environmental Policy from the University of California San Diego. She is an eco-musician, environmental policy professional, eco community developer, founding director of EcoArts Foundation and a partner and affiliated artist at the Climate Science Alliance. She collaborates with companies, nonprofits, and eco-artists to spark important conversations on environmental topics, including via her podcast Let's Talk About the Weather.

DAVID STONE received his PhD in Environmental Science from the University of Arizona, where his research focused on the "creative corrosion" of iron. He has continued to explore the patterns, forms, and aggregations driven by this entropic process, and he contributed to the emergence of a new sub-field within chemistry called chemo-brionics, which investigates certain classes of self-organized growing structures. For the past eight years Dr. Stone has been project director in the Office for Sustainability at the Tohono O'odham Community College, where he applies his expertise toward the development of green, carbon-negative building materials that would be suitable for the physical construction of a new ecological civilization.

YOSHIHIKO WADA is professor of ecological economics at the Faculty of Economics, Doshisha University in Kyoto. He is also director of Doshisha University EU campus office. Wada received his PhD in planning from the University of British Columbia, Canada. He specializes in Ecological Footprint analysis and ecological impacts of mining and also involved in studies of "conscience" and is director of the NGO, Ecological Footprint Japan.

www.ingramcontent.com/pod-product-compliance
Lightning Source LLC
Chambersburg PA
CBHW051716020426
42333CB00014B/1004